Dickens and the Workhouse

D. Maclise, R.A.   R. Graves A.R.A.

CHARLES DICKENS.

ÆT. 27.

FRONTISPIECE. Young Dickens. A fine engraving by Robert Graves for the 'Nickleby' portrait painted by Daniel Maclise in 1839, when Dickens was 27. This image is from the 1875 American edition of Forster's *Life of Dickens*, published in Boston by Osgood.

RUTH RICHARDSON

DICKENS
· AND THE ·
WORKHOUSE

OLIVER TWIST
AND THE LONDON POOR

OXFORD
UNIVERSITY PRESS

OXFORD

UNIVERSITY PRESS

Great Clarendon Street, Oxford ox2 6DP

Oxford University Press is a department of the University of Oxford.
It furthers the University's objective of excellence in research, scholarship,
and education by publishing worldwide in

Oxford New York

Auckland Cape Town Dar es Salaam Hong Kong Karachi
Kuala Lumpur Madrid Melbourne Mexico City Nairobi
New Delhi Shanghai Taipei Toronto

With offices in

Argentina Austria Brazil Chile Czech Republic France Greece
Guatemala Hungary Italy Japan Poland Portugal Singapore
South Korea Switzerland Thailand Turkey Ukraine Vietnam

Oxford is a registered trade mark of Oxford University Press
in the UK and in certain other countries

Published in the United States
by Oxford University Press Inc., New York

British Library Cataloguing in Publication Data

Data available

Library of Congress Cataloging in Publication Data

Data available

Typeset by SPI Publisher Services, Pondicherry, India
Printed in Great Britain
on acid-free paper
by Clays Ltd, St Ives plc

ISBN 978-0-19-964588-6

1 3 5 7 9 10 8 6 4 2

For All who love Dickens
*& **everyone** who helped save the*
Cleveland Street Workhouse from demolition
&
Most especially for my darling parents.

ACKNOWLEDGEMENTS

My primary thanks are to my darling parents, Hilda and Billy Richardson, who kept wonderful books on lower shelves, and encouraged early reading.

I cannot find words enough to thank my Brian, sweetheart of thirty years, and our lovely boy Josh who has helped with hardware, software and transcribing.

I should also like to thank my headmistress, Mrs M. H. Saunders at Lancaster Road LCC Infants' School, who generously gave me the Oxford University Press edition of *Oliver Twist* (with a preface by Humphry House) when I left infants' school at the age of 6. It is an enormous pleasure, now that I am grown, to be writing about Dickens, and to be published by Oxford University Press. I know she would be pleased.

I should also like to thank all those involved in the Cleveland Street Workhouse Campaign, especially Nick Black, Aimery de Malet, Peter, Peter Higginbotham, Kitty, Lucinda Hawksley, all our local supporters, and participants of Howard House and Cleveland St (north) Neighbourhood Watch, and other friends. Thanks above all to Heidi, that very special person who tracked me down, and recruited me to the campaign. What a fine team we have all been!

A very special thank you goes to the Dickens Rare Books specialist Dan Calinescu of Boz and Friends Rare Books of Toronto, who in true Dickensian fashion has been our staunch supporter, a kind friend, and the most helpful correspondent in the world.

Everybody at Oxford University Press with whom I have had the honour to work deserves my thanks: Luciana O'Flaherty, Matthew Cotton, Latha Menon, Emma Barber, Phil Henderson, Kate Farquhar-Thomson and Kirsty Doole, Fo Orbell, Mary Worthington, Gail Eaton, Wilbur Wright, and three unnamed Readers whose comments have been enormously encouraging and helpful. Thanks also to the unknown designers, typesetters, printers, bookbinders, and others who have brought this book to press.

I owe an enormous debt of gratitude to Dickens scholars, most especially to Paul Schlicke, who has encouraged my researches so kindly, and has addressed my ignorance with great forbearance. I greatly regret that I did not make the discovery about the Workhouse when Kathleen Tillotson was alive: she would have been glad to see me such a keen Dickensian, and I know she'd have put me right on a host of matters. Thanks also to friends and colleagues on the DickensForum, and to Michael Allen, Malcolm Andrews, Norman Page, John Drew, Audrey Jaffe, David Paroissien, Michael Slater, David Perdue, Joan Dicks, Judith Flanders, Lucinda Hawksley, Bill Long, Patrick Macarthy, Herb Moskovitz and the BuzFuz e-newsletter, Mitsu Matsuoka, Robert Newsom, Bob Patten, Andrew Sanders, and staff at the Dickens Museum at 48 Doughty Street. Also to historians of the workhouse system and the lives of the London Poor, above all Norman Longmate, Anthony Brundage, Simon Fowler, David Green, Peter Higginbotham, Tim Hitchcock, Elaine Murphy, Simon Fowler, and Tony Wohl.

Acknowledgements

Most of my work for this book has been done at the British Library, in the Rare Books Room, and the Maps Room, Manuscripts, and the old Official Publications Library. Like Dickens, I was very young when I was granted the privilege of a Reader's Ticket. I should like to thank every individual member of the staff there, including all those who have recently been made redundant, for their unfailing courtesy, kindness, and helpfulness. Thanks, too, to all the staff at the old British Museum Round Reading Room, the old North Library, the unseen delivery staff, the academic staff at the Library, whose scholarship is priceless, the staff in Book Preservation, and the Security Staff who care for the building. And while thinking of this great institution, I salute the memory of Robin Alston, and his life's work.

Staff in charge of that extraordinary and rich resource, the British Museum Prints and Drawings Collection, deserve real thanks for putting the collection online and making it freely available.

Many archivists have been extraordinarily helpful, and I would like to salute their fine work: particularly those at the Bishopsgate Institute, the London Metropolitan Archives, at Westminster City Archives, and the Camden Local History Library, Barnet Local Studies, the University College Hospital Archives, the Wellcome Collection, and the Harry Elkins Widener Collection, Houghton Library, Harvard University.

Staff at English Heritage put up with enthusiastic nuisances like me asking about things not fully understood, with courtesy and forbearance during the campaign to save the Workhouse. I have nothing but thanks and respect for their work and for their scholarship. Thanks, too, to staff at the Department of Culture Media and Sport, and especially the Ministers, Jeremy Hunt and John Penrose, who countermanded the daft decision of the previous government concerning the Workhouse, and listed it.

Staff at the Museum of London made me welcome, and kindly shared their resources: many thanks to Julia Hoffbrand, Beverley Cook, and Alex Werner. Andrew Potter, at the Royal Academy Library, and Philip Athill of Abbott and Holder, kindly helped me concerning Mr Gaugain.

I should also like to thank Clare Brant and Hope Wolf and friends at King's College London Strandlines Project, Ann Saunders [Cox-Johnson] and the London Topographical Society, The Georgian Group, the Soho Society, the Marylebone Society (especially Gaby Higgs and Victoria Lochead), the Camden History Society, the Friends of Highgate Cemetery, the Friends of St George's Gardens, and the City of Westminster Guides.

I also thank friends and colleagues Susan Armstrong, Adrian Autton, Alison Backhouse and her *Worm Eaten Waistcoat*, Mr Baveystock, Betty Bostetter, Helena Cronin, Francis Eames, the Eddy family, Jan Farrow, Fiona Godlee, Lindsay Granshaw, Tim Hitchcock, Annie Janowicz, Kiran Jatania, Rory Lalwan, Annie Lindsay, Elaine Murphy, Gerhard Lang, Josh Loeb, Jayne Joso, Bridget MacDonald, Helen MacDonald, Lynn McDonald, Natasha McEnroe, Professor Gordon McMullan, the current inhabitants of Norfolk Street, Peter Razzell, John Richardson and Helen English, Glenys Roberts, Maureen Rose of Taylor's Buttons, Piloti, the Publican and staff at the 'King & Queen' opposite the Workhouse, Doc Rowe, Katie Sambrook, Ian Smith, Guy Speranza, Gavin Stamp, Robert Thorne, Gillian Tindall for inspiration, various booksellers, most especially Jarndyce of Museum Street, Jane Wildgoose, Alison Wood, and Malcolm Young.

Acknowledgements

I have tried to do justice to Dickens's own writings by way of illustration, and the work of other scholars, but draw most heavily upon my own original researches in archival resources in London repositories. In the time there was to research and write this book, in order to allow the Press sufficient time to have the book ready for Dickens's 200th birthday, I was unable to dig as deeply as I'd have wished into the vast resource of Dickens scholarship. If in my haste I have missed giving proper credit to anyone, I ask forgiveness, and should like to be informed of omissions/errors so that due corrections may be made.

I thank the *Dickens Quarterly* for permission to reproduce passages from my article 'Charles Dickens and the Cleveland Street Workhouse', published in the journal in June 2011, 28/2: 99–108.

Thanks too, to *The British Medical Journal* for permission to quote from the article I wrote with Brian Hurwitz, 'Joseph Rogers and the Reform of Workhouse Medicine', published in the journal in 1989, 299: 1507–10.

CONTENTS

Contents

LIST OF ILLUSTRATIONS

George Cruikshank

Introduction

OLIVER TWIST AND THE WORKHOUSE

OLIVER TWIST RESEMBLES Frankenstein, in that everyone knows the gist of his story. Oliver is the poor boy who asks for more, who sings 'Food, glorious Food!' and who is taught to pick pockets in Victorian London. Most people know him from the original book by Charles Dickens, or from the spectacular opening scene of the twentieth-century musical, where the chorus of neglected boys belt out their lust for food in the echoing workhouse hall.

Readers and scholars have puzzled over the whereabouts of the original workhouse which inspired Dickens, and why he chose such a grim setting for this major early novel. The location of the workhouse at the centre of Oliver's story is extremely vague, but an intriguing recent discovery has thrown fresh light on Dickens's preoccupation with the bleak workhouse at the heart of the book.

FIGURE 1. The defunct Middlesex Hospital Outpatients' Department—the old Strand Union Workhouse—boarded up to keep out vandals and squatters. Photographed in 2011 from Foley Street, by the artist Gerhard Lang.

In October 2010 I was asked by a group of local people to join their campaign to save an old workhouse, which stands on Cleveland Street, just by the foot of London's Telecom Tower. They had found an article that I'd written years ago, which concerned a doctor who had worked there in the nineteenth century. I hadn't known the building was under threat, and agreed to help.

By what now seems a rather circuitous journey, and at the eleventh hour, I made the remarkable finding that before he wrote *Oliver Twist*, Charles Dickens had lived for several years only a few doors from this particular workhouse. To discover such a close geographical association between a surviving workhouse and the creator of *Oliver Twist* was a most extraordinary and unexpected surprise.

Remarkably, too, the actual house in which Dickens and his family had lived still stands on the next block.

You'd think that nearly 150 years after his death, and after countless biographies and articles, there was nothing more to be known about Charles Dickens. But it turns out that fresh discoveries about him can indeed still be made.[1] This book shares the story of what has been unearthed about Charles Dickens's associations with the neighbourhood of the Cleveland Street Workhouse. We look first at how little is known about Dickens's London childhood, at the unexplained silences about his family's association with the street, and how the discovery was made.

By carefully examining the area and what its history holds, it is hoped to reinhabit Norfolk Street, shedding new light on Dickens's early life and his development as a novelist. The book weaves together the story of the street, the house, and the Cleveland Street Workhouse as we follow Dickens's life from his family's arrival in London in 1815, to the publication of *Oliver Twist* in 1838.

Much of the research for this book was done while the Cleveland Street Workhouse* was under threat of demolition, and while the local campaign group was mounting an appeal to the British government for a reconsideration of the building's listed-building

---

*   To avoid confusion, in this book a lower-case 'w' is used for the nineteenth-century workhouse as an institution and as a system, and also for Poor Law workhouses in general. The Cleveland Street Workhouse near Dickens's home, and shortened references to it, have a capital initial letter.

status, and while we were running what rapidly became a world-wide and—happily—eventually, a successful campaign to save this extraordinary place.

CHAPTER I

Discovery

THREAT, PUZZLE, SILENCES

C HARLES DICKENS IS just about the most famous literary figure in London's history, apart from Shakespeare. Yet when the Cleveland Street Workhouse was under imminent threat of demolition in 2010–11, the house in the same street, in which Dickens had lived, carried no plaque or sign whatever to announce this important fact of its history. Had there been a marker on his old home, the relationship of the two places would have been obvious to anyone who knew that the old Outpatients' Department of the Middlesex Hospital nearby was originally a workhouse. None of the local campaign group, including myself, knew of the association at the outset, and nor did English Heritage, the government body which recommends the 'listing' of buildings to protect them from demolition.

The fact that Dickens had lived in this part of London, east Marylebone, had been known to scholars of his life and work as an obscure snippet of biographical data. In 1951, Leslie Staples, then

Editor of *The Dickensian*—the journal of the Dickens Fellowship and an excellent source of detailed information about Dickens's biography and writings—published a brief article about the house in which the Dickens family had lived, along with a photograph of the place.[1] Biographers do mention the address, but they have invariably paid greater attention to Dickens's long-demolished home in Bayham Street, Camden Town. Neither *The Dickensian*'s Editor nor any other of Dickens's biographers—so far as I have been able to discover—has ever noticed that Dickens's family home stood within doors of the Cleveland Street Workhouse.

Dickens's novel *Oliver Twist* memorably opens in the lying-in (maternity) ward of a workhouse. Workhouses were publicly run institutions funded by local taxation ('poor-rates'), which provided minimal accommodation and sustenance for the desperate poor. The baby Oliver is born on the novel's first page, an illegitimate parish orphan. *Oliver Twist* is well known as Dickens's major attack on the New Poor Law of 1834, and its worse than miserly treatment of the poor. Once it was discovered, the likely importance of the proximity of Dickens's early home and this particular workhouse was therefore grasped immediately by Dickens readers and the international press. The existence of a workhouse doors from Dickens's home suggested that *Oliver Twist* might not be wholly fictional, that like some of Dickens's other works, it might have roots in a real place. Many people knew that in Dickens's childhood his father had been imprisoned for debt, but a workhouse standing right by his home: that was news!

Quite why the house had no plaque to commemorate its most famous resident is a mysterious puzzle which appears to have no answer. It seems to originate in very old silences, which shroud

Dickens's association with the entire neighbourhood in which the house stands.

Charles Dickens's first London home is mentioned only once, and only very briefly, in the great biography written by his best friend John Forster, soon after Dickens's death in 1870.[2] Forster's biography, which provides the basis for all subsequent books on Dickens's life, mentions the address within a discussion of a document known to history as the 'autobiographical fragment'. This was an unfinished manuscript Dickens himself wrote about his early life, apparently only ever seen by Forster. Parts of it were eventually incorporated into Forster's biography of Dickens. Concerning Dickens's first childhood home in London, Forster reports as if from the 'autobiographical fragment':

> When his father was again brought up by his duties to London from Portsmouth, they went into lodgings in Norfolk Street, Middlesex Hospital; and it lived also in the child's memory that they had come away from Portsea in the snow. Their home, shortly after, was again changed.[3]

The story of the writing of the 'autobiographical fragment' is important. Forster described it as having been provoked by a personal question concerning the 'blacking factory' period of Dickens's childhood. This was a deeply traumatic period for Dickens's family, when in 1824 his father John Dickens fell into debt, and was imprisoned in the Marshalsea Debtors' Prison, near London Bridge, where Dickens's mother Elizabeth and the smaller children joined him. At that time, debtors who could not pay off their creditors often found themselves arrested and imprisoned.

The young Charles Dickens had already been taken away from school. While his family was in the Marshalsea, he lived in lodgings, and was sent to work in a factory situated near the Strand, manufacturing and packaging shoe-polish, or 'blacking'. Forster explained:

The incidents to be told now would probably never have been known to me, or indeed any of the occurrences of his childhood and youth, but for the accident of a question which I put to him one day in the March or April of 1847.

I asked if he remembered ever having seen in his boyhood our friend the elder Mr. Dilke, his father's acquaintance and contemporary, who had been a clerk in the same office in Somerset House to which Mr. John Dickens belonged. Yes, he said, he recollected seeing him at a house in Gerrard Street, where his uncle Barrow lodged during an illness, and Mr. Dilke had visited him. Never at any other time. Upon which I told him that some one else had been intended in the mention made to me, for that the reference implied not merely his being met accidentally, but his having had some juvenile employment in a warehouse near the Strand; at which place Mr. Dilke, being with the elder Dickens one day, had noticed him, and received, in return for the gift of a half-crown, a very low bow. He was silent for several minutes; I felt that I had unintentionally touched a painful place in his memory; and to Mr. Dilke I never spoke of the subject again. It was not, however, then, but some weeks later, that Dickens made further allusion to my thus having struck unconsciously upon a time of which he never could lose the remembrance while he remembered anything, and the recollection of which, at intervals, haunted him and made him miserable, even to that hour.

Very shortly afterwards I learnt in all their detail the incidents that had been so painful to him, and what then was said to me or written respecting them revealed the story of his boyhood. The idea of *David Copperfield*, which was to take all the world into his confidence, had not at this time occurred to him; but what it had so startled me to know, his readers were afterwards told with only such change or addition as for the time might sufficiently disguise himself under cover of his hero. For the poor little lad, with good ability and a most sensitive nature, turned at the age of ten into a 'labouring hind' in the service of 'Murdstone and Grinby,' and conscious already of what made it seem very strange to him that he could so easily have been thrown away at such an age, was indeed himself. His was the secret agony of soul at finding himself 'companion to Mick Walker and Mealy Potatoes,' and his the tears that mingled with the water in which he and they rinsed and washed out bottles.

It had all been written, as fact, before he thought of any other use for it; and it was not until several months later, when the fancy of *David Copperfield*, itself suggested by what he had so written of his early troubles, began to take shape in his mind, that he abandoned his first intention of writing his own life. Those warehouse experiences fell then so aptly into the subject he had chosen, that he could not resist the temptation of immediately using them; and the manuscript recording them, which was but the first portion of what he had designed to write, was embodied in the substance of the eleventh and earlier chapters of his novel. What already had been sent to me, however, and proof-sheets of the novel interlined at the time, enable me now to separate the fact from the fiction, and to supply to the story of the author's childhood those passages, omitted from the book, which, apart from their illustration of the growth of his character, present to us a picture of tragical suffering, and of tender as well as humorous fancy, unsurpassed in even the wonders of his published writings.[4]

David Copperfield was published in instalments during 1849–50, a couple of years after the 'fragment' had been drafted. Contemporary readers may indeed have wondered about the derivation of parts of the story, but no one beyond Dickens's own close family circle, apart from Forster, knew that the hero's experiences were so very closely modelled on Dickens's own life. The factory experiences of the book's hero are based on those of Dickens himself as a boy, and the Micawbers' imprisonment for debt in the King's Bench prison approximates to that of his own parents in the Marshalsea.

Materials from the manuscript 'autobiographical fragment' were never made public during Dickens's lifetime.[5] Knowledge of the dark time when young Dickens was a factory boy and his father a prisoner Charles Dickens said he kept even from his wife.

These parts of his life are thought by many scholars to have scarred Dickens's soul, caused him deep sorrow and shame, and created a well of resentment against his parents' fecklessness, which seems to have been lifelong. Dickens mellowed towards both his parents as he grew older, recognizing and even saluting their valiant merits as he matured. But as he developed as a famous writer he was careful to keep these dark days from public view, and they remained publicly unknown until after his death.

Since his death, however, Dickens's personal mortification about the debtors' prison and the blacking factory has not prevented his association with the Marshalsea Prison or the whereabouts of the blacking factory from becoming very generally known. Hungerford Stairs, near the present Hungerford Bridge, where the factory was first situated, has since disappeared, swept away when the Victoria Embankment was being built in the 1860s. But plaques currently mark as significant locations in Dickens's biography the remains of the Marshalsea Debtors' Prison and the factory's subsequent site in Chandos Street, Covent Garden. London has more than twenty plaques commemorating Charles Dickens's associations with various places in the metropolis. There is even a plaque for one of his more obscure characters (Mr Kitterbell, in his *Sketch* 'The Bloomsbury Christening') on a house in Great Russell Street. So it seems quite incomprehensible that no plaque or sign whatever marked the house which had been Dickens's first home in London, and where he had lived for more than four years before he wrote *Oliver Twist*.

Until late in 2010, it seems to have been almost forgotten that Dickens had ever lived there. Indeed, an urban legend was circulating to the effect that out of Dickens's many homes in London, only a single survivor was still standing: the house in Doughty Street, which is now the Dickens Museum. An otherwise excellent online 'Camden Dickens Walk' stated this as if it was a fact in November 2010: '48 Doughty Street is the only surviving one of Dickens's main London homes.'[6]

The urban legend cannot entirely be blamed on those who have given it currency by repetition, because both Dickens and Forster were hardly forthcoming about the time the Dickens family spent in the house by the Workhouse. Historically, Norfolk Street has been submerged to a degree even deeper than the blacking factory. References to debtors' prisons and shoe-blacking emerge sporadically in Dickens's writings, but the street in which his first home stood does not, and there is no further mention of it in Forster's book.[7]

Who was responsible for the lack of emphasis upon Dickens's Norfolk Street home in Forster's biography isn't clear, but Forster would surely have been more forthcoming if Dickens had written at any length about it, so it is likely that Dickens himself downplayed its significance. Whether this was because it really was insignificant, or because he regarded it as such, or for some other reason; or, because he actually wanted to keep it obscure as a location of importance in his own biography, we shall see. If the latter is the case, Dickens succeeded for nearly 150 years.[8] Forster's treatment of Norfolk Street, which has influenced all biographies of Dickens to date, might be rooted in his own ignorance or neglect; after all, the two men did not become friends until 1836, when Dickens was already married, and living in Furnival's Inn, on High Holborn, and about to move into 48 Doughty Street. Forster may never have perceived the locality as important, or Norfolk Street as significant, or he may have picked up Dickens's unwillingness to mention it.

But, since the proximity of the Workhouse has been recognized, the question has emerged: what if this neglect was a studied neglect, or if Dickens deliberately kept Forster ignorant of the street's importance? These notions would indicate to modern eyes that— just as Dickens's lifetime embargo on the factory/prison episode revealed—Norfolk Street might actually be a matter of some considerable significance. Either way, a reconsideration of Norfolk Street as a location in Dickens's life is of value in reassessing a neglected part of his biography, and perhaps uncovering traces of things he might have wanted to conceal.

For many people it is almost impossible to think of the workhouse regime of the Poor Law without thinking also of Dickens's novel *Oliver Twist*, and it is probably true to say that modern-day conceptions of the workhouse as an institution have been fundamentally influenced by the novel. That such a strong influence should have persisted is hardly strange, because *Oliver Twist* has always been one of the best known and most widely read of all Dickens's novels ever since it was first written, and in our time the story has been given wide added currency in other media: children's books, film and TV versions on video and the internet, not to mention the famous Lionel Bart musical *Oliver!*

Oliver Twist; or, The Parish Boy's Progress was originally published in monthly parts. It appeared in a new magazine called *Bentley's Miscellany*, which Charles Dickens edited under his pen name, 'Boz'. *Oliver Twist* offered a marked contrast to the existing work for which 'Boz' was known: his many short and clever *Sketches*, and *Pickwick Papers*, which by then had become a publishing sensation. *Pickwick* had begun publication by Chapman and Hall in March 1836, appearing monthly in its own wrappers. Sales took off during midsummer 1836, when Dickens introduced the wonderful Cockney character of Sam Weller. Pickwick was a phenomenon, there was a *Pickwick* fever, and a snowstorm of plagiarisms and unauthorized merchandising, cashing in on the story's huge popularity.[9] *Oliver Twist* began in February 1837, when *Pickwick* was at its height, and the two stories ran in parallel for the next nine months, until *Pickwick* concluded in October 1837.[10] *Oliver Twist* continued publication until March 1839, by which time Dickens was already more than halfway through his next novel, *Nicholas Nickleby*.

While *Pickwick* was a loose cluster of adventures interspersed with stories, light-hearted and picaresque, from the outset *Oliver Twist* was altogether a more serious and tightly plotted novel. It opens with a birth and a death, the mother unmarried and the child illegitimate, or, as Dickens describes him, a burden on the rates. Dickens's style in the opening chapters of *Oliver Twist* is satirical and knowing, he exposes the small-minded meanness and cruelty of the workhouse regime, the ways in which the innocent were treated, and pillories the entire inhumane system. There is a satirical edge to his voice in the book, which is quite unlike *Pickwick*, and which probably disconcerted some readers, who were expecting more light-hearted fun from Boz's pen. The prose is witty, but it is also highly political and extremely topical.

The older system of support for the poor went back to Elizabethan times, and was organized at a parish level. Recognizing that wages were low, especially for working people with families, parishes provided family support subsidies and poor-house accommodation for the sustenance of those who could not provide for themselves: orphans, deserted women, sick, disabled, insane, and injured people,

the infirm, and the elderly. In times of recession parishes often provided help for the unemployed to earn their bread through publicly
funded work projects, like road-mending. It wasn't an ideal system,
but it was rooted in Christian charity, and recognized the humanity
of the poor: valuing family ties and endeavouring to keep families
together. The new system enshrined in the New Poor Law of 1834
instead repudiated traditional responsibilities towards the poor,
refusing all help unless it be inside the workhouse, where families
were separated, and harsh conditions were deliberately cultivated
so the poor would not seek to enter. Inmates had to wear uniforms
and were forced to work for the meagre diet provided. Harsh punishments for 'refractory' behaviour were instituted, including the
withdrawal of food. The system was under the centralized control
of the Poor Law Commission. The new workhouses were effectively a sort of prison system to punish poverty.

Like many other people at the time, Dickens thought the New
Poor Law cruel and deeply unchristian. His subtitle for *Oliver Twist*—
The Parish Boy's Progress—was taken from John Bunyan's allegory,
The Pilgrim's Progress. But Oliver's progress was to London, not to a
Celestial City: 'a dirtier or more wretched place he had never seen'.
In place of angels to greet him, he fell into the clutches of Fagin.

Dickens was not writing documentary history. Both the magazine format and the treatment of the workhouse in *Oliver Twist*
clearly presented the story as fictional, and Dickens located the
story in a geographically indeterminate town and set the story a
little back in time. However, once the Workhouse in Cleveland
Street is recognized to have been a possible source of inspiration for
Oliver Twist, it becomes evident—as we shall see—that Dickens
probably did have a particular workhouse in mind. But, like the

English artist William Hogarth, who famously elevated Drury Lane into allegory as 'Gin Lane', Dickens transformed a place he knew into a symbolic workhouse, recognizable by everyone, something that stood for the cruelties of the system as a whole.

The discovery that Dickens had lived close to the Cleveland Street Workhouse came about during the height of the campaign to save the Workhouse and while it was under imminent threat of demolition. It happened because I had approached the subject from the direction of the Workhouse, rather than from Dickens's biography. Much later in his life, when he was a great and famous Victorian novelist, Dickens had publicly supported an organization founded by Joseph Rogers, the reforming doctor about whom I'd written, who for years had worked as the Poor Law Medical Officer inside that Workhouse.[11] In seeking new evidence to support the building's preservation, I wondered how far back Dickens's knowledge of the Cleveland Street Workhouse actually went. I began to wonder about the precise location of the blacking factory, and whether it might have been within the parish of St Paul Covent Garden, the parish which had originally built the Workhouse in the eighteenth century, and which was still responsible for running it when Dickens was a factory boy. If the blacking factory had stood inside the Covent Garden parish boundary, I thought it could be possible—even likely—that Dickens had worked alongside parish apprentices sent out from Cleveland

Street, and so could well have heard far more about the place than had previously been supposed.

I had an image in my mind's eye of a plaque marking the site of the blacking factory, somewhere near the Strand. I remembered having been puzzled when I'd first seen it, because of a vague memory that the factory had been right by the River. So I went in search of the plaque. I eventually found it quite high up on a fine late-Victorian building which stands on the south-western corner of the junction of Bedford Street (which runs down to the Strand from Covent Garden Market) and what is now Chandos Place (Chandos Street in Dickens's day). When I found it, it was evident to me that it was an *unofficial* plaque, placed there by someone who loved Dickens, and who wanted to mark one of the most momentous periods of his life: it had not been erected by English Heritage or any of the older 'official' sponsors of the blue plaques of London, such as the London County Council or the Society of Arts. 'Official' plaques in London are nowadays placed only on original buildings, which explains why English Heritage had not erected it: the site might be right, but the building isn't the one Dickens knew. Looking at the plaque critically, as a historian, I knew that I would have to double-check its truth before I could be certain that it was reliably in the correct position; and that meant more research.

This is how one thing leads to another in historical research. Ransacking biographies and bibliographies, the *Surveys* of London, chronologies, volumes of Dickens's letters, I scoured the internet, and pored over maps and microfilms. In the process, it emerged that the factory had changed site during the period of Dickens's employment. It had originally occupied an old building at the bottom of old Hungerford Stairs, right beside the River Thames. Then the manufacturing part of the business was moved uphill to No. 3 Chandos Street, Covent Garden, which the 'unofficial' plaque exactly and correctly marks. Forster quotes a carefully described passage from Dickens himself from the 'autobiographical fragment', which provides the topography pretty near perfectly:

> the blacking-warehouse was removed to Chandos Street, Covent Garden...Next to the shop at the corner of Bedford Street in Chandos Street are two rather old-fashioned houses and shops adjoining one another. They were one then, or thrown into one, for the blacking-business; and had been a butter-shop. Opposite to them was, and is, a public-house, where I got my ale, under these new circumstances. The stones in the street may be smoothed by my small feet going across to it at dinner-time, and back again.[12]

Crossing the same road to take a photograph of the plaque, I realized that—almost two centuries later—there was still a public house opposite.[13]

A careful examination of old maps and other sources concerning the parishes around the Strand revealed that when Dickens was working there, the blacking factory on Chandos Street was situated just north-east of a nest of 'rat-deserted' narrow alleys known as 'Porridge Island' at the back of St Martin's Church, and it was just inside the boundary of the parish of St Paul Covent Garden.[14] The parish boundary passes in a jagged line just behind the backs of all the houses in that row. So it was quite possible that if parish apprentices had been employed in the factory, Dickens could have heard inside stories from the Cleveland Street Workhouse. Each of the Strand parishes had their own workhouse when Dickens was a

FIGURE 2. Chandos Street from Bedford Street, Covent Garden. This is
where, as a child, Dickens worked in the blacking factory window. The factory
is out of view on the left-hand side, a couple of shops further along from the
corner nearest the viewer, having moved here from Hungerford Stairs. The
corner shop may not be the one Dickens knew, but several of the old buildings
opposite would have been familiar to him in the mid-1820s, as part of the
prospect from his workbench. Beyond here, on the left, was a maze of small
streets known as 'Porridge Island'. This street is now called Chandos Place.
Watercolour by T. C. Dibdin, *c*.1851.

factory boy, but you couldn't just walk in and take a look—they
were more like prisons than anything else, and they had their own
fearful shadow. The young Dickens would have been aware of these
places: but had he been threatened with the workhouse when he
was in Chandos Street (and that was a common threat for working-
class children even in the 1950s, as I well recollect) it would not have
been a local one that would have been meant, but the Covent
Garden Workhouse in Cleveland Street.

FIGURE 3. Church Lane, a back alley leading west from the direction of Chandos Street towards St Martin's-in-the-Fields, through the poor district of Porridge Island. Dickens would have explored little alleys like this when he was a factory boy in the Strand area, and he might have enjoyed discovering book-shops like the one shown here. Such alleys were of course places where pick-pockets could make an easy getaway. A few very narrow alleys survive to the east of St Martin's Lane even today, but the Strand improvements swept away Church Lane and most of the warren of Porridge Island. Watercolour by George Scharf, 1828.

With this well-gleaned knowledge of the Covent Garden parish boundary verified, I felt a lot happier about saying that Dickens could well have known more about the threatened workhouse than had previously been thought. But, by that stage something else had caught my eye.

While researching the correct location of the blacking factory, I had wondered where Dickens had been living while he was working there. It turned out that he'd not lodged locally, but first in Camden Town, and then south of London Bridge with a family in Southwark, closer to the Marshalsea Prison. Seeking out his home addresses at that time in his life alerted me to a curious fact: the Dickens family had been extraordinarily itinerant. My notes included at least seventeen different addresses for Dickens before he established an independent home of his own at the age of 22, and there were probably more: I wasn't certain I'd noted down every known one of them, or indeed, that all of them are actually known. Even seventeen made the average stay in any one place only about 15 months. Many of the dates of arrival and removal are still vague or unknown.

The family had moved usually to follow John Dickens's employment but, on occasion, to evade importunate creditors. This itinerancy was an interesting phenomenon in itself, but one of the addresses called double attention to itself, because the family had lived there twice: sometime before and sometime after the Marshalsea Prison episode. The address was: 10 Norfolk Street, Middlesex Hospital.

The Middlesex Hospital part of the address made me sit up, because I knew the Workhouse was close to that hospital. But Norfolk Street was not a street name with which I was familiar. I've lived in London all my life, and have been immersed in London's history for much of that time, so my ignorance of it made me curious. That part of London, Marylebone, has always been an expensive district, so it seemed an unlikely place for this impecunious family to settle. Even more intriguingly, not long before their second stay in Norfolk Street, the family had been evicted from a house in Somers Town, north of King's Cross, which was a poorer and more peripheral part of London. I couldn't figure out how the family could have made the transition to Marylebone.

The current London *A to Z* lists no Norfolk Street in that district now, which explained why I didn't know it. Might it have been bombed or redeveloped, or erased for some ugly housing estate or a busy road? The archives beckoned again, now, urgently. I knew that Cleveland Street itself bordered onto Marylebone, and that since the address included the words 'Middlesex Hospital', there was a good chance that Dickens might have known the area around the Workhouse from having to pass through on his way somewhere. It seemed to me that since the family had lived there twice, there had to be something about the street which brought them back. The two periods of Dickens's life during which he was there—as a child and as a near-adult—seemed to me to be likely to have been significant for reasons of his personal development. At that stage, these were hunches, no more.

Nothing in my wildest dreams prepared me for what came next. Poring over an old map with a magnifying glass in the Westminster Archives, after several false starts, I at last found the words 'Norfolk Street', and nearly fell off my chair. The words were actually placed along the southernmost arm of Cleveland Street itself, the very same street as the Workhouse! Norfolk Street had not been bombed or redeveloped, but simply *renamed*. It formed one boundary of the block occupied by the Middlesex Hospital. What remains of it now lies alongside the eastern flank of the vast field of broken bricks which marks where that great hospital stood for 250 years. Norfolk Street was the same street as Cleveland Street. So, Dickens had inhabited the same street as the Workhouse . . . and twice!

Knowing that I might have found something really important for the Workhouse, at this stage I deliberately restrained my excitement, because it was imperative that everything should be verified. A rigorous double-checking process had to be done, to prove to myself that all the details I had were genuine and really correct, and also to find out if anyone had done all this before. The work had to be reliable: no wishful thinking!

So off I went to the British Library, checked all the sources I could lay my hands on, examined more maps, checked the internet, requested all the biographies I could find, and avidly read them through to see if anyone had done this work before. It turned out that most of Dickens's biographers had paid scant attention to his life in Norfolk Street. If they mentioned it at all it was usually just as Forster had done: describing the street as Dickens's first London home for a brief period in his infancy. The place was apparently unimportant to his biography. Most of Dickens's biographers glide over the early period in a sentence, many of them passing straight from Portsmouth to Chatham, missing out his initial two years in London entirely; they generally ignore the second period in Norfolk Street by focusing elsewhere—looking at his working life, not his domestic setting at all. In this way the period of four or more years Dickens spent in Norfolk Street has become, until now, a peculiar biographical void.

The best work I found for my purposes was Michael Allen's beautiful little book *Charles Dickens' Childhood*, which has a good short chapter on his first stay in Norfolk Street, but sadly stops before the second. But not a single writer could I find who mentioned the proximity of the Workhouse.[15]

At this stage the work felt ready to share, and I decided to take it first to Heidi, the remarkable local woman who had recruited me to the campaign. I took all my evidence down to her home in Fitzrovia. With the maps and the other documents laid out on her kitchen table, I talked her through the whole process behind the discovery, explaining exactly what I'd found. Her excitement rose as my narrative unfolded. We both knew in our bones that this evidence might save the Workhouse.

The exact whereabouts of the house in which the Dickens family had actually lived seemed from existing sources to be No. 22 Cleveland Street, at the corner with Tottenham Street, but once again, it was crucial to be certain. We couldn't go public with information of such importance without having verified it properly for ourselves.

It was clear from the first old map I had examined that Norfolk Street was not lengthy as London streets go, only a block in extent, whereas Cleveland Street was (and still is) a very long street of many blocks and intersections. The western side of what was Norfolk Street—the Middlesex Hospital side—has now completely disappeared, and only a handful of the original houses are left standing on the other side of the way, one of them being No. 22. But there was no plaque to mark it, and we wondered why not. Dickens is so famous that it seemed inexplicable: surely the house would have had a plaque if it really was his old home? Perhaps the attribution of the street number in our sources was wrong, or perhaps there was some other kind of uncertainty.

My colleague and I arranged to meet up again at the Westminster Archives to try to verify exactly where No. 10 Norfolk Street had stood. I can still see her beautiful finger with its long red fingernail pointing to the house number on the old map that the archivist dug out for us, when we asked if there was such a thing as a map of the right historical period which showed house numbers. We had checked the rate-books already and knew that the landlord's name was correct. It turned out that No. 10 really did occupy the corner of Tottenham Street, so the stories were correct: that it is indeed now No. 22 Cleveland Street. Remarkably, the old house is still standing. The landlord in Dickens's time was a man called John Dodd, a cheesemonger and grocer, who kept the corner shop. When we counted, we found that the Workhouse was only nine Georgian doors away.

There was clearly a lot more research to be done concerning the history of the Workhouse and Dickens's residence in Norfolk Street, but these discoveries were enough, we felt, to transform our position from beleaguered small fry to confident and fearless campaigners. We knew that we now had something of inestimable value with which to defend the Workhouse.

Dickens never actually finished the autobiography he had begun, and the manuscript 'autobiographical fragment' remained forever incomplete. This is in many ways a pity, but as Forster knew, its contents re-emerged in a different form. Like other writers before

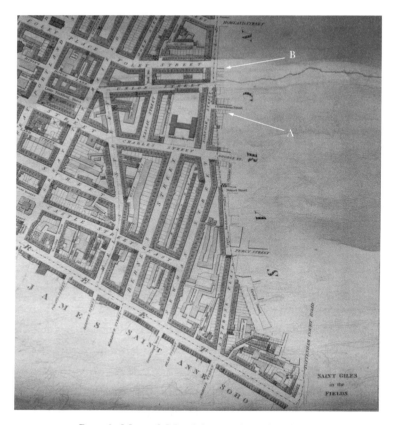

FIGURE 4. Potter's Map of Marylebone, 1832, showing Norfolk Street with all its house numbers. The long boundary—between St Pancras (shown blank on the right) and St Marylebone—runs the length of Cleveland Street, and passes directly behind the rear wall of No. 10 Norfolk Street, on the south-eastern corner of Tottenham and Norfolk Streets (A). The Workhouse itself is not shown, since it stood over the border in St Pancras, but its site is marked with a dark line just opposite Foley Street (B). Peter Potter, Cartographer, 1832.

and since, Dickens drew on his own autobiography in his work, and while transmuting his own life experience into fiction, he concealed it in obvious places. As Forster put it: 'the idea of *David Copperfield*...was to take all the world into his confidence'. Taking 'all the world into his confidence' was not a process of truth-telling in a factual sense, but fiction-spinning. The world grew to know that this extraordinary man had a very wide swathe of observation: that, as his Editor at the *Morning Chronicle* newspaper once observed, Boz 'has spent his time in studying life'.[16]

There must, of course, always be extreme caution about stating as fact that this or that event related by Dickens corresponds with this or that event in his life. But it is known that many episodes in his writings do so correspond. Forster knew this in Dickens's lifetime, and revealed some of what he knew after his death. He says in the extract quoted above that parts of the autobiographical fragment more or less became passages of *David Copperfield*, and that Dickens had disguised himself under cover of his hero.

In the years since Dickens's death, the reading world has continued 'in his confidence', as far as *David Copperfield* is concerned. Yet the silence about Norfolk Street in the autobiographical fragment as reported by Forster meant that at the time we were endeavouring to preserve the Workhouse, no one had thought to mark the house in which Dickens first experienced London, and in which he had spent several important years of his life. The world was 'in his confidence', yet Norfolk Street was an inconsequential location in his biography.

Dickens was never incarcerated inside a workhouse himself, and nor was he ever a pickpocket, so he clearly did not make the same direct transcription from life to tale in *Oliver Twist* as he did later in *David Copperfield*. But where did his passionate writing in that book come from, why did he choose to write on such a painful and powerful topic at such an early stage in his writing life? From where did he acquire his inside knowledge of the workhouse? Could his time living only doors from the Cleveland Street Workhouse have influenced his writing? I think the answer to that last question must be the same as others would give to questions concerning the influences wrought by his time in Chatham or in Chandos Street: it must be yes.

As a young man, Dickens trained himself to become a shorthand writer. His work was to transcribe present events into code, for later decipherment. This may have been a role he sustained in altered form for the rest of his life. Dickens's great inclination was for theatre and fiction, and his own code hid within his splendid fictions, characters, and events re-presented to the public as deeply familiar and satisfying transcriptions of the realities he perceived around him.

Fiction is never a straightforward transcription of reality, and great swathes of his work were replayings and confections drawn from his own imaginative life. Yet tucked in amongst his writings there are nuggets of autobiographical transcription, transformed into tales, or elements of tales. Dickens's transformations of reality take many forms, and numerous critics have expended great and unremitting efforts to decipher and interpret the nature of his genius. Biographers have spent their own lifetimes pulling together hints and images to help understand and elucidate his life and work.

Dickens's tales play knowing games with the reader's credulity, and we read them and enjoy them knowing that his stories are stories; they tell only so much, and take the reader into the author's confidence only so far.

In reality, Dickens was a very private and rather secretive person, who came from a private and secretive family. It is said that after their period of incarceration in the Marshalsea Debtors' Prison the family never spoke of it, that Dickens told no one about either the prison or the blacking factory, and that his own children were surprised to learn of the story after his death.[17]

At certain points in his life Dickens burned vast quantities of private letters and other personal materials. The interminable roll-call of the letters he destroyed or caused others to destroy, which is recounted in the opening pages of the great Pilgrim Edition of his collected letters, reads like a long wail of scholarly dismay. Until the mid-twentieth century it was not widely known that towards the end of his life Dickens had a long-term relationship with the actress Ellen Ternan, and even today, whether or not they lost a child is a matter of dispute. His private life Dickens wished to remain strictly private.

Yet we also know that Dickens certainly used autobiographical materials in his work, and moreover that he often presented such materials to the public (as in *David Copperfield*) as if they were in his own voice, inviting or enticing identification. His playful art of whimsical confabulation is part of the reason Dickens has been and is so greatly loved. Readers often become deeply involved in his writings not just because they are compelling and satisfying fictions full of brilliant observation, indignation, remarkable imagery, good-heartedness, and wit, but also because they present rich and many-layered fictions, which can engender processes of recognition and anticipated identification in his readers.

Readers' reactions often include the desire to know more about the material basis for the stories, especially since so many of them intriguingly have apparently real places at their heart. Numbers of his locations—like Seven Dials, or the City of London Guildhall—appear in his writings as real places, which his contemporaries would personally have known, or would have known genuinely existed, either from having witnessed them or by repute, perhaps from factual writing, such as guidebooks. The stories which include such locations depend upon a stratum of public knowledge and understanding about the real world which his readers shared, and can still share today.[18] Places described in Dickens's books—such as Jacob's Island, an important location in *Oliver Twist*—often have a solid topographical basis, which Dickens was careful to research and, occasionally, forthright to defend.[19] In other instances, his topography is deliberately vague, or concealed in some way. In *Pickwick Papers*, Dickens introduces his coverage of Mr Pickwick's record of the election at that puzzlingly unknown place called Eatanswill with the following important words:

> Mr. Pickwick, with that anxious desire to abstain from giving offence to any, and with those delicate feelings for which all who knew him well know he was so eminently remarkable, purposely substituted a fictitious designation, for the real name of the place in which his observations were made.[20]

Dickens is describing his own practice here. He, too, often disguises by renaming, or by a process of deliberate transposition—lifting a place from its actual location into some new geographical position, so as to preserve its personality, but alter its identity. When he wrote this passage Dickens was still signing his works with his pen name 'Boz', and clearly gained writerly pleasure by sharing with his readers the open secret that Mr Pickwick gives real places fictitious names, just so that they know. These in-joke transformations partake of his love of the flying carpet from the *Arabian Nights*, and sometimes more seriously of the work of William Hogarth. As one commentator has noted: 'This was part of Boz's system; he supplied the thing accurately enough and the locality, but shifted or transposed the name—generally by design.'[21]

A very brief but characteristic instance has the Pickwickians on a fast coach galloping towards Dingley Dell at Christmas time. Rattling through ill-paved streets, they are about to change horses at an inn-yard, when:

> Mr. Winkle, who sits at the extreme edge [of the coach's roof], with one leg dangling in the air, is nearly precipitated into the street, as the coach twists round the sharp corner by the cheese-monger's shop, and turns into the market-place.[22]

That sharp corner could have been any shop—a bookshop or a barber's—but it's a cheesemonger's, like Mr Dodd's, which has the air of a kindly in-joke for the friends of 'Boz', because he has just been reminiscing about family Christmases, and has only just noticed a family throwing an extra log on the fire in preparation for their father's return.[23] Examples of this kind arise repeatedly in Dickens's work, and have been noticed by readers and scholars over the years.[24] Indeed, a great deal of writing on Dickens concerns itself with the topography of his novels, such as, for example, the actual route of Little Nell's final journey in the *Old Curiosity Shop*, or the real location of Dickens's original for the graveyard in *Bleak House*, which are likely to be difficult to trace because they are from the geography of his imagination.

But Dickens also sometimes mentions places he knew as a child quite straightforwardly. He had been living away from Norfolk Street for almost thirty years, when on 1 January 1859 he published an essay in his own magazine *Household Words* on the theme of New Year's Day. The exchange of gifts often traditionally took place on that day when he was a child, rather than on Christmas Day, and Dickens described in some detail being taken on a childhood walk by a rather formidable elderly woman in black mourning. The object of the journey was a visit to the 'Soho Bazaar', which was a well-known semi-charitable indoor emporium or hypermarket of many stalls, selling a wide variety of handmade goods. It was situated at the north-west corner of London's Soho Square, near to the junction of Oxford Street and Tottenham Court Road. The essay typifies Dickens's style in so far as it ranges widely around its theme in a series of entertaining episodes. At its heart is a memorable description of this childhood excursion. These are Dickens's own words:

> When I was a little animal revolting to the sense of sight (for I date from the period when small boys had a dreadful high-shouldered sleeved strait-waistcoat put upon them by their keepers, over which their dreadful little trousers were buttoned tight, so that they roamed about disconsolate, with their hands in their pockets, like dreadful little pairs of tongs that were vainly looking for the rest of the fire-irons); when I was this object of just contempt and horror to all well-constituted minds...when I was this

exceedingly uncomfortable and disreputable father of my present self, I remember to have been taken, upon a New Year's Day, to the Bazaar in Soho Square, London, to have a present bought for me. A distinct impression yet lingers in my soul that a grim and unsympathetic old personage of the female gender, flavoured with musty dry lavender, dressed in black crape, and wearing a pocket in which something clinked at my ear as we went along, conducted me on this occasion to the World of Toys. I remember to have been incidentally escorted a little way down some conveniently retired street diverging from Oxford Street, for the purpose of being shaken; and nothing has ever slaked the burning thirst for vengeance awakened in me by this female's manner of insisting upon wiping my nose herself (I had a cold and a pocket-handkerchief), on the screw principle. For many years I was unable to excogitate the reason why she should have undertaken to make me a present. In the exercise of a matured judgement, I have now no doubt that she had done something bad in her youth, and that she took me out as an act of expiation.

Nearly lifted off my legs by this adamantine woman's grasp of my glove (another fearful invention of those dark ages—a muffler, and fastened at the wrist like a handcuff), I was haled through the Bazaar. . . . I was put before an expanse of toys, apparently about a hundred and twenty acres in extent, and was asked what I would have to the value of half-a-crown? Having first selected every object at half-a-guinea, and then staked all the aspirations of my nature on every object at five shillings, I hit, as a last resource, upon a Harlequin's Wand—painted particoloured, like Harlequin himself.

Although of a highly hopeful and imaginative temperament, I had no fond belief that the possession of this talisman would enable me to change Mrs. Pipchin at my side into anything agreeable. When I tried the effect of the wand upon her, behind her bonnet, it was rather as a desperate experiment founded on the conviction that she could change into nothing worse, than with any latent hope that she would change into something better. Howbeit, I clung to the delusion that when I got home I should do something magical with this wand; and I did not resign all hope of it until I had, by many trials, proved the wand's total incapacity. It had no effect on the staring obstinacy of a rocking-horse; it produced no live Clown out of the hot beefsteak-pie at dinner; it could not even influence the minds of my honoured parents to the extent of suggesting the decency and propriety of their giving me an invitation to sit up to supper.

The failure of this wand is my first very memorable association with a New Year's Day.[25]

I have given this passage at length here because it is an important piece of reminiscence and storytelling from Dickens's pen, which relates to a real place in the vicinity of his first childhood home in London. From his description of his own height (the woman nearly lifted him by his muffler, her pocket was near his ear) Dickens was probably quite a small child when this experience occurred, which seems to date it to the family's time in Norfolk Street, when he was between the ages of almost 3 to almost 5.

The lady in black, Michael Allen has suggested, is likely to have been Dickens's paternal grandmother, who lived just around the corner from the Soho Bazaar. To visit her at home would have involved being taken for a walk down Norfolk Street, crossing Charles Street (now Mortimer Street) and passing down the entire length of Newman Street in the direction of the tower of St Anne, Soho, still visible today above the houses. Across Oxford Street, a little way east, another Charles Street led south into Soho Square.

Grandma Dickens lived a few doors further along Oxford Street towards St Giles's Church.

Dickens refers to the woman as a Mrs Pipchin, and it seems to be widely understood among Dickens scholars that the character of that name in *Dombey and Son* was based upon a Mrs Roylance, a widow of the family's acquaintance, with whom Dickens later lodged miserably for a while when he was in the blacking factory. But the discovery that Dickens's grandmother was living only a few doors from Soho Square at that time means it is much more likely that she was the person in question. Whoever she was, and however much of her description is subsequent elaboration, her punitive manner of wiping his nose certainly feels real enough.

Oxford Street was a busy shopping street, and the difficulty of navigating it safely with an active and perhaps wayward child may well have been what provoked the shaking in the by-street. The Soho Bazaar had first opened its doors in the spring of 1816, so the date of this expedition is most likely to have been at the turn of the next new year in 1817, when Charles Dickens was nearly 5, perhaps only days before the whole family left London for Sheerness and Chatham.

This is the description by an adult of a childhood memory. One of the most interesting things about it is the level of detail the child apparently noticed and the adult recollected: the smell of the woman's clothes, the clink in her pocket, the humiliation of being shaken in a by-street, his desire for the more expensive toys, and for vengeance. How much of this is the *post hoc* elaboration of a man who was by that time the father of a large family himself is difficult to tell, but the atmosphere of this journey, the rapid revision of expectations, and the character of the relationship between old woman and young boy has the feel of authentic memory. The sheer powerlessness of the child in the hands of this curiously munificent but aggressive adult is a strong theme of the essay, along with the impotence of magic to improve matters: despite the child's concentrated investment in the power of the wish.

Beneath the reminiscence, we are permitted to see that this is fundamentally a lucky child. Although the piece makes evident the fact that Dickens's parents were not 'carriage-folk', he presents the boy as well dressed, he is taken individually to have half-a-crown spent upon him, he visits as a purchaser the emporium of toys exhibited for sale in the Soho Bazaar, he already knows who Harlequin is, and there is both a rocking horse and a beef-steak pie at home. When the essay was written, the child had survived the high infant mortality of London to be able to reminisce over forty years later about these events from the safe retrospect of his own journal. Though clearly a child deprived of much personal agency—and taken off-street to be given a good shake if he exhibited any—the young Charles Dickens as presented here was emphatically not deprived in the sense the young Oliver Twist was.

So where did Dickens's empathy with the plight of the bereft orphan workhouse boy come from? Might he have witnessed or overheard something at an early age, which made him ponder his own fortunate position, the blighted possibilities of poorer lives, experiences more bitter than his own?

CHAPTER 2

Vicinity

ENVIRONS OF GENTILITY, ENVIRONS OF POVERTY

W HEN DICKENS LOOKED back from adulthood to recall his first experience of London, he associated it with snow: 'it lived also in the child's memory that they had come away from Portsea in the snow. Their home, shortly after, was again changed.'[1] This is Forster's version of Dickens's written recollections, and the way it is composed conveys the impression that the family had not stayed very long. But it was actually a full two years before Dickens's father was transferred away again.

Charles Dickens was almost 3 in January 1815 when the family first arrived in London, and when they left in January 1817 he was nearly 5 years of age. These are important years in any child's life: the years a child becomes aware, begins to develop an understanding of the world, learns to read, write, and draw, begins schooling. Readers of Dickens are aware how pre-eminently important the years of childhood are in his work. In these years, too, Dickens's baby sister, Letitia, was born at 10 Norfolk Street, and (unlike his little baby brother who had died the previous year) proved sturdy enough to survive. There is no reference to the arrival of this new baby in Forster's rendering of the autobiographical fragment, and no recollections whatever of the period the family spent in Norfolk Street. So this chapter looks at what Dickens might have been aware of on the street and in London more generally between the years 1815 and 1817.

We have seen how alert and aware the child Dickens was when he visited the Soho Bazaar, near the end of this first stay in Norfolk Street, and how much he was able to recall years later, when he came to write about the experience of childhood in his own magazines. Although detailed memories from these years have not come down to us via Forster, echoes of them surely supply detail, colour, and sensibility to other of Dickens's writings. I have often wondered, for example, where the wallpaper and flooring were to be found which Dickens describes in the perception of the boy in *Dombey and Son*:

> He loved to be alone; and in those short intervals when he was not occupied with his books, liked nothing so well as wandering about the house by himself, or sitting on the stairs, listening to the great clock in the hall. He was intimate with all the paperhanging in the house; saw things that no one else saw in the patterns; found out miniature tigers and lions running up the bedroom walls, and squinting faces leering in the squares and diamonds of the floorcloth.[2]

Dickens has a facility for relating experiences, which feel so truthful and authentic that it is not difficult to believe that he is remembering his own experiences and insights as a child. It is well known that

Dickens surprised his own family with the vividness of his early recollections.[3] The memorable clarity of this passage from *Dombey* reminds me very much of some particular lino in the flat where I spent my own childhood, where I remember noticing all sorts of images (especially faces) when I was small. I do not think such experiences are unusual in childhood. Dickens places himself as if his eyes are those of the child in the story, seeing those very things, recognizing that no one else perceived them but the child himself, and he somehow relates the experience in such a way that he almost places us there too, with our own child eyes, imagining that kind of child intimacy with one's surroundings and one's own pattern-making perceptions, forming dragons and faces on a wall in our own adult imaginations in close sympathy with the child in the book. The intimacy of the perception is put into words (and such words!) which encourage the reader to recollect those sorts of sensations, in amongst our own memories, to identify and sympathize with the fictional child of the story, almost to see as he does for a moment or two in the power of a recollection almost our own. Henry James described Dickens's power as that of creating near-hallucination, but I think it lies rather in evocation/suggestion, a form of persuasion.[4] We may not see the wallpaper, but we remember the sensation he describes. Somehow, he activates the mind's imaginative eye.

Most grown-ups have largely forgotten these sensations until reminded, but part of Dickens's singularity as a writer is the adept way he both remembers and reminds. I mention this passage not to suggest that Dickens saw such wallpaper or such floor coverings in Mr Dodd the cheesemonger's house at Norfolk Street. There is no scope for any certainty at all on this score—even if wallpaper archaeology were to reveal the early wall-coverings of Norfolk Street—and especially not when we remind ourselves how many homes the Dickens family actually lived in. But, that said, Dickens was a child for two years in Norfolk Street, and he wrote later with a child's perception of such things, so it must remain a possibility.

Given Dickens's ability to recollect and portray events and images from memories laid down before the family's years in Norfolk Street, and the boasted robustness of his memory, these years of his childhood should have been noteworthy, especially as the district itself looks to have been important to Dickens on several counts, and the times in which he was there were memorable for other reasons. Why these childhood years in Norfolk Street were left blank is intriguing.

Within a month or so of the family's arrival in London, for example, shortly after Dickens's third birthday, in early March 1815 the alarming news spread that Napoleon Bonaparte had escaped from exile in Elba, had cleared Italy, and was amassing a new army in France. Cartoons in London announced in alarm: 'BONEY BROKE LOOSE!'[5] War was declared later that month. Having believed Napoleon safely out of harm's way, and having already celebrated the end of the long years of war, the rest of Europe had now to remobilize hurriedly, and then await—with fearful anticipation—the military showdown that must come. This tense time was the period later known as the 'Hundred Days', which culminated in June 1815 with the battle of Waterloo. The outcome was not at all a foregone conclusion.

Dickens's father was employed as a clerk in the Navy Pay Office in Somerset House, and would probably have been personally involved in some of the urgent preparations to ship men, money, and equipment out to Belgium, and it is not unlikely that some of this would have been talked about at home, either because he was working late nights, or because of the general level of anxiety. Prospects for the future if either side won—foreign invasion as against a prospective slump in work—might have been mulled over by Mr and Mrs Dickens. How much of all this a small child might have grasped is doubtful, but the rising tension probably communicated itself.

As soon as news of the victory arrived from the battlefield, London was engulfed in celebration. A 'general illumination' on the night of Friday, 23 June 1815 saw candles set in every window. It is very likely that candles would have been lit at 10 Norfolk Street, the shutters folded back, and little Charles held up, or stood up on a chair, to gaze down from an upper floor at the gleaming lights in the windows of the houses across the road, and perhaps further afield.

After his defeat, Napoleon had made for the western coast of France, hoping to embark for America. But the folly of the idea becoming evident, in July 1815 he surrendered to the captain of the blockading British flagship *Bellerophon*, and was shipped first to Plymouth Sound, and subsequently (without having set foot in Britain) to the distant island of St Helena. Celebrations of the peace in Europe were still continuing in London the following January, and again on the anniversary of the battle in June 1816, with parades and church services. To the delight of many, Napoleon's great carriage captured at Waterloo was put on public display in Piccadilly, and was crawled over by all and sundry. Lord Byron ordered a close copy of it to be made by a London coach-master, and travelled across war-torn Europe in it during the *Frankenstein* summer of 1816.[6] George Cruikshank's cartoon of the Piccadilly exhibit is entitled 'A Swarm of English Bees hiving in the Imperial Carriage … A Peep at the Spoils of Ambition', and both he and Thomas Rowlandson portrayed a level of excitement and hilarity which feels like the elation of victory, as well as the indulgence of curiosity. It seems odd that Dickens does not appear to have reported remembering anything of this atmosphere in London when he was a child.

Then there was the weather. The year after Waterloo was known as 'the year without a summer'. The extraordinary weather of 1816 is now thought to have been caused by a volcanic eruption on the other side of the world, resulting in below-average temperatures (and very fine sunsets) for quite some time. It is perhaps unsurprising that Dickens recollected the snow, which probably merged in his memory with this chilly, dull year in London.

The lack of sunlight prefigured other forms of dearth. Catastrophic harvests across Europe (and indeed the rest of the world) brought food shortages and high food prices. The government had recently enacted the Corn Laws, which kept prices artificially high for English farmers, and slowed imports: so prices rose considerably, generating inflation at a time when wages were static or falling. The final end of the Napoleonic Wars in 1815 brought floods of demobbed soldiers back to London, many of them wounded or disabled, seeking work, begging on the street, or claiming an honourable subsistence, and of course in the aftermath of Waterloo, thousands of women discovered themselves widows, and their children fatherless. Along with the high food prices and poor weather, the end of the war brought with it an industrial slump, as demand vanished for battle supplies like iron for armaments and textiles for uniforms. Industrial districts were pitched into recession, and workers from these places often found their way to London, seeking work where artisans were already unemployed. Famine in Ireland also swelled existing communities in London, such as the district around St Giles's. Poverty, hardship, and hunger became widespread.

For the moment, the Dickens family was in the fortunate position of having a breadwinner in full employment. Charles's father would have had to walk daily to Somerset House and back through the heart of Regency London. Streets a modern Londoner might use nowadays did not then exist: in 1815 New Oxford Street, Charing Cross Road, Kingsway, and Trafalgar Square had yet to be created, and the Nash 'improvements' to London's fabric—such as the construction of the new Regent Street—were only just under way. Walking was how most people navigated London: there were no buses, no railways of any kind, and the old hackney cabs were costly. Central London was densely inhabited, and there were clusters of really bad slums, the character of which encouraged most people to avoid them—districts Jonas Hanway had described as 'a kind of separate town or district, calculated for the reception of the darkest and most dangerous enemies to society'.[7]

We do not know what route John Dickens habitually took to work, but the quickest way from Norfolk Street would have been through the rough and poor districts of High Street St Giles and down the length of Drury Lane, or down the less seedy Castle Street (now part of Charing Cross Road) or St Martin's Lane and along the Strand. It may have been his parents' knowledge of St Giles and Seven Dials, and family stories of earlier 'tumults', which intrigued Charles Dickens with those districts: it was in St Giles that forty members of the 'republic of thieves' had been captured in 1780 at the end of the Gordon Riots, fighting among themselves over their looted booty.[8] That period, like sedan chairs and ruffles, was still very much in living memory in 1815, and it would not be at all surprising if the young Dickens had heard tales of it. His novel *Barnaby Rudge* certainly has the feel of local knowledge, and parts of the book take place in the fields beneath what later became Cleveland Street.

They went up Parliament Street, past Saint Martin's church, and away by St Giles's to Tottenham Court Road, at the back of which, upon the western side, was then a place called the Green Lanes. This was a retired spot, not of the choicest kind, leading into the fields. Great heaps of ashes; stagnant pools, overgrown with rank grass and duckweed; broken turnstiles; and the upright posts of palings long since carried off for firewood, which menaced all heedless walkers with their jagged and rusty nails; were the leading features of the landscape: while here and there a donkey, or a ragged horse, tethered to a stake, and cropping off a wretched meal from the coarse stunted turf, were quite in keeping with the scene, and would have suggested (if the houses had not done so sufficiently, of themselves) how very poor the people were who lived in the crazy huts adjacent, and how fool-hardy it might prove for one who carried money, or wore decent clothes, to walk that way alone, unless by daylight.[9]

FIGURE 5. Roque's Map of London *c.*1725, showing 'The Green Lane' (where Cleveland Street now runs) and the fields and farms of eastern Marylebone and Bloomsbury, before the Middlesex Hospital and the Covent Garden Workhouse were built. The map pre-dates the New Road (now the Marylebone and Euston Roads) and the modern laying-out of most of the streets and squares. John Rocque, Cartographer, *c.*1725.

Whether the adult Dickens knew about the character of the fields beneath Cleveland Street from local information or folklore, or recollected descriptions overheard in childhood, or transposed observations of similar neighbourhoods of his own era, he had evidently pondered what the area had been like before he'd arrived there. He may well have known that the local militia had stored its arms and ammunition in the lobby of the new workhouse in 1779–80 during the Gordon Riots, and had vacated the space when the riots were over.[10] Dickens was certainly firm in his conviction in the book that the story is based on fact.[11] No organized police service existed in London in 1815, apart from the local parish watchmen, though there was a watch-house on Cleveland Street when the Dickens family lived there.[12] Street lighting was variable—gas light in Pall Mall and soon other major streets, but oil lamps elsewhere. John Dickens would have had to be careful of the route he took returning to Norfolk Street at night. He might possibly have chosen a longer but more familiar way home, such as through Soho and up Newman Street.

The district the Dickens family settled upon for their first home in London is worth examining, as its character very much suited the family's fortunes. Cleveland Street's special geography is important, as it marked (and still marks) a major London boundary. A long-standing historic demarcation passed right down the centre of the street's entire length, then turned south-eastwards at Norfolk Street, to run behind the houses at an angle towards Rathbone Place. The rear wall of 10 Norfolk Street was part of this demarcation. The boundary separated the ancient parishes of St Marylebone and St Pancras, and demarcated landed estates, too.

FIGURE 6. The St Pancras Parish marker 'St P x P 1830' (or 1839?) fixed on 49 Tottenham Street, the house which directly abuts the back of Mr Dodd's house, No. 10 Norfolk Street. The wall on the left here is in St Pancras Parish, whereas that on the right, which is the rear wall of Dickens's old home, is in the parish of St Marylebone. Photographed by the author 2011.

Dickens's old home was on the Marylebone side, while the adjacent house at the back still carries the old parish boundary marker demonstrating that the edge of St Pancras passed right along the Dickens family's back wall.

After passing behind Norfolk Street and down the length of Rathbone Place, this boundary arrived by a diagonal just above the important junction now known as Centre Point, at the intersection of Oxford Street, Tottenham Court Road, and High Street St Giles's. There, a number of parish boundaries converged: Dickens's own parish of St Marylebone met with St Pancras (the parish directly behind his home), St Anne Soho, south of Oxford Street, and St Giles in the Fields and St George's Bloomsbury to the south and east.

Standing back from the map, one can see that the part of St Marylebone in which the Dickens family lived almost touched St Giles's, one of those places many people would not care to walk, and would warn servants to avoid: a parish famous for its desperate poverty, overcrowding, high mortality, crime, and prostitution, with historic associations as the location of Gin Lane, and (in the days before hangings were removed to Newgate) of the public house where condemned prisoners had their final drink before execution at Tyburn. The contiguity of these parishes perhaps helped keep this eastern part of Marylebone affordable for marginally viable families like the Dickenses.

Oxford Street itself had previously been known as the Tyburn Road, or the Oxford Road, and was the major thoroughfare giving access and egress from London to the west. By the early nineteenth century it and Tottenham Court Road were busy shopping streets, known especially for furniture and fabrics. The Dickens scholar Michael Allen has done careful work on this locality, and suggests reasons why the district should have been highly memorable to Dickens: he has shown that the Dickens family had close relatives who were shopkeepers on Oxford Street, near this junction of thoroughfares and parishes. John Dickens's older brother, William, ran a coffee-shop on the south side of Oxford Street at No. 35, very close to Charles Street, Soho Square, and a cousin had a draper's shop directly opposite.[13] It now seems fairly clear that Dickens was the child of Londoners, and that both his parents already knew the

region of London known as Marylebone well when they arrived in
Norfolk Street: that they each arrived with local foreknowledge. On
his mother's side, the Barrow family had local connections in eastern
Marylebone. One of her brothers lived nearby on Berners Street,
which runs next to Newman Street between Oxford Street and the
Middlesex Hospital, and her great-aunt Charlton ran a lodging
house in the same street.

Dickens's father, John Dickens, had been born and christened in Marylebone. Dickens's paternal grandparents, from
the servant aristocracy, had been settled thereabouts for years:
butler and housekeeper for the Crewes, an aristocratic family
considered among the cream of high society, whose town house
was on Grosvenor Street, one of the most upmarket streets of
Mayfair, between Grosvenor Square and Bond Street.[14] Neither
John Dickens, nor his son Charles, ever knew Grandfather
Dickens, as he had died very soon after his younger son John
had been born. But at the time the Dickens family was in
Norfolk Street Grandmother Dickens was still alive and living
locally in her retirement with her eldest son William, above his
Oxford Street coffee-shop. She later died there in the summer
of 1824, while John Dickens was being held in the Marshalsea
Debtors' Prison.

It is not known if the disgrace of his imprisonment for debt accel-
erated her death, or if she had ever conveyed to her little grandson
her own fears of ending up in a workhouse. Nor do we have any
knowledge of her funeral. Not a great deal is known about her, or
the nature of the relationship she had with her youngest son John,
but it seems quite likely that in that department she was braced for
disappointment. She thought him lazy.[15] Her stern attitude towards

her young grandson Charles (if it was indeed she that bought him the Harlequin wand) may have been associated with her estimate of his parents. Yet she is also said to have been a wonderful and a compelling storyteller.[16]

Grandmother Dickens must have been well aware of her own son John's character, so she would perhaps have been shocked but not surprised at the family scandal, which had erupted soon after his marriage, associated with her son's new father-in-law.[17] When John Dickens had married Elizabeth Barrow in the summer of 1809 at the church of St Mary-le-Strand near Somerset House, everything had appeared hopeful.[18] Elizabeth's father, Charles Barrow, occupied a position of high status and trust: 'Chief Conductor and Paymaster of Contingencies' in the Navy Pay Office.[19] The son of top servants married a top civil servant's daughter. But even before the first of the young couple's many children arrived, Charles Barrow had fled into exile abroad, having been discovered by the Admiralty to have embezzled over five and a half thousand pounds, a colossal sum, nearly four hundred times a woman house servant's annual wage.[20] At that time, sentences of death were routinely handed down for far smaller thefts.[21] Charles Barrow's sudden disgrace was probably a very great shock to the young couple, who were now thrown entirely on their own resources for the future, John Dickens losing an important supporter within the career structure of the naval civil service, and Elizabeth Dickens losing the prospect of paternal financial assistance in the event of difficulty, and any possibility of a legacy later. Charles Dickens was their second child, born into a family trying to live down the stigma and shame of scandal. He was named after this fugitive grandfather. How much he knew of this as a child remains unclear, nor do we know when he learned of it, as Forster did not discuss the matter at all.

Despite the stain on the family's reputation, Dickens's parents had social pretensions. It cannot have been easy for them to settle in lodgings in a London street like Norfolk Street without misgivings. They had previously occupied a modest house; here they were in lodgings above a shop. Yet at the christening in the Old Marylebone church where he himself had been baptized, John Dickens signed the register characterizing himself as a 'Gentleman'.[22] Examining the possible alternatives to such a status, it's clear that it would not have suited his temperament to register as anything less genteel. Of course, we do not know who decided upon the categories—other fathers on the same pages were listed as: Attorney, Esqr. (esquire), Labr. (labourer), Mechc. (mechanic), Schoolmaster, Servt. (servant), and Victualler (publican). Some of these are occupational descriptions, but 'clerk' does not feature in Mr Dickens's description. 'Esquire' and 'Gentleman' were not simply courtesy titles at that time: each had social meaning, too. An *esquire* was historically a male attendant upon a knight, and a *gentleman* someone of high birth and dignity, someone belonging to the gentry. Both designations implied membership of one of the professions, real social status, or a private income. In reality Dickens's father had none of these.

A radical strand in English culture held that *anyone* might be considered a gentleman—'When Adam delved and Eve span, who was then the Gentleman?'—and this may be where Dickens's father reasoned from, but it is equally possible that he had absorbed the social aspirations and loyalties of his own parents. Upper servants notoriously identify with their employers' values, and the Crewes were a very eminent Whig aristocratic family.[23] There is something valiant in the self-delusion of the fatherless child of an upper servant who presents himself as a Gentleman, but also an element of pathos in the rhetoric of his social posturing. The Marshalsea episode makes clear that John Dickens's income never matched his aspirations.

There is poignancy in Dickens's depiction of his parents as Mr and Mrs Micawber in *David Copperfield*, making the rhetorical best of every adverse circumstance. But he was able to smile only at a distance: Dickens himself shared the family sensitivity about their real social circumstances. Many local people gave their address as 'Norfolk Street, Middlesex Hospital', but, as we shall see, he—when he later had his own calling card especially printed—chose to give his address as '10 Norfolk Street, Fitzroy Square'—associating his street address with the elegance of Fitzroy Square at the very northernmost end of Cleveland Street, almost half a mile away, rather than with the hospital whose flank wall stood behind the houses opposite. In later life Charles Dickens rejected the pretence of gentility derived from his parents, and requested in his will that his tomb bear the simple inscription of his name in plain English letters, 'without the addition of "Mr" or "Esquire"'.[24] Yet to the end of his life he had remained unforthcoming about his family's two eras in Norfolk Street. Was this social insecurity, or something else?

London's social geography is a difficult thing to map, not only because real change occurs over time, but the attitudes which characterize an area as desirable or not also vary. People who know London well are aware of the way in which socially conscious inhabitants (and estate agents) concern themselves about addresses, which can often be matched very precisely to social classifications, or aspirations. There has only ever been one serious attempt to map London from this point of view, by the social investigator Charles Booth in the late nineteenth century. He and his teams of researchers chronicled and charted the social status of London's inhabitants, and presented their results using colour-coding to show the distribution of its wealthiest and its most desolate crime-ridden streets, in gold and black respectively. In between there were shades of red darkening into purple and blue, showing the various mixes of middle, lower-middle, working, and casual labour-ing classes.

Had such colouring been applied to a map in Dickens's child-hood, Norfolk Street would certainly have been 'mixed', and prob-ably blushing towards the purple end of the red spectrum. What such colourings could not reveal was whether an area was going up- or down-market at any one time, or whether—like Norfolk Street—it was never likely to rise. A street with a workhouse in it would never be a 'good' address: could never be elegant, stylish, chic, or fashionable. Just to the south, Newman and Berners Streets preserved a little of their faded gentility, tinted with the raffishness of the artists and the professionalism of the doctors who congregated there; but Norfolk Street ran alongside a hospital, and led to a workhouse. It could never be other than an unexceptional eighteenth-century London street of smallish houses over smallish shops, with few grounds for pretension among its inhabitants.

To be sure, there were some extremely wealthy districts within a few minutes' walk. Cleveland Street was a border area, occupying the ancient fault line between the great manorial farms of Maryle-bone, Tottenham Court, and Bloomsbury. It served as a divide between Bloomsbury to the east, with its fine housing for the professional classes around the British Museum on Bedford and Bloomsbury Squares, and the socially elite district of Marylebone to the west, which boasted Cavendish and Portman Squares. Directly south of Oxford Street was the lively trading district of Soho, while to the south-west was Mayfair, with its aristocratic settlements around Hanover, Grosvenor, and Berkeley Squares right down to St James's. Cleveland Street was a sort of no man's land on such a map; on one map I came across, the street even lacks a name.

During the family's first stay in Norfolk Street when Dickens was small, the Regent's Canal was nearing completion to the north, running through the farms and pasturelands of Middlesex, and plans for a new street linking St James's Palace to the Marylebone Road and the Crown Lands at Marylebone Park were just coming off the drawing board. The clearance of land for the construction of Oxford Circus and the area to its north was probably going on while young Dickens was in Norfolk Street. A London map of 1814 shows the original street pattern, while one of 1817 shows the whole of the new street superimposed, and the old mansion of Foley House cleared for the building of Portland Place. William Henry Wills, who worked with Dickens for many years on his magazines *Household Words* and *All the Year Round*, was two years older than Dickens, and could remember the houses along Regent Street still in their scaffolding.[25] By the time the family returned again to Norfolk Street in 1829 when Dickens was a young man, both the Regent's Canal and Regent Street were completed, and the lovely Nash church of All Souls in Langham Place showed to good advantage in the guidebooks.

But the rural hinterland of London wasn't far away. Thomas De Quincey described being able to look up the long straight streets running north from Oxford Street to the countryside. He would 'gaze from Oxford Street up every avenue in succession which pierces through the heart of Mary-le-bone to the fields and the woods... travelling with my eyes up the long vistas which lay part in light and part in shade'.[26]

Little Charles was probably taken for walks in all directions from Norfolk Street, but probably avoiding St Giles. He might well have been taken northwards, towards these fields, to look at the landscaping which would soon transform the old pastures and cow-folds of Marybone Park Farm into the Regent's Park.[27] In later life Dickens lived opposite one of the gates into the Regent's Park, and he probably recollected what it had been like in the making, living with past and present before him.

FIGURE 7. Portland Place, Marylebone, a rather arid but elite street. The view looks north up towards Dupper's Field at the street's northernmost end, and the farmland beyond, which would shortly be landscaped to become Regent's Park. The image dates from 1815, when the Dickens family was first living in Norfolk Street, only a few blocks east of here. Aquatint after a watercolour by T. H. Shepherd.

The adult Dickens covered great distances on foot, but we do not know whether this was a habit that originated when he was small, or how far afield he might have been taken as a child. It is certainly likely that he was taken for outings to Primrose Hill, as local children still are, to look down over the heart of London from that wonderful height. A local ballad, 'The Middlesex Farmer' described the nightingales and larks of its surrounding fields, and the splendid view from there:

> From the top of the primrose hill
> How many proud buildings I see,
> Let the lords of 'em envy who will,
> My ease and my cottage for me.[28]

Despite the recent rapid encroachment of London, parts of the area within a brief walking distance of Norfolk Street were still quite rural in 1815. Haymakers worked in fields near Baker Street into the 1820s, and beyond the New Road (now the Marylebone Road) to the north, lanes still intersected pastures and farms which would have been in the process of disappearing by the time the family returned to the district, and mostly gone within a generation.[29] Walking or being pulled in a little go-cart or chariot around the nearer vicinity would have given the little Dickens a grasp of the contrast between Cleveland Street and some of the more austere, more arid genteel streets in the neighbourhood, like Harley Street, where he later housed Mr Merdle, the crooked financier in *Little Dorrit*. Quite a number of exclusive gated roads existed in Marylebone and Bloomsbury: these were supervised streets from which through-traffic was excluded, and 'trade' vehicles and other wheeled visitors (even funerals) and hawkers were barred, unless permission had been granted from a specific address in the vicinity. Gower Street was one such gated road, and others kept the great squares—like Bedford, Mecklenburgh, Harrington, Oakley, Tavistock—exclusive. Few of these protected areas survive in London now, but one can get a sense of their dignified exclusivity by glancing at the gated road known as Millionaire's Row which borders the western extremity of Kensington Gardens today. The Outer Circle at Regent's Park remains gated, even today, and although traffic is allowed through the gates (no 'trade' vehicles) the gates are still closed at night. Both wide highways are lined with magnificent houses, and each preserves that sense of unhurried and decorous wealth to which other gated roads aspired.[30]

Such streets, one hopes, yielded large donors to the medical charities of Marylebone, although many of those who gave funds were clustered in much less fashionable districts, and often far afield. The Marylebone Dispensary, for example, in Wells Street—close to Norfolk Street—had been founded by local philanthropists in the 1780s to provide a walk-in clinic and community care for those unable to obtain hospital treatment. Supported by 'contributions from the Nobility, Gentry, and others', it endeavoured to help poor people in affliction from the 'degrading necessity of seeking assistance within a parish workhouse', recognizing that over-subscribed hospital provision was often 'inadequate to relieve the afflicted', and that treating sickness or accident swiftly could prevent long-term 'torment' or untimely death 'from want of assistance'. The Dispensary provided home care in childbirth within a two-mile radius to help prevent infant and maternal deaths among the poor, and in times of dearth the doctors gave food as well as medicine in desperate cases. Affluent and benevolent donors were sought to help those loaded with the 'complicated Misery of Sickness and Poverty'.[31]

When Dickens was a boy, such benevolence towards poverty was shifting among the moneyed classes. He would later witness for himself the parliamentary debates soon after the Great Reform Bill received its passage, which brought in the harsh New Poor Law.

CHAPTER 3

Institutions

HOSPITAL AND WORKHOUSE

T HE SOUTHERN END of Norfolk Street ran south into a short street, which connected Mortimer and Goodge Streets. In Dickens's day it was known as Charles Street, and it was an important street because on it stood the great institution, the Middlesex Hospital. Historically, Middlesex is an important county, the ancient country of the middle Saxons, embracing almost the entire London region north of the Thames, outside the City of London itself. The county boundary encompassed a large hinterland as well as Westminster, and most of the population of London outside the City.

Knowing Dickens's interest in names, it seems likely that as a child he would have relished having an important street nearby named Charles Street, as it were for himself, or at least for himself and his fugitive grandfather. As he grew older, traversing London or looking at maps and street directories, young Dickens would have become aware that London had quite a number of other streets—like the one leading to Soho Square—that carried his first name.

In this chapter we'll look at the two large institutions which stood close to Dickens's home: the hospital and the workhouse. The Middlesex Hospital dominated Charles Street. Contemporary images make clear the importance of the place in its vicinity: taller and larger than any building in sight. There being no other hospital in that part of West London, the hospital had been founded in 1745 to meet the unmet needs of the burgeoning population who could not afford private medical care. It had originally occupied a private house in nearby Windmill Street (just off Tottenham Court Road) but had grown rapidly, and in 1757 moved to a new purpose-built building in Marylebone Fields.[1]

The catchment area for the Middlesex Hospital—both in terms of patients and patrons—was extensive. When the Dickens family was living in Norfolk Street in the few years before 1820, the hospital was treating thousands of patients a year. Though it went through periods of crisis, it was an institution adept at raising funds from private donors, and in generating strong loyalty among staff, patients, patrons, and local inhabitants.[2]

The Middlesex was an innovative hospital, and is said to have been the first in London to introduce a ward for married lying-in patients in 1747. The building on Charles Street was originally built as a large H block, on a site enclosed on three sides by housing plots, it gradually acquired and demolished over time as the institution expanded to occupy almost the entire field in which it stood. In the early twentieth century, to allow further expansion, the Workhouse building on Cleveland Street (also originally designed on an H block plan) was purchased and modernized

FIGURE **8**. The devastated site of the Middlesex Hospital, seen looking northwards towards the Telecom Tower, from Mortimer Street. Photographed by the author, 2011. The right flank of the site was once the western side of Norfolk Street, its far corner occupied by Mr Baxter's pawnshop, diagonally between Dickens's old home (A) and the Workhouse (B), both of which are visible here. The hasty demolition of the Hospital was a scandalous pity, as it destroyed a fine edifice with a profound history on the site, reaching back to the fields beneath. The same fate awaited the Workhouse in 2010.

for an annexe. It was this acquisition by the great hospital on the next block that served to preserve the Workhouse building as a functioning health facility into the twenty-first century.

Maps of Dickens's day show the hospital with a large garden or orchard at the rear: land which much later was built upon for the Medical School. Right up until its closure in 2005–6 the Hospital preserved a garden within its central core, with shrubs and shady trees, and benches for patients and visitors. Historically, it was a large and very busy general hospital, as well as a centre for clinical innovation: a focus of medical, surgical, and nursing expertise, and forward-thinking. The garden provided an oasis of greenery at the centre of that work.

In pondering what Charles Street and its neighbourhood were actually like in Dickens's day, we have to bear in mind that past views of the Hospital—perhaps understandably—tend to aggrandize the institution by focusing the eye upon it, and ignoring or editing out its surroundings. I had hoped that it might be possible to glimpse what Norfolk Street was like from such images, but none of those who created pictures of the old Middlesex Hospital seem to have shown much interest in its urban context. So, as yet, it has proved impossible to find a view which takes in Norfolk Street in a way that is at all informative about the shops and houses—or indeed the Workhouse—that stood there in Dickens's day: the focus always veers towards the grand building on the adjacent block.

I live in hope that a beautiful watercolour of Charles Street will somewhere be found, showing the Hospital and Norfolk Street in perfect detail and glorious technicolour. But until then, the best image of the street I've yet found is a very small diagram dating from the 1830s, which appears in Tallis's *Street Views* of London.[3] John Tallis's speciality was in the presentation of linear diagrams of the grand streets of London, like the Strand or Piccadilly, so it is unsurprising that the interest here is very much upon the great institution on Charles Street: the Middlesex Hospital. But next to the Hospital, this little view also includes within it a small vista looking up Norfolk Street from Charles Street. Because there is so little else to guide us in an understanding of the street and its vicinity when Dickens knew it, although the view is peripheral, it is important. We can imagine Dickens walking down his little street, or returning this way after an outing, and looking up to see the great institution which stood behind the houses opposite his home.

Tallis is not accurate in showing a single frontage as the termination of the vista up Norfolk Street: this seems to have been a device applied to other streets in his *Street Views* such as Berners and Nassau Streets, on the same page, where a slight bend eventually obscures the view. A map (on the same page) shows that the prospect northwards up Norfolk Street should extend much further, more like the streets De Quincey mentioned running north off Oxford Street. Cleveland Street is unusually long and straight, as London streets go. But where Tallis is extremely helpful is in the attention paid to the environment on Charles Street itself, most especially in the relative heights of buildings, and in his record of the unpretentiousness of the local housing. We shall look at this view a little more closely in the next chapter.

The life and busyness of the area around the Hospital go entirely unrecorded by Tallis's clean lines, since he drew his streets without inhabitants of any kind. He does not show, for example, the claret-faced woman ballad-seller, who we know usually occupied a regular pitch beside the Middlesex Hospital's gates. It was she who directed the antiquarian ballad collector Sarah Banks of Soho Square to a printer in Long Lane, Smithfield, to purchase a rare song she lacked among her own stock of half-penny ballads, strung up against the hospital's front wall.[4]

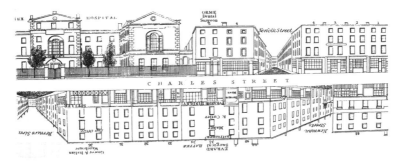

FIGURE 9. The dignified central and eastern wings of the Middlesex Hospital, seen from Charles Street (now Mortimer Street), with Norfolk Street forming the Hospital's eastern flank. The houses opposite (shown upside down) include the archway to Berners Mews. From John Tallis, *Street Views of London*, 1830.

Knowing about this encounter somehow gives us permission to revive the bustle of the place in imagination, and it helps to know that Charles Street was the name given to a short section of a much longer thoroughfare of many names, from west to east: Upper Seymour Street, Portman Square (south side), Lower Seymour, Edward Street, Wigmore Street, Cavendish Square (north side), Mortimer, Charles and Goodge Streets. This road was a major lateral artery more or less midway between Oxford Street and the New Road, connecting the great northerly roads north-west out to Edgware (Shrewsbury, Liverpool) and north-east to Camden Town (York, Newcastle, and Edinburgh), busy with traffic and the usual business of many shops, its adjacent business areas (generally south, towards Oxford Street) and residential areas branching off to the north, and the New Road.

In front of the Hospital, as well as the ballad-seller, there would have been much added bustle from passers-by, and the sheer number

FIGURE 10. The view northwards up Norfolk Street (now Cleveland Street) in 2011, from a position similar to that taken by Mr Tallis. Photographed by the author, 2011.

of visitors to the Hospital—walking sick and lame, nurses, students, clerks, cleaners, porters, relatives, medical men—or governors arriving in their gigs, patients arriving on stretchers or ladders, in wheelbarrows, or in hackney cabs, and of course there would have been the traffic arriving with deliveries of food and other supplies for the Hospital. Hovering about, hoping to capitalize on this activity, there would surely have been other street-hawkers and beggars, fruit and flower sellers, and, in the right season, the portable ovens of the baked potato sellers or the vendors of roasted chestnuts, providing a grateful sight (and smell and warmth) to passing Londoners on freezing days. Local bookshops, coffee-shops, bakehouses, pie-shops, and stalls catered to visitors; print-shops and other shops displayed their wares to passers-by.

FIGURE 11. A Cleveland Street coffee-shop, drawn by George Sharf in the 1820s. Scharf was an acute observer of the details of ordinary London lives at the very time Dickens was growing up in this part of London: here, both the man reading his newspaper, and the woman cooking on an open fire at the back, might regularly have walked past his door.

In the 1870s, the author of *Old and New London*, a huge encyclopedic work on the history of the metropolis in six volumes, described a busy street market in Charles Street, and used a mid-nineteenth-century passage from Henry Mayhew concerning the liveliness of the market at the New Cut (near Waterloo) to illustrate the same kind of atmosphere near the Middlesex Hospital:

> The southern side of Charles Street, which is continued by Goodge Street into Tottenham Court Road, presents a busy appearance, especially on Friday and Saturday evenings; and as

one of the few street markets remaining at the West-end, and probably destined at no long interval to disappear, may claim a short notice. To the long row of stallkeepers on its southern side, who display their stores of fish, fruit, and vegetables in hand-barrows and baskets, and on movable slabs, we may apply the words of Henry Mayhew:—'The scene in these parts has more of the character of a fair than of a market. There are hundreds of stalls, and every stall has its one or two lights; either it is illuminated by the intense white light of the new self-generating gas-lamp, or else it is brightened up by the red smoking flame of the old-fashioned grease lamps. One man shows off his yellow haddock with a candle stuck in a bundle of firewood; his neighbour makes his candlestick of a huge turnip, and the tallow gutters over its sides; while the boy shouting "Eight a penny pears!" has rolled his dip in a thick coat of brown paper, that flares away with the candle. Some stalls are crimson with a fire shining through the holes beneath the baked chestnut stove...while a few have a candle shining through a sieve. These, with the sparkling ground-glass of the tea-dealers' shops, and the butchers' gas-lights streaming and fluttering in the wind like flags of flame, pour forth such a flood of light, that at a distance the atmosphere immediately above the spot is as lurid as if the street was on fire.[5]

So far, I have been unable to verify whether there was a street market in Charles Street in Dickens's day, but the fact that Marylebone Market developed there perhaps suggests that the street by the Hospital had a liveliness and a large enough working-class population to sustain a growing number of street stalls.

London is a curious city. One can go a couple of blocks from an area that is down-at-heel and be in the most exclusive streets. Local inhabitants know where the divisions fall. It may be that Norfolk

Street fell on the wrong side of a divide: south of the street market was still an 'acceptable' address, north, not at all, at least not until you got to Portland Place. Dickens's silence about Norfolk Street may show a Londoner's tender sensitivity to such territorial markers. William Makepeace Thackeray recorded a conversation he had once with a barrister, who apologized to him for knowing people who lived in Brunswick Square! How much worse Norfolk Street might have seemed to such a small-minded snob we do not know.[6]

Near the Hospital, too, there were cutlers and surgical instrument makers, bandage and dressing makers, medical bookshops and manufacturers of flock mattresses and feather-beds, all with skills and stockrooms to be called upon when required by the institution and its staff. There would also have been call for the local dentists, and certainly the local undertakers. A good proportion of the vehicles and people on Charles Street would have reached there via Norfolk Street: the area was not a quiet backwater, but a back thoroughfare from Tottenham Court Road, and northwards the street was effectively part of Cleveland Street which connected directly to New Road.

Dickens would have become familiar with this locality as a small child watching from the window, and from the journeys on which he would have been taken along the various streets. We do not know whether the windows of the wards of the Middlesex Hospital were visible over the roofs of the houses opposite. It certainly looks from the Tallis view up Norfolk Street that the top storey of the Hospital was higher than the houses on Norfolk Street, so the glimmer of candlelight might have been visible from them on winter evenings. Many years later, when he had become a writer, Dickens described imagining the interior of a hospital from outside:

> In my rambles through the streets of London, after evening has set in, I have often paused beneath the windows of some public hospital, and pictured to myself the gloomy and mournful scenes that were passing within. The sudden moving of a taper as its feeble ray shot from window after window, until its light gradually disappeared, as if it were carried further back into the room to the bedside of some suffering patient, has been enough to awaken a whole crowd of reflections; the mere glimmering of the low-burning lamps which when all other habitations are wrapped in darkness and slumber, denote the chamber where so many forms are writhing with pain, or wasting with disease, has been sufficient to check the most boisterous merriment. Who can tell the anguish of those weary hours, when the only sound the sick man hears, is the disjointed wanderings of some feverish slumberer near him, the low moan of pain, or perhaps the muttered, long-forgotten prayer of a dying man? Who but those who have felt it, can imagine the sense of loneliness and desolation which must be the portion of those who in the hour of dangerous illness are left to be tended by strangers,—what hands, be they ever so gentle, can wipe the clammy brow, or smooth the restless bed, like those of mother, wife, or child?[7]

In that vicinity it was probably not a rare occurrence to see genuine objects of charity in a pitiable condition, having been refused access to the great institution which stood there. The Middlesex Hospital, like other charitable (or what were called 'voluntary') hospitals, took in treatable casualties and those whose ailments were considered potentially curable. But—except for the care of cancer, in which the hospital had a specialist interest—the chronic sick, the infirm, the mentally ill, and the dying poor were turned away. This was because the great charitable hospitals of London, of which the Middlesex was one, depended for their income entirely upon private charitable 'voluntary' donors. To keep the money flowing in, it was important for the Hospital to keep up a rolling programme of 'successful' care. To take in the dying, who would make the Hospital's statistics look poor, or those who might be a serious long-term drain on the institution's resources (what we might now describe as 'bed-blockers') would skew the Hospital's statistics in an undesirable direction.

High rates of cases successfully treated (and beds ready when necessary to accommodate well-off subscribers' domestic servants) were crucial to keep donations flowing, without which such institutions would fail. Later in life, when Dickens was a celebrity, he described to his friend Douglas Jerrold what he had witnessed in attending a public fund-raising dinner for one of these hospitals, and it makes for fascinating reading:

> Oh Heaven, if you could have been with me at a hospital dinner last Monday! There were men there who made such speeches and expressed such sentiments as any moderately intelligent dustman would have blushed through his cindery bloom to have thought of. Sleek, slobbering, bow-paunched, over-fed, apoplectic, snorting cattle, and the auditory [i.e. the audience] leaping up in their delight! I never saw such an illustration of the power of purse, or felt so degraded and debased by its contemplation, since I have had eyes and ears. The absurdity of the thing was too horrible to laugh at. It was perfectly overwhelming.[8]

Those who subscribed money to the hospital were given letters (larger donors received more letters) to distribute annually to 'worthy' recipients of hospital care. Unless they were taken in as casualties, new patients were expected to obtain one of these letters. Even in the case of casualties, hospitals demanded signed documents of financial security against burial costs in the event of death, and actively investigated marital status. A distinction was made between 'worthy' objects of charitable medical oversight and others, such as unmarried mothers and paupers, who were sent elsewhere. The local Marylebone Dispensary would have accepted some of them, but it, too, eventually went over to subscription letters. Those rejected for treatment often had nowhere to go for help but the final fall-back of the parish doctor and the parish workhouse.

But the Poor Law was organized in such a way that individuals had to apply to their own home parish for succour, so although the Cleveland Street Workhouse was right around the corner from the Hospital, it was an outpost of a distant parish a mile to the south in Covent Garden. A news report dating from 1810 will illustrate what these demarcations could mean for individuals:

> A scene, most shocking to humanity, was witnessed on Wednesday evening near Fitzroy Square. A poor woman, actually in labour, and attended by her midwife, was delivered of a child at the door of a poor-house, to which she in vain requested admittance. A crowd was naturally collected, and the utmost indignation was expressed at the brutal indifference shewn by the officers of the poor-house, for while the poor creature was labouring in agony, they remained inexorable. The infant perished during this inhuman scene. At length the people broke open the doors of the house, and carried the unhappy mother into one of the wards.[9]

This event looks to have taken place outside the front gates of the Workhouse in Cleveland Street, since there was no other poor-house in the vicinity. Most likely the poor woman had been turned away at the Middlesex Hospital because she was unmarried, or had no subscriber's letter, and was not eligible for help from the nearby Dispensary either. She was doubtless refused entry at the Workhouse because she did not belong to the parish of Covent Garden. Workhouse gatekeepers were employed to be particularly vigilant not to accept the financial burden of additional illegitimate children, which birth-entitlement entailed. What lay behind the tragedy in this case was probably the peculiar primacy of parish boundaries in the culture of the day: born outside the gates, the child was the responsibility of St Pancras; across the road, of St Marylebone; within the Workhouse gates and walls an island of exclusive governance belonged to the distant parish of Covent Garden.

A disjunction is strongly marked in this news report between the feelings of decency and humanity among those who inhabited Cleveland Street, as against the petty officiousness of the minions of Covent Garden parish. The morality of the street prevailed: an institution normally shunned was deliberately invaded, and forced to provide the care it had tried to shirk. It would not be at all surprising if the story of this sad case, involving the unseemly exposure of a poor woman's childbirth travail in the street, and the death of an innocent child, was still circulating by word of mouth in the area when the Dickens family arrived less than five years later: it is the kind of shocking story that local women might confide to newcomers (especially pregnant women like Mrs Dickens) or that men might discuss over their cups in the local public house. The humane indignation of the inhabitants of Cleveland Street would surely have been appreciated by Dickens's parents, and later, by Dickens himself.

On early maps of Marylebone, Norfolk Street is first shown as Upper Newman Street.[10] Its naming indicates the way in which the street developed in the late eighteenth century—northwards from the centre of London, at first simply a northern extension of Newman Street. It soon acquired its own distinct name, and the even younger Cleveland Street subsequently developed north-wards from it, eventually reaching all the way along the old 'Green Lane'. At the inception of this process, when building began on the street that would become the Dickens family's first home in London, a view up this way would have shown the Workhouse standing alone, ahead of the encroaching houses. When it was first built, the Workhouse is said to have been 'insulated in the fields'.[11]

The main front four-storey H-shaped block of the Workhouse was originally erected in the mid-1770s on land owned by the Duke of Bedford, bordering on a part of that estate already sold to a Mr Goodge, after whom Goodge Street is named. Old records suggest the Workhouse had initially been conceived as developing from a little right of way called Bedford Passage from Charlotte Street rather than from Cleveland Street, which for years was still a leafy country lane, even while new streets were encroaching from the south, and rising on either side. The field on which the Work-house was erected had been known as 'Culver Meadow', meaning a field of doves. Before it was acquired by the parish of St Paul Covent Garden, it had been (probably for centuries) a pasture for cattle.

The Churchwardens of St Paul Covent Garden had purchased the land in the 1770s because the parish itself was landlocked. Carved out of, and surrounded by, the larger parish of St Martin-in-the-Fields, St Paul Covent Garden was a very densely populated central district, which had run out of burial space for its poor. The parish was a unit of local government as well as an ecclesiastical entity, and it was also seeking ground on which to erect a workhouse in which to house its infirm elderly parishioners and other poor dependants, to employ its unemployed and to house its homeless in times of dearth. There was no vacant land within the parish for such a purpose: buying land at a distance was the only solution.

At about the same time, during the last quarter of the eighteenth century, population pressure on inner-city graveyards led a number of London parishes to seek distant fields as 'additional' burial grounds for their own poor. They were not popular places for burial, being so far from their communities, and being vulnerable to predation by body-snatchers supplying the medical schools of London. Covent Garden was enterprising in using the purchase of Culver Meadow for the double purpose of erecting a new workhouse and providing a new graveyard.

Being the great landowner, the Duke of Bedford was the parish patron, who had the power of nominating its churchmen. He it was who sent meat from his own herds for the churchwardens' annual venison supper.[12] The Duke was also the developer of the still rural lands he owned to the north of the built-up centre of London, although he held out for a long time against any building between

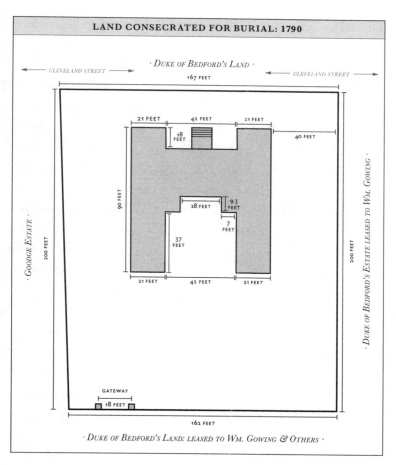

LAND CONSECRATED FOR BURIAL: 1790

· DUKE OF BEDFORD'S LAND ·

CLEVELAND STREET — 167 FEET — *CLEVELAND STREET*

· GOODGE ESTATE ·

· DUKE OF BEDFORD'S ESTATE LEASED TO WM. GOWING ·

21 FEET · 42 FEET · 21 FEET

18 FEET · 40 FEET

90 FEET · 200 FEET · 200 FEET

28 FEET · 9·3 FEET

7 FEET

37 FEET

21 FEET · 42 FEET · 21 FEET

GATEWAY

18 FEET

162 FEET

· DUKE OF BEDFORD'S LAND: LEASED TO WM. GOWING & OTHERS ·

FIGURE 12. A plan of the Workhouse and its consecrated burial ground, from measurements taken at the time of consecration in 1790. All the ground, except that actually under the footprint of the Workhouse, was consecrated—and presumably used—for burial. Dr Rogers reported that burials went very deep. Redrawn from the consecration records of the Church of England, held at the London Metropolitan Archives.

his own back windows and the fields of Bloomsbury to the north, to preserve the view.

Initially the land at Culver Meadow had been acquired from the Duke on a 99-year lease, and the Workhouse was designed and erected between 1775 and 1777. But the Anglican Church declined to consecrate the land around it for burial unless the parish of Covent Garden owned the land outright. Anglican consecration cannot be limited by leaseholds as it holds in prospect a far longer time-span than any human document can encompass: until the Last Trumpet on the Day of Resurrection. So the meadowland was eventually negotiated for and purchased on more secure terms. In April 1790, the entire plot—except for the area actually occupied by the Workhouse itself, which by then had been inhabited for over a dozen years—underwent the official process of consecration.

The great parchment describing the consecration ceremony survives. It records that after a religious service at the mother church in Covent Garden, the Bishop of London—with a retinue of worthies from church and parish—journeyed to the new site. There, seated under a special tent, he was ceremonially presented with the title deeds. He then consecrated the whole of the ground not occupied by the Workhouse, announcing that it was henceforth to be separated and consecrated from 'all common and profane uses whatsoever', and dedicated to the burial of the parishioners of St Paul Covent Garden, for them to rest in peace, preserved from all indignities for ever.

Living inside an austere building whose garden was a walled graveyard where you knew that you yourself would eventually be buried cannot have been a very cheering experience for those inside the Workhouse, even if the Consecration Day's events were commemorated with extra food for the inmates—perhaps the 'pease and bacon' they were permitted once a season.[13] The enclosing brick wall might have offered a wry kind of comfort to some in the House, in terms of the security provided from body-snatching for the local medical students, but in general the confinement and the lack of a hopeful vista cannot have been comforting. Other charitable institutions, like the great Hospital for old soldiers at Chelsea—were surrounded by graveyards intended for their own inhabitants, so this arrangement—which might seem rather insensitive and objectionable today—was not unusual for the time.[14]

The poet George Crabbe—a country vicar known as 'the poet of the poor'—is often thought of as an eighteenth-century figure, but he was still composing during Dickens's childhood and youth. In one of his poems, Crabbe describes a country workhouse. The parish workhouse of St Paul Covent Garden differs from the one he described, being newly purpose-built on the edge of countryside—the rural nature of the old Green Lane was fast disappearing. Yet Crabbe's description characterizes the sense of hopelessness these places could generate for their inmates even before the enactment of the New Poor Law:

> Theirs is yon house that holds the parish poor,
> Whose walls of mud scarce bear the broken door;
> There, where the putrid vapors flagging play,

And the dull wheel hums doleful through the day;
There children dwell who know no parents' care;
Parents, who know no children's love, dwell there;
Heart-broken matrons on their joyless bed,
Forsaken wives and mothers never wed;
Dejected widows with unheeded tears,
And crippled age with more than childhood-fears;
The lame, the blind, and—far the happiest they!—
The moping idiot and the madman gay ...
Here too the sick their final doom receive,
Here brought amid the scenes of grief to grieve,
Where the loud groans from some sad chamber flow,
Mixed with the clamors of the crowd below;
Here, sorrowing, they each kindred sorrow scan,
And the cold charities of man to man.
How would ye bear in real pain to lie,
Despised, neglected, left alone to die?
How would ye bear to draw your latest breath
Where all that's wretched paves the way for death?[15]

Records concerning the regime operating in the Covent Garden Workhouse under the Old Poor Law are scanty and fragmentary: very little has survived. But from what there is, an idea can be gleaned of the kind of place it was. Numbers of deaths, especially of the elderly poor, and of unmarried mothers (like Oliver Twist's mother) and/or their babies, took place inside the Workhouse on Culver Meadow.[16] It is not known if the surrounding land had been used covertly for their burial before the consecration, or if not, where the dead from the Workhouse were taken for burial before 1790.

After the consecration ceremony, notes of burials appear occasionally in the Minutes of the Trustees of the Poor. In 1791, for example, a woman called Anne Hawkins was delivered of a 'Dead Male Bastard Child' (the poor child was dead, but its illegitimate status and his mother's shame must of course be explicitly noted). While his little body was awaiting burial, another inmate, Robert Prince, died in the Workhouse. The Trustees' minutes record: 'they was both buried in one Coffin this day.'[17]

In the bleak midwinter night of 23 December 1791, Abigail Allen, John Rawson, and James Kempton all died, and were later buried 'at this House'. All had missed enjoying the annual change on Christmas Day from the usual year-long sugarless gruel: two days later 'veal, plumb pudding & porter' were served to the surviving inmates.[18] The parish undertaker petitioned in 1793 for money in advance, and higher fees were agreed: ten shillings for each adult coffin, and half price for a child.[19]

In the 1790s Mrs Owen, the retiring House Midwife, was rewarded with three guineas 'in consideration of the great trouble and inconvenience she had been put to and the singular illness she has laboured under from attending upon many foul women in the House'. In other words, she had probably caught syphilis, or some other infection from infected women whom she had helped give birth. How many others might have acquired disease from her, nobody knew. A new midwife, Mrs Harrison, was appointed soon afterwards, being paid the usual fee of 5 shillings for each labour; she left within the year, and was again replaced.[20]

In these pages, the fathers of illegitimate children are searched out and chivvied for contributions for their maintenance. Prices of goods for the workhouse are negotiated for: good and sweet Butchers' Meat, sweet Butter and Cheese, Beer, and Coals. Old folk are admitted lame or ill, lunatics confined, people are discharged when well, sometimes being given clothes, shoes, a 'Rugg' or a blanket as they go. It feels rather like a modern refugee camp in a disaster zone, thin pickings, but with a degree of benevolence. Quarterly payments are made to the Tinman (presumably for mending kettles, pots, metal dishes, and other objects), the Tallow Chandler (who provided cheap tallow candles and rushlights), the Baker, and the Corn Chandler. People were checked for hiding food about their persons and then complaining of shortage, and the meat had to be checked before it went into the great copper for boiling, in case the butcher had sent it maggoty, rancid, or underweight.[21] Handbills were printed and distributed offering cheap labour:

> The Churchwardens acquaint the Inhabitants of this Parish that Plainwork, Mangling, paper Bagg making, Cotton winding, Silk winding, and Quiltmaking are done at the Workhouse...in the best and cheapest manner possible.[22]

Various Workhouse Masters and Matrons were discharged from their positions of power over the Workhouse—for being 'by no means competent' or for systematic fraud—and new ones appointed.[23] One parishioner, Ann Ellis Atkins, came to appear especially before the Board of Trustees to 'return thanks for the great care and services rendered to her during her illness in this House'.[24] Another, Mary

Wilson, presumably recovering from an amputation, was provided with a new wooden leg, and granted a Shift, a Gown, an Apron, a Handkerchief and a Shoe.[25] A Mr Burrows was instructed to 'make a proper erection for Beating Carpets upon', which was to prove a long-term and lucrative funding stream for the Workhouse, and a source of noise and filthy dust in the environment of the Workhouse until Dr Rogers's time there in the 1860s. Carpet-beating was one of the jobs adult men were required to do at Cleveland Street, in return for their bed and board. The paupers—including the children—were instructed in various remunerative forms of labour by the schoolmaster, who was also the superintendent of the Workhouse on-site 'Pinheading Manufactory', and who received a small percentage of the profits.

Older children were put out individually to apprentice—after a trial 'on liking'—and larger groups of girls and boys were disposed of by being sent over 150 miles away from the Workhouse to a Calico Manufactory in Macclesfield. These children seem not to be heard of again. For the authorities at Covent Garden Workhouse, silence from Macclesfield was probably welcome, as the unremitting responsibility of finding funds to support unmarried mothers and their children was a constant headache, worsening in times of dearth. The documentary silence about the fate of these factory children has echoes of the story of Robert Blincoe, who as a child of 7 was sent from St Pancras workhouse in the 1790s into 'cotton-mill bondage' in an isolated factory near Nottingham, where severe physical cruelty and abuse, unprotected dangerous machinery, and malnutrition caused deaths and deformities among the children, which were never adequately investigated. He survived but others didn't.[26]

The four-storey Workhouse in Cleveland Street and its burial ground were in active use throughout both periods when Dickens was living only doors away. Like the Regent's Park up the road, the Workhouse inhabited an enclosed space. But it was not an entirely closed institution: what went on there influenced the locality in more ways than we can imagine. The front gateway, for example, carried a stern message, recorded by a Victorian observer as a 'sermon in stone'. In its brick pediment there stood a sculpture ... which broadcast its judgemental warning continually to passers-by, and to all who entered there: 'an ideal figure of an old man holding and pointing to a piece of drapery, with the motto: "AVOID IDLENESS AND INTEMPERANCE" '[27]

Cleveland Street was not unique in this; other Georgian work-houses carried these kinds of messages too: the frontage of the Bishopsgate Workhouse, for example, carried two figures in niches, and the legend: 'GOD GIVES PEACE TO INNOCENCE AND PLENTY TO INDUSTRY'.[28]

The many windows of the Cleveland Street building's frontage overlooked the street, so from across the road faces might be seen behind the glass, and perhaps human voices heard. The life of the entire institution was coordinated by the regular jangle of the workhouse bell, which punctuated the working day within the institution at the hour of rising, working, dining, and sleeping.[29] A great workhouse bell intended to be heard in every ward and across the backyard and forecourt of this large institution can hardly have been inaudible in the surrounding streets. Other sounds might also have escaped beyond the walls of the institution: both the lying-in ward and the ward for lunatics were at the front of the building, so on occasions moans and wails might have mingled and merged audibly outside.[30] The overpowering smell of the place, which even Poor Law correspondents, who generally understated institutional shortcomings, referred to as 'fetid exhalations' (something apparently generic, of which the poet Crabbe was also unpleasantly aware), was commented upon by Dr Rogers, who also spoke with disgust of the choking clouds of dust from the paupers' carpet-beating and stone-breaking, particles from which must surely have freighted the ambient air of nearby streets.[31]

The Workhouse gate was usually kept firmly shut.[32] The gateman, whose double gatehouse stood on each side of the entrance, inside the Workhouse front wall on Cleveland Street, was expected to keep firm control over access. The stout gates (most likely of panelled timber) probably had a smaller inner door or wicket and perhaps a barred visor set within the gate, rather like the secure sub-door in the great gateways of prisons, allowing the gatekeeper to observe applicants for entry, preserve security while examining their documentation, and permit one person in or out at a time.

The gateman required a written order from arrivals before opening the gate, searched visitors individually for 'spiritous liquors' as they entered, accepted and documented deliveries, checked all those who left the House, and noted everything in a great ledger. We do not know whether he was summoned by bell or knocker, but both would have been audible on the street as well as inside his gatehouse. Tradesmen, visitors, pauper funerals arriving for the graveyard, and pauper applicants for admission would all have had to wait outside until he verified their credentials. There would have been times, no doubt, when the queue was long.[33]

We do not know what attitudes he may have shown to the poor inmates on entering or departing; nor with what obsequious bowings and scrapings the gateman might have welcomed the parish Beadle, or the august personnel attending or departing from the monthly meetings of the management held in the Workhouse Board Room upstairs. Nor do we know—when the gates were locked at night, and the great keys carried indoors by the Workhouse master—what shouts or pleadings might have punctuated the stillness of the night.

·CHAPTER 4·

Home

HOUSE, LANDLORD, SHOP,
INSIDE, UPSTAIRS, DOWNSTAIRS

I F YOU STAND in the street today to take a good look at
Charles Dickens's first London home from the outside, you
notice first of all that it's quite tall. There's a basement below
the street-level shop, and three storeys above it. The house is also
rather wide, being three windows across. It's a Georgian row-house,
what Londoners would now call an end-of-terrace, not so grand in
its dimensions as the fine houses in Bloomsbury, or those further
west in Harley, Wimpole, and Welbeck Streets, but emphatically not
a mean house. This house was home to the Dickens family twice:
when Dickens was a child between 1815 and 1817, then again
between 1829 and 1831, when he was in his late teens, and earning
his living in London.

No. 10 Norfolk Street stands on a corner, facing into what is now
Cleveland Street. Its side flank around the corner has a wide area
of wall above the side shop window, and a single window on each

85

FIGURE 13. Dickens's old home and the adjacent Georgian shops, looking south towards Charles Street (now Mortimer Street). Mr Dodd's bow shop window is in the immediate foreground. On the far side of the house front door, the next shop, Taylor's Buttons, with the circular sign, was Mr Dodd's 'back' parlour. Above them the house is three windows wide. The railed area allowed natural light down to Mr Dodd's basement kitchen, but the lodgers' kitchen (below the button shop) remains very dark because the great flagstone under the parlour window has only the original iron grating listed in the 1804 Schedule. Mr Dodd's corner house and the next three houses occupy the wider part of the vacant wedge of land shown on the Horwood map. Photographed by the author, 2011.

floor near the rear of the building looking onto Tottenham Street. In this chapter we'll look at what can be discovered of the history of the house, meet the landlord, and learn a little about him, and then we shall enter the front door and have a look around inside.

The front door on Cleveland Street has a neat Georgian doorway, designed for an earlier, more slender silhouette than the Victorian crinoline. The little fanlight looks old, but the number 22 in the glass probably dates from the 1860s when the separate naming and numbering of Norfolk Street disappeared, and this part of the road was merged with the rest of Cleveland Street.

The six-panel front door looks old too, despite having lost its original furniture. The area was inhabited by numbers of medical students long before there was an officially established medical school at the Middlesex Hospital, and Victorian medical students were notoriously rowdy; for some obscure reason they seemed to think it fun to wrench door knockers from street doors, so perhaps it's not surprising that only one door in the street seems to have anything resembling original door furniture.[1]

To the right of the house door, a small domestic window starts at about hip-level, which brought daylight to the shop's parlour, placed at the side rather than at the rear of the shop because of the curiously shaped site this house occupies. This room is now a small and delightfully quaint button shop, quite separate from the café, which currently occupies the corner. It is run by a lady called Mrs Rose, and is lined from floor to ceiling with shelves piled high with little boxes, each with a button attached outside, to show its contents. The shop feels curiously ancient, as though it's been there for ever, and reminds Dickens-lovers who have seen it of Mr Pumblechook's seed shop in *Great Expectations*, of which Pip thought: 'He

FIGURE 14. The corner house at 22 Cleveland Street (10 Norfolk Street). Originally Mr Dodd's corner shop, and Dickens's old home. From this direction, the entrance to Mr Dodd's shop and his side windows on Tottenham Street are visible, as well as those of the three upper storeys. Photographed by the author, 2011.

must have been a very happy man indeed, to have so many little drawers in his shop.'[2]

To the left of the front door the building has a very large bow-fronted shop window, which curves round in a wide shallow arc to the shop door at the corner. This great window was probably originally a typical Georgian shop window: composed of many smaller panes of glass, and supported by a curved grid of glazing bars. The same is probably true of the other large shop window round the corner, which faces onto Tottenham Street, but there is no sign that that one was curved.

The character of the house finds echoes in the design of the adjacent run of three Georgian shops, which lead south towards what used to be Charles Street, and the front of the Middlesex Hospital. Each has a similarly wide bow-fronted shop window with classical denticulated detailing along the top, and separate doors for shop and house. Each looks originally to have had a railed area at the front for light and access to the basement, which survives in three of the four, though their railings are assorted.[3] The houses in this little row are in various states of repair, and are painted various colours, but they have a kind of unity of dimension, style, and detail which suggests that they may be the work of the same builder. Who that builder was isn't certain, but their history is curious and offers clues to who it might have been.

This little group of Georgian shops is all of a piece, originally Nos. 7 to 14 Norfolk Street, later additions to the rest of the street, being afterthoughts. Old maps show that they were individually designed to fit on a curiously wedge-shaped piece of land on the east side of Norfolk Street which straddled Tottenham Street, left vacant when most of the houses on both side streets were already

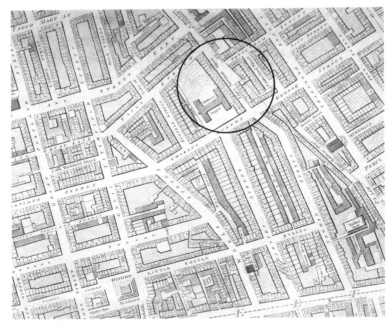

FIGURE 15. Horwood's Map of London, 1799, showing the 'H' block of the Middlesex Hospital and its garden, and the southern wing of the 'H' block of the Workhouse (centre top). The fields of Rocque's map had already disappeared under streets and houses, but the old field boundaries are often still discernible in the street-plan. Oxford Street runs along the bottom of the map, and Tottenham Court Road clips the corner at the top right. The wedge of land on which Dickens's future home would be built is still vacant, between the east wing of the Hospital and the estate/parish boundary, which runs top left to lower right. Norfolk Street was still regarded as a northern branch of Newman Street at this date. Richard Horwood, Cartographer, 1799.

built. The older houses at the rear—on what is now Goodge Place—and others infilling the land on the St Pancras side of the boundary, were on land belonging to a different owner: the Goodge estate. Several had windows or gardens running tight up to the parish boundary behind Norfolk Street.

The vacant wedge of land, by contrast, was on the Marylebone side of the boundary, and was part of the Berners estate. For some reason—perhaps from some disagreement concerning access rights or light—this wedge of ground had been left empty when the rest of the block was built. Yet it must have possessed considerable value. A large folded parchment deed survives in the archives concerning the smaller northern half of this site.[4] It shows that in the 1790s the thin end of the wedge above Tottenham Street was sold by Charles Berners to developers John Johnson and William Horsfall, the second of whom was a local builder who lived on the opposite side of Norfolk Street, and who had workshops in a mews on Tottenham Street.[5] In the deed's margin is a tiny sketch plan of the plot of land, with its detailed dimensions. It shows it was widest at the south, but that above Tottenham Street it tapered sharply to less than six feet in depth. The houses eventually erected on it had street frontages as wide as those that remain, but there was so little depth to the site that it seems curious they were ever built at all.

These peculiarly shallow houses have all since disappeared; in the twentieth century their site was absorbed by a large building which juts into the pavement on Cleveland Street south of the Workhouse wall, following the outline of the old wedge of land. The pavement on Cleveland Street at this point still exhibits a shallow bend to accommodate those extra six feet, and this bend marks the historic northernmost tip of Norfolk Street.

It seems likely that the men named in this old deed were also responsible for building the four houses which still stand on the wider part of the wedge of land, including the corner house in which the Dickens family lived. Sadly, every single one of the other houses on Norfolk Street, which pre-dated them, has disappeared, leaving only this late cohort of four Georgian houses as the only remnants of the street Dickens knew.

The odds against their survival were high, especially when we consider that besides the expansion of the Middlesex Hospital—which removed the opposite side of the street—and the encroachments of twentieth-century property 'developers', which took the rest, there has also been the London Blitz, when bombs rained down all around. Second World War London Bomb Damage maps show that bombs fell in a line up Charlotte Street, the next street along, at Goodge Street, Tottenham Street, and Howland Street, and that a landmine obliterated Whitfield's Tabernacle on Tottenham Court Road, including its vaults where that 'celebrated fanatic' Lord George Gordon (instigator of the Gordon Riots, the central theme of Dickens's novel *Barnaby Rudge*) had been buried, and decimating its churchyard monuments.[6]

But the old house that Dickens knew has endured. Despite the destruction and change evident all about, from this house and its few neighbours we can try to visualize the street as it was, and be grateful for the enormous good fortune that these modest Georgian houses, and most especially the one on the corner, have survived.[7]

The Dickens family's landlord at 10 Norfolk Street was a cheese-monger and grocer: Mr John Dodd. Little is known about him or his family. We do not know how the Dickens family found Mr Dodd, but there may have been some family or other contact which put them in touch with one another—one seeking tenants, the other seeking an affordable home in London. It's possible that Dickens's relatives in Berners Street knew him, or that he was a supplier to William Dickens's coffee-shop, or that other mutual friends lived nearby.

Mr Dodd had been settled in Norfolk Street for over a decade when the Dickens family arrived in 1815, and was still there during and after their second stay in the 1820s. Records fix him at that address for over twenty-five years between 1804 and *c*.1830. Not much is known about him, but there is a strong possibility that he was local to Marylebone as a boy.[8] If this was the case, it could mean that John Dodd and John Dickens had known each other since their schooldays. Later, in 1824, when John Dickens was imprisoned in the Marshalsea Prison, Mr Dodd was one of John Dickens's creditors, so it looks as though the Dickens family had not paid him all the rent they owed him from living in Norfolk Street when Dickens was a child. But it is also known that Mr Dodd was not responsible for triggering the proceedings against John Dickens, which were begun by a Camden Town baker to whom John Dickens owed £40.[9] Furthermore, in the later 1820s, Mr Dodd took the Dickens family back into his home for a second time after they had been incarcerated in the debtors' prison and after they had been evicted from their home in Somers Town. So it appears that he was a forgiving landlord, and perhaps a good friend.

It may be that this kindness contributed to Mr Dodd's own rocky financial times, as he was himself nearly bankrupted in 1816, and fully so in 1825. We do not know what caused his first crisis, which looks to have occurred while the Dickens family were living in the house.[10] In the second instance, Mr Dodd's difficulties may have been precipitated or exacerbated by the failure of a bank. A banking crash in 1824–5 forced the closure of nearly eighty banks, and many people lost their entire savings. I have found evidence which shows that Mr Dodd lost the sum of £101 (twice the annual rateable value of his house) in the crash of a local bank, in which his savings were lodged. He may well have lost other money he had carefully saved elsewhere.[11]

Dodd is not a rare name, even within the confines of the parish of Marylebone, and it has been devilishly hard to try to work out anything about Mr Dodd more personal than his money problems. Henry Dodd, the 'refuse collector and philanthropist' (and would-be patron of decayed actors), who much later became the model for the 'Golden Dustman' in *Our Mutual Friend*, is not likely to have been of the same family, but Dickens may have been well disposed towards his name when they became friends in the 1860s.[12]

There are tantalizing hints of the possibility of connections in the local arts world: but it is not known as yet if John Dodd was anything to do with Mr Dodd the famous singer, who had entertained visitors a generation earlier at Drury Lane Theatre and in the open air at the Marylebone Gardens, with Garrick's song from *Harlequin's Invasion*:

> Thrice happy the Nations that Shakespeare has charm'd
> More happy the bosom his genius has warm'd

Nor do we know if the Dodd brothers, famous for their violin bows, who made musical instruments and sold harps in Berners Street, were associated with him.[13]

When Mr John Dodd of 10 Norfolk Street was listed for bankruptcy in 1816, the official *London Gazette* described him not only as a cheesemonger, but also as a dealer and a chapman.[14] The description 'dealer' is unfortunately too vague to be helpful: it simply means that he made deals in goods other than cheese; but a *chapman* is more specific—Mr Dodd sold cheap literature. Of course we have no idea how extensively he traded the little books called chapbooks, or what sort of chapbooks they may have been.[15] The range of cheap books available for purchase in Regency London was very wide, from children's books of nursery rhymes, fairy tales, or alphabets and reading primers, to reading materials for adults who could not afford bound books: almanacks, stories of shipwrecks, murders and other crimes, letter-writers, fortune-tellers, or dream interpreters, caricatures, religious or political pamphlets, or moral tales such as the 'Cheap Repository Tracts' designed to suppress political activity among the poor.

Chapbooks were made from one large sheet printed on both sides, folded in half several times down to a smallish booklet, sewn across the final fold and the edges cut to make the pages. They invariably had an interesting woodcut illustration or a loud exclamatory headline on the front cover to attract attention. Some of Dickens's earliest reading matter may have been chapbook versions of traditional tales like Dick Whittington, Robin Hood, Aladdin, and Cock Robin, novels abridged for children's reading such as *Gulliver's Travels*, *Moll Flanders*, or *Robinson Crusoe*, comic alphabets or little books of songs, jokes and riddles, or London cries.

To ponder what illustrated books and chapbooks, or indeed pictures, Mr Dodd might have had about the shop and inside the house, or perhaps framed on the stairs, leads to another realization: that Norfolk Street stood in a district rich in printed, painted, and sculpted imagery. Just to the south, Berners and Newman Streets were well known as a hub of artistic industry. Dotted along Charles Street and around the cluster of small streets surrounding the Middlesex Hospital were the workshops and studios of artists, sculptors, picture-frame carvers and gilders, engravers, lithographic and copperplate printers, wood engravers, and skilled tinters of finished prints.[16] The famous sculptor Nollekens was living just round the corner on Mortimer Street when Dickens was a child, as renowned for his miserliness as for his tombs.[17] On the next corner up from Mr Dodd's shop, past the Workhouse, was another sculptor's studio. The men who worked there—the Gahagans, father and son—made busts, and standing statues, and small maquettes, many blackened to look like basalt—Nelson, Wellington, George III, all gazed out with their blank eyes, and amid the dust and straw of the studio, one might have seen hands and feet in stone or plaster lying about waiting to be fixed to their bodies.[18] There were also musical instrument makers, piano tuners, timber yards, timber benders, cutlers, all sorts of practical workers, as well as oil and colourmen selling paints and sundries for artists and carvers, and for the scene painters at the theatre on Tottenham Street.

A much stronger connection with the art world is with the artist Philip Augustus Gaugain, son of a family of engravers, who gave 10 Norfolk Street as his studio address on a number of occasions when he exhibited at the Royal Academy and at the British Institution in the early 1820s, between the Dickens family's two stays there.[19] There was also a dynasty of Dodds who worked as artist-engravers in Marylebone.[20] If John Dodd was related in some way to these engravers, there's a possibility that he owned some of their work, and that as a child Dickens might have seen the lad climbing into a waggon from *Roderick Random*, or the *Fatal Bridge* from the melodramatic production of the *Blood Red Knight* at Astley's Amphitheatre, or even more mournful images, such as the poor prisoners near Newgate after the Gordon Riots, from the *Newgate Calendar*.[21]

As a child, Dickens might have been aware of the artiness and the busyness of the creative industries of the area only at a marginal level, but the visuality of his perceptions suggests that he could well have been interested from an early age in the pictures displayed in shop windows, or for sale in boxes or portfolios out on the street.

Just a little way up the road at No. 9 Cleveland Street, for example (directly opposite the Workhouse), was the printing workshop of Thomas and William Daniell, artists and prolific aquatint etchers, famous not only for their *Picturesque Voyage to India by way of China*—accurately recording Chinese and Indian landscape and architecture (like the Taj Mahal) with the precision of the camera lucida—but also for fine views of London from the River. Some of their work is likely to have been displayed in the shop window.[22] William Daniell began his most famous work, *A Voyage Round Great Britain*, just before the Dickenses moved in with Mr Dodd, and was busy etching and printing the plates from the first tranche of his great coastal survey

97

from Land's End to Dundee via Holyhead. His press room may perhaps have been visible to passers-by from the street. The work on this huge project—which resulted in a splendid set of 308 etchings in eight volumes, and took in the entire circuit of the coastal topography of the British mainland—continued through the Dickens family's first stay in Norfolk Street, and beyond.[23]

Just around the corner from the Daniells, the entire Landseer family was living and working at 33 Foley Street, which branches off Cleveland Street opposite the Workhouse. A series of exceedingly beautiful prints of human body parts by Edwin Landseer (then training under Benjamin Robert Haydon) was printed and published by John Landseer from that address between 1814 and 1818, while Dickens was living in Norfolk Street.[24] In Tottenham Street, the street onto which Mr Dodd's other shop window faced, were the premises of at least two other important picture printers. When Dickens was a small boy, the Havells—world-famous now for their spectacular series of over 400 coloured aquatints of Audubon's *Birds of America*—were creating a fine series of coloured vignettes of historic English costume and architecture, some by Dickens's future cousin by marriage, Richard Cattermole.[25] Another printer on Tottenham Street was John Dixon, known for his large mezzotint portraits like that of the great actor David Garrick, and society beauties like the Crewe sisters (the employers of Dickens's grandmother).

While the Dickens family was living at 10 Norfolk Street, Dixon had been creating smaller etchings, of Waterloo (by Thomas Bewick's pupil Luke Clennell) and scenes from most of Shakespeare's plays.[26] It is not known if the porcelain figurine of David Garrick in the actor's most famous role as Richard III, which was based on Dixon's print of him, was actually on sale in the Staffordshire chinaware shop round the corner in Cleveland Street, or indeed, if it had been inspired by prints on display in Tottenham Street.[27]

There was probably a brisk market for theatrically themed goods in the vicinity, because of the well-known theatre on Tottenham Street, which, when the Dickens family first lodged in the area, was called the 'Regency Theatre'.[28] The theatre features in an 1802 cartoon by Gillray of an irate Sheridan—dressed hilariously as Harlequin—followed by other legendary actors invading the theatre when aristocratic amateurs calling themselves the 'Pic-Nic Club' took over the place for their own shows, attracting wealthy friends away from the regular theatres.[29]

Originally, the theatre had been 'The King's Concert Rooms', a concert hall specializing in ancient music, and numerous musical instrument makers continued to work in the surrounding streets. A view of the theatre's interior in 1817 shows its auditorium to have been modest in size, with benches for the audience in the pit, boxes, two balconies, and people leaning over a bar in the 'gods' above, watching a scene from *Othello*.[30] We do not know for certain if Dickens was taken there as a child but it seems quite a likely possibility, and he would have seen the printed playbills and the place so even if he didn't enter, he would probably have been intrigued by it.[31]

The presence of all this vibrant engraving and printing in the immediate area of Norfolk Street leads to the hope that somewhere

FIGURE 16. Butter-paper from the shop of John Wrigley, Grocer. Artist unknown.

there may exist a more prosaic production of the printing press: a butter-paper from Mr Dodd's shop. London grocers often had their own personalized papers for wrapping the butter and cheese they sold.[32] Such ephemeral things are extremely elusive, and relatively few examples of them survive, so one from Mr Dodd's shop may never be found. But if such a thing existed, it might perhaps have shown the shopfront as it then was, with Mr Dodd's name in large letters, his address less prominently, some swags or flourishes, and perhaps a list or an illustration of the things he wanted customers to know about his stock-in-trade.

Other cheesemonger-grocers enumerated a considerable array of goods on their papers—these were not shops containing only a variety of fresh and smoked cheeses: they also dealt in fresh butter, eggs, cream, sausages, poultry, fresh lard, and also preserved or smoked meats such as bacon and hams, as well as traditional baked pork pies and cold pies with other fillings. They often also sold other provisions which did not deteriorate quite so swiftly: dried goods like teas, coffee, cocoa, and sugar, dried or crystallized fruits, ginger, nuts, rice, pulses and grains, bottled jams and marmalades, as well as sauces, salted and pickled fish, pickles and other relishes, spices, treacle, oils, and vinegars. Some grocers sold starch and laundry blue. A considerable part of a grocer's stock might also be in bottled drinks—wines, ales, cider, ginger ale, soda water, lemonade, and barley water. We do not know how extensive Mr Dodd's stock might have been (bearing in mind that some shops were quite sparsely stocked) or whether he served, as some grocers did, as a wholesaler, or if he dealt in stationery, books, or newspapers alongside his chapbooks, sold confectionery, tobacco, or snuff, or if he had other sidelines.[33]

How Mr Dodd navigated being landlord to the Dickenses and surviving near bankruptcy during the two years they were first living in the house is not known. When Dickens's father was later under pursuit by creditors, he went to ground, disappeared to other lodgings, suffered the indignity of being shouted for in the street, and he was also arrested and locked up in what was known as a 'sponging house', a sort of private holding facility for arrested debtors, in Cursitor Street, off Chancery Lane. We simply do not know whether Mr Dodd had to flee his shop, or saw his stock impounded by bailiffs. The Dickenses were lodgers, and almost no documentation survives for the period, but it is possible that the shop was closed, or kept running by a loyal assistant, or managed by means of a ruse—in the name of Mr Dodd's wife or a friend, for example. All we have to go by at the moment is that in the February of 1816 Mr Dodd's imminent bankruptcy was announced in the press.[34]

Yet it is also clear that Mr Dodd traded from the same shop long afterwards, so he must have been able to raise the money to clear his debts relatively swiftly. These crises suggest that Mr Dodd could have become inveigled into extending himself—perhaps laying out on stock—from greater creditors. Possibly he had clients to whom he had delivered goods, who had failed to pay, which was a constant headache for all London shopkeepers and craftsmen, including even Lord Byron's coachmaker.[35]

It may have been a misfortune of another kind that caused Mr Dodd's difficulties. Prosecutions by grocers during this era show that they were often going after untrustworthy staff rather than shoplifters, and although no record of any legal proceedings by Mr Dodd has yet been found, we do not know if such might have been the case: it may be that he was too kind to prosecute. Nevertheless, to have survived as a cheesemonger, grocer, and chapman on the corner of Norfolk Street for a quarter of a century suggests that John Dodd was an able shopkeeper, and that he had a loyal clientele.

London grocers frequently used as a shop sign the conical solid old-fashioned sugar loaf, or a tea canister, and had a custom of standing tea-chests (which in those days had Chinese lettering) outside the shop. Unlike many other shopkeepers—such as greengrocers, furniture brokers, pawnbrokers, or linen drapers—a cheesemonger might not have the opportunity to display goods outside for fear of theft, perishability, and street dust, so Mr Dodd's two windows on the corner were probably important to attract customers inside. It is most likely that for the display of fresh cheeses Mr Dodd would have used the shaded interior of the shop, while the Cleveland Street window (which receives some direct sunlight in the afternoon) would be suitable for lighting the interior, for publicity, and perhaps for the display of bottled and packeted goods less easily spoiled by exposure.

The window displays of this era are an under-researched area, but shelves inside the bow-fronted window probably created a little shade, and allowed the display of imperishable objects—such as a display of boiled eggs in straw to look new-laid, or baskets or stacks of mock cheeses—as well as small tableaux of farm folk or mandarin figures, pot plants, or notices in some of the panes of glass promoting the goods sold. The adult Dickens seems to have had an interest in advertising and billboards, which may date from exposure to Mr Dodd's window-dressing.[36]

Life for a cheesemonger in the days before refrigeration probably focused to an extraordinary degree on the storage and preservation of perishable goods, and would have entailed care in their protection from London dust, and the constant cultivation of coolness. A through-draught would have been valuable in summer, less welcome in winter. Flies (especially as there were stables across the road in the mews behind Tottenham Street) and, doubtless, mites and mice were also attracted to the food, and there would have been odours in the hall and rising upstairs: mixed odours of freshness and rancidity, of cheese and smoked bacon—that slightly fusty smell one can still encounter in small delicatessens, despite refrigeration, but to a more concentrated degree.

Even within living memory, stone or glass slabs and damp butter-muslin cloaking cheeses were the stalwarts of the cheesemonger for coolness. Fresh leaves or cut paper were probably used for platters under cheeses, and other paper wrappers used for cones or twists of sugar or salt, tea, and other dry goods. Cheesemongers were evidently also known to utilize recycled paper, as there is a story that one of Dickens's favourite actors, Charles Mathews, was able to obtain some manuscript letters of the playwright Sheridan from a colleague who had discovered them among a heap of manuscripts sold as waste paper to a cheesemonger.[37]

We do not know if Mr Dodd or his corner shop had any profound influence upon Dickens's imagination, as it may have done in its owner's love of order and his entrepreneurial and presentational flair. But we do find Dickens occasionally employing grocerly imagery, which catches the attention. Might the badging and ticketing of Oliver as a pauper infant, which I discuss later in the context of pawnbroking, derive or share something from the date/source derivation of pickles, cheeses, and other foods, wines, or the stock-taking of deliveries? In *Barnaby Rudge*, a vast cheese is the emblem of John Willet's hospitality; in *Pickwick Papers,* Dr Slammer's bottled-up indignation effervesces from all parts of his countenance and Mr Pickwick pauses, bottles up his vengeance, and corks it down. David Copperfield's lessons in arithmetic are conducted in cheeses: 'If I go into a cheesemonger's shop, and buy five thousand double-Gloucester cheeses at fourpence-halfpenny each, present payment.' The most memorable of these images appears in *Oliver Twist*, when Dickens takes a moment out of the narrative to employ streaky bacon to describe dramatic practice:

It is the custom on the stage: in all good murderous melodramas: to present the tragic and the comic scenes, as in regular alternation, as the layers of red and white in a side of streaky, well-cured bacon.... Such changes appear absurd; but they are not so unnatural as they would seem at first sight. The transitions in real life from well-spread boards to death-beds, and from mourning weeds to holiday garments, are not a whit less startling.[38]

Food and drink, and shopping for them, are so essentially domestic and general that it is impossible to assign their many appearances in Dickens's fiction to his having lived above a shop. Yet several of these images are hardly domestic slices or cut measures, rather wholesale items, great cheeses and sides of bacon; it's the scale that suggests they maybe derive from cheesemongery.

Another image which haunts, when one ponders what it might have been like to live in a food shop—especially in a street by a workhouse—is one in which Dickens describes 'pale and pinched-up faces hovered about the windows where was tempting food; hungry eyes wandered over the profusion guarded by one thin sheet of brittle glass—an iron wall to them'.[39]

A comic print of 1828 by Henry Heath in the British Museum collection shows the interior of a cheesemonger's shop, with the counter at right-angles to the front window, much as it probably was in

FIGURE 17A&B. 'What a treat' and 'I wish that you may get it'. This delightful double cartoon shows two shop interiors, a cheesemonger on the left, suggestive of the kind of shop Mr Dodd might have inhabited, and an oilman/tallow chandler on the right. The images show the nature of contemporary retail display, and the poverty in London in the 1820s. Note the boy's badly chipped china, and the girl's pattens, to keep her feet out of the mud and muck of the streets. Etched by Henry Heath and hand-coloured by unknown artist(s). Published by Gans, London, 1829.

Mr Dodd's shop.[40] A rather gaunt boy has come in with a badly chipped plate, asking for two penny's-worth of scrapings. The well-fed shopkeeper, just patting some butter into shape, looks askance at the boy—but for us it is the rest of the image that is revealing: the cage-basket for eggs, the shelf in the window bearing goods on display, great cheeses on other shelves behind the counter, scales and weights on the counter, the shopkeeper's bright white sleeve-covers and apron, and paper bags (or butter-papers?) on their hook. The companion piece shows a scrawny girl sent out to try to borrow money from another shopkeeper by a verbal ruse and a doubtful promise. The bottle under her apron suggests where the money would go were it to be given, which from the shopkeeper's expression seems unlikely.

One wonders whether the living was quite as thin as this in Norfolk Street. I doubt that it was—there were plenty of poorer areas in London, and although Norfolk Street was not as wealthy as central Marylebone or Bloomsbury, there was a large middling population in the vicinity, so a trustworthy grocer should have been able to make a fair living. The fact that Mr Dodd kept his shop for so long—despite plenty of competition nearby—suggests that there were good times as well as bad.

The working day would have been long, with early in-deliveries for fresh goods, out-deliveries to prepare and send to private customers' homes, and, of course, customers visiting the shop. Before the Ten Hours Act of 1847 (which only limited the length of the work day for women and children) working days for everyone were long, so if Mr Dodd wanted to cash in on evening custom, he would have had to remain open late. In one of the *Sketches by Boz*, Dickens describes a cheesemonger's shop at night:

the ragged boys who usually disport themselves about the street, stand crouched in little knots in some projecting door-way, or under the canvass window-blind of the cheesemonger's, where great flaring gas lights, unshaded by any glass, display huge piles of bright red, and pale yellow cheeses, mingled with little five penny dabs of dingy bacon, various tubs of weekly Dorset, and cloudy rolls of 'best fresh'...It is nearly eleven o'clock, and the cold thin rain which has been drizzling so long is beginning to pour down in good earnest; the baked-'tatur man has departed—the kidney-pie merchant has just taken his warehouse on his arm with the same object—the cheese-monger has drawn in his blind—& the boys have dispersed.[41]

Mr Dodd might well have provided an indoor welcome in the form of chairs, or—as in the Heath cartoon, an upended barrel—for customers to rest upon while waiting for purchases to be assembled and packaged up, and perhaps while passing the time of day.

The sociality of shops is evident from cartoons of this period, which sometimes feature two- or three-way conversations which include the shopkeeper. The semi-domestic/semi-public interior of shops seems to have partaken of the informality of the parlour, and something of the conviviality of the ale-house without its boisterousness, and is often used in droll cartoons to provoke laughter through comment on the times. If Mr Dodd was a witty or a friendly shopkeeper, conversations and laughter may often have been audible on the house stairs. If the Dickenses purchased ingredients for their suppers from him, commentary on national affairs as well as local news would have passed upstairs, too, just as they would in conversations had by Mrs Dickens or the family servant elsewhere in the house, or elsewhere in the street.

The permeability of the house might also have been a problem, in terms of interlopers. Mr Dodd would have had to keep a sharp eye on the interconnecting door to the hall, which led up and down to the rest of the house. Burglary was a common problem in London, and opportunist thieves as active then as now: a corner shopkeeper would have to be alert, or he might find his home and lodgers robbed.[42]

Looking at the rest of the house from the inside, we find that in the basement below the shop and parlour were two kitchens, one of them fairly extensive. How much of the produce that may have been sold upstairs in the shop (like baked pies and pickles) was actually made on the premises isn't known, but it's likely that the larger of these kitchens was designed to serve the shopkeeper and his household, and the smaller the lodgers on the upper floors.

It's genuinely a surprise how much can be deduced about the inside of 10 Norfolk Street, and not only from the building as it survives. At some time in the mid-twentieth century, a kind archivist at the British Records Association discovered an old inventory listing the fixtures in the house, and arranged for it to be donated to the Westminster Archives. This document, which calls itself a 'Schedule', was taken down in 1804, in a beautiful clear longhand script. It names Mr Dodd, and specifies the location of his house on the corner of Norfolk and Tottenham Streets.[43] As you read, it's not difficult to imagine the assessor passing through the house looking attentively at everything, even the bolts and latches on the doors, choosing the appropriate terminology, and carefully noting down the details.

The listing goes from the basement methodically upwards to the attics (though sadly missing the final sheet/s) and begins by itemizing the fixed equipment of each kitchen, including a large eleven-foot dresser with pewter-topped shelves, fixed cupboards ten feet tall with strong locks, lead-lined oak sinks, water cisterns with ballcocks, water service pipes, waste pipes, and cooking ranges with sliding spits, trivets, and fenders.

There was a 'copper' for laundry in the north kitchen, which was presumably a facility shared by both households. A copper was a curious thing, quite unfamiliar today. We can glimpse one in use in a contemporary Fairburn cartoon featuring Dickens's favourite clown, Grimaldi, who in the role of a coachman accidentally falls down some steps into an open basement, straight into a barrel of suds, and comes out singing: 'I laugh'd he!he! he! and the Washer-woman laugh'd ha!ha!ha!'[44] The copper is the heavy barrel-shaped object behind the laundress, a brick-built furnace with a fire in its belly (notice the small door and the coal lying by it on the floor), a heavy wooden lid, and a stirring stick protruding from the copper vessel embedded over the fire, which held water for boiling and starching laundry. The famous Cruikshank illustration of Oliver asking for more also features a copper: this one, in the workhouse, was used to heat the paupers' gruel and soup.[45]

We do not know who inhabited these basement kitchens. There may have been a cook and skivvy serving the shop and Mr Dodd's household upstairs, and for the Dickens family a maid-of-all-work who probably spent time down here preparing food and laundering for the growing family upstairs, when she wasn't minding the children.

The Schedule of Fixtures ... ... referred to by the above written Indre

Basement Story

South Kitchen

A Dresser 11f Long with a Two Inch deal top & Four draws
under D⁰ & pit board Compleat — W⁰ 8 dutch rings & One Lock to draws —
Three lengths of pewter shelves 11f long with 2 butt Standards and boards
Linings behind the Shelves — Oak Sink lined with lead copper Grate
and Lead Cockett under D⁰ into drain 1 brass cock & Service pipe —
Two Shelves over sink and boarded linings back of D⁰ A 5½"
banted partition with door in D⁰ from foot of stairs 1 Sash over door
with 15 Square. A deal Pass 7f high & 2f wide — with folding doors
N⁰ 5 Shelves in D⁰ 18" wide — a 5" full waxed dead Lock 1 Letter Lock
One 6 light Sash to partition to passage. A 45" Kitchen range with
... ...
handle & Two swing trivets One Iron Return fender 6f 3 Long
Portland Stone Chimney, inside door a round paneled thumb latch &
1.9" round barrel bolt — 1.7" three bolt brob Lock to inner door —

North Kitchen

A dresser 9f long with 2" deal top, 4 draws under D⁰ & pit board W⁰ 8
dutch rings & One Lock — Three pewter Shelves over dresper with cut standar
& brick lined with deal — 1 Oak Sink lined with lead brass Grate & lead
Cockett to D⁰ and into drain lead pipe ... & brass sink A 4"
A cistern over D⁰ lined with lead 1½" lead waste pipe & lead to sink
1 standing waste in cistern & brass washer a Bell Lock to service pipe
from Street to supply the cistern — W⁰ 2.9" Cockett bolts to outer door &
1.10" spring bolt to D⁰. 1 Large thumb latch. A Pass 7f high & 2f
wide & a 5½" three pannel door 5 Shelves in D⁰ 18" wide — a 5" full
waxed dead Lock — 1 Standard Grate 2" long drop bars ... ...
and sliding Shut backs — 1 iron return fender 5f 6 long — a 17" coffee ...

One cannot fail to ponder whether as a child Dickens found his way down here for breakfast, or for little snacks with the maid-of-all-work, and what conversations might have been had here while pastry was being rolled or pot-herbs chopped, what stories passed on. The smaller kitchen was a dark room even then, because although its tall window opens onto the front yard, at this point the street pavement passes above it on stone slabs, the only direct daylight being provided by an iron grating fixed into the stone, and listed in the Schedule. Another window opens at the back of this room onto the stairwell, but it's a long way down from the first window on the stairs, and would surely have been gloomy, just as it is now without the lights on.

When I was first researching the Dickens family's association with the house, I was astonished to find this inventory, and spent some time transcribing it in detail.[46] No such document survives in the archives for any other house on Norfolk Street, so we must consider this extraordinary manuscript—like so much that has survived for the history of 10 Norfolk Street—as an unexpected gift from the past. I have been fortunate enough to be invited into the house by the current inhabitants, and can report that quite a surprising proportion of the materials listed in the Schedule can still be found *in situ*. We went round the house with the transcript, and as I read it out loud, we looked about us. All of us had an extraordinary feeling of the past flooding through the words.

FIGURE 18. (*Left*) The extraordinary Schedule, or inventory, of Mr Dodd's fixtures and fittings at No. 10 Norfolk Street, many of which survive today. The document dates from 1804.

FIGURE 19. Inside No. 10 Norfolk Street: 1. The curved ripples in some of the panes in this slanted partition, mentioned in Mr Dodd's Schedule of 1804, show it to be probably original hand-blown Georgian glass. Photographed by the author, 2011.

In the basement passage, for example, the Schedule describes 'a canted partition with door from foot of stairs' with a glazed panel over it of '15 squares'. This door and its upper panel were likely to have been important for preventing cooking and laundry smells and steam rising up through the house. The door itself has disappeared, but the door's frame remains, exactly as it says, at a slant, at the bottom of the stairs, and remarkably the fifteen panes of glass above it are still there too, some of the glass showing by its curved undulations to be hand-blown and therefore likely as old as

FIGURE 20. Inside No. 10 Norfolk Street: 2. The staircase down to the basement: the original treads of the stairway still *in situ*. Photographed by the author, 2011.

the house, despite everything the Luftwaffe dropped on the neighbourhood.

This passage-way lies under the hallway on the ground floor above, and runs between the two basement kitchens. It leads from the foot of the stairway in the rear of the house to the open area in the front yard, where there is still a locked coal-hole and a water closet (just as there was in Dickens's day) as well as a lockable vault, under the street pavement. The Schedule lists a large lead-lined water tank, or 'reservoir', raised upon York stone supports, presumably operated by gravity and hand-pump to serve the basement water closet and both kitchens as well as the laundry copper and other facilities upstairs: a very important provision in the days before a constant and pressurized water supply.

The two basement kitchens in the house have of course been modernized in the intervening two hundred years, and denuded of most of what was listed for them in 1804. But, as we turned back into the house from looking at the front yard, we saw that the shelves of an old dresser survive in the passage, and although the pewter coverings, and the long work surface listed below it have gone, the deal backing described in the Schedule still survives; and, it measures eleven feet long.

The artist George Scharf, a contemporary of Mr Dodd, painted the basement kitchen in his own home in Francis Street, only a few blocks east of Cleveland Street. The room has similar dimensions to the larger kitchen in Norfolk Street, so the painting provides a good idea of how the kitchens in Mr Dodd's basement might have appeared at the time.

Scharf's fine watercolour shows a wide stone-flagged floor with painted matting in its centre. A very long dresser (it could easily measure eleven feet) occupies the longest wall. The woman who worked there stands before it, proud of the neatness and good order of the room. The dresser is loaded with dishes and tureens, willow-pattern serving plates, dinner plates, jugs, and bowls, a cruet, coffee grinder, trays, and other dining equipment, with cooking pots, kettles, a trivet, gridiron, and various sieves stowed underneath. It is quite possible that both dressers in Norfolk Street were used in a similar way.

Looking at this household equipment, one realizes that if the Dickenses had belongings of this kind they had probably been

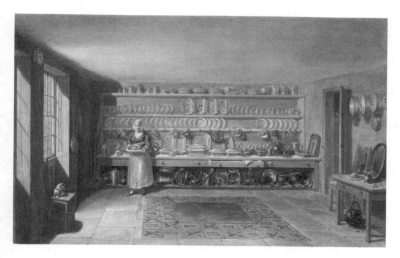

FIGURE 21. Basement kitchen in Francis Street, Tottenham Court Road, by George Scharf. This delightful interior gives a good sense of the kitchen of a comfortable middle-class home. Mr Dodd's and the Dickens family's kitchens at 10 Norfolk Street may have been more sparsely furnished with movable goods, but might have aspired to something like this. The woman's pride in the domestic display is evident. Watercolour, 1846.

received as wedding gifts, and would be just the kind of things they would have had to pawn when Mr Dickens was later threatened with being arrested for debt. For now, this is the kind of room (and perhaps the kind of inhabitant) with which young Dickens might have been familiar below Mr Dodd's shop.

At the very back of the house in 10 Norfolk Street is a basement room entirely without windows. It lies partly under the stairwell, tucked away behind the smaller kitchen. It is described in the Schedule as a wine vault, with its own door and 'full warded lock'. It is still the coldest and darkest room in the house, and still has deep apertures set three by three, into the depth of a very thick wall, which the writer of the Schedule described as '9 brick catacomb wine binns'.

Cold wine racks are rarely described today as 'catacombs', which we associate with the idea of burial. So it is intriguing to think Mr Dodd would have stored his bottled drinks for the shop upstairs (and perhaps some for his own consumption) here, as well as other shop stock which needed to be kept secure and cool.

The stairway up through the house still has its original handrail, and the original sturdy stair treads—thick slices of heavy hardwood, shiny with age and much varnishing—remain in daily use on the first flight of stairs up from the basement to the shop level. They were designed to last in the 1790s.

The Schedule provides a good idea of Mr Dodd's shop fittings, describing four shelves in each shop window, and window shutters outside. Both inner walls of the shop were furnished with units of multiple shelves supported on ornamental columns, and nests of drawers. One cannot fail to wonder if Dickens was thinking of them when he described the 'delightful rows of green bottles and gold labels, together with jars of pickles and preserves, and cheeses and boiled hams, and rounds of beef, arranged on shelves in the most tempting and delicious array' in *Pickwick Papers*, or the very different ones elsewhere in the same book bearing dummy stock, and half of whose drawers had 'nothing in 'em, and the other half don't open'.[47]

Mr Dodd had three counters, a lockable mahogany writing desk and till drawers. No trace of them remains. The little parlour across the passage, which is now the button shop, had a fireplace, tall cupboards, and windows shutters, all now disappeared, as has the brass doorknocker listed in the Schedule. But the little foot-scraper listed outside still stands.

FIGURE 22. Inside No. 10 Norfolk Street: 3. The staircase up from the kitchens, showing the original handrail. Many other details from the Dickens era survive in the house. Photographed by the author, 2011.

The inventory continues for upstairs, but has less to report. Perhaps the most interesting item is the description of the 'patent water closet' on the wide first landing, with its mahogany seat, as it was when Mr Dodd and the Dickenses lived there, with a sink in the separate multi-shelved china closet beside it. This would have been an unusual but crucial facility in the house at 10 Norfolk Street, because unlike most other houses, there was no backyard for the usual London outdoor 'necessary', or cesspit. A modern toilet and cupboard now occupy the same landing.

In most of the remaining rooms the listing simply mentions door locks and window shutters, built-in cupboards, and fireplaces with marble 'slips' (slabs lining the hearth) firestone hearths, and wooden 'dressings' (which I take to mean mantelpieces) but it does not go into details. In almost all instances, these old fittings are gone, but the best room in the house—the first-floor front, what would probably have been Mr Dodd's sitting room—still has all its window shutters, and a perfect Georgian mantelpiece.

The survival of the Schedule allows us to perceive the house in a very different way from how one might otherwise regard 10 Norfolk Street today. When the listing was noted down in 1804, the house was still quite new—perhaps less than ten years old—and its details help us recognize how very modern and commodious it must have felt when Mr Dodd took it over, with its ornamental shop-fittings and excellent water closets. Ten years afterwards, when the Dickens family first arrived, Mr Dodd was settled in, the shop well established, and domestic arrangements with previous lodgers are likely to have been well worked out.

As one would expect with any London house now divided into separate flats, there has been a great deal of modernizing and obliteration. Yet much survives, and this extraordinary inventory helps us imagine and confirm what Dickens would have known intimately everywhere within this unique London house. One can imagine his child's hands holding tight on the square balusters as he laboriously climbed up step by step on chubby toddler's legs, or later, as a teenager racing up the same stairs, two or three steps at a time.

CHAPTER 5

Street

LOOKING DOWN AND AROUND

W E'VE LOOKED AT the maps for a bird's eye view of the district, glanced at the big institutions in the neighbourhood, the local environment, and the house from outside and in, so in this chapter we're looking down at the street from inside the house, as Dickens would have done, as a child, from an upstairs window. What might a curious little boy have observed, gazing down on the street life of this part of the metropolis from the warmth and safety of his home?

The main difficulty is that we don't know for certain on which floor or floors the Dickenses lived at 10 Norfolk Street, but the most likely possibility is that Mr Dodd, as the owner and householder, would have kept the main floor above the shop for himself, and rented out the upper storeys.[1]

Upper floors in London—being less easy of access and with lower ceiling heights—have always been cheaper to rent than the grander first-floor rooms, and that would also have suited Dickens's parents. In being posted to work at Somerset House, John Dickens's income—curiously—had suddenly dropped: special port allowances due to him for his work in Portsea now ceased, and it appears there was no recognition in the Navy Office pay structure of the higher costs of living in central London.[2] The Dickenses, faced with supporting a growing family on a reduced income, were probably glad to take Mr Dodd's lodgings, especially since the locality was familiar and close to the homes of the extended family on both sides.

We do not know if the Dickens family had one floor or two, or if there were other lodgers in the house at the time. Close-living, or what we might regard as overcrowding, limited in scale but comfortable (as Dickens described it) was an accepted part of ordinary life for most Londoners.[3] The Dickens family household now comprised his parents John and Elizabeth Dickens, the children Fanny and Charles, and soon the new baby Letitia, who was born at Norfolk Street in April 1816. Mary Allen, Elizabeth's widowed sister, seems to have lived with the family until she remarried in 1821, and there was probably also a maid-of-all-work, whose name has not come down to us.[4]

Each of the floors of Mr Dodd's house had three rooms: in the Schedule/inventory mentioned in Chapter 4, these rooms were termed 'Sitting room', 'Bed room', and 'Breakfast room'. It is possible that there were four rooms in the attic storey at the very top of the house; the Schedule/ inventory was sadly cut off after its first mention of the 'Atticks', but, commonly, although there is less height, there is more floor space at the top level of the house, because there is no need for a long landing to get to a higher level. If the family had only one level, the best room (the large front room) is likely to have been chosen as the family parlour, perhaps with a sofa-bedstead, and another the parental bedroom. The two older children may have shared a room with Aunt Mary and/or the family servant.[5]

If this, or something like it, was the arrangement, little Charles is likely to have slept on the very top floor of the house or the one below it, and perhaps played up there too. Kneeling or standing on a chair, he would have been able to look out from high windows over the housetops, into the rooms opposite, and down onto the streets which formed his corner.[6]

Thinking about what Norfolk Street might have been like in the years leading up to 1820, we have to imagine all its original houses back in place, including those across the road, which would have filled his view. No. 10 Norfolk Street has a wide frontage, with three well-spaced windows, so, obliquely right and left his vista could have taken in most of the opposite side of the street, perhaps down almost to Charles Street looking left, and as far up the street the other way as the shining shop sign of the three golden balls at the top end of Norfolk Street, and the City of Hereford public house facing it from the next corner up, at the start of Cleveland Street.

Dickens himself was a coastal boy before he became a metropolitan one, and he always loved and appreciated the countryside, especially within reach of tidal waters. He later wrote a conversation in which Sam Weller commented that a rural view 'beats chimbley pots'.[7] It is possible that Dickens was aware of the aridity of Norfolk Street as a child. Although the little house the family had just left in Portsea was also urban, it did have sea spray in the air. The air of

London was laden with smoke and dust, and the houses in Norfolk Street were taller than those he had left behind, so the canyon between them was correspondingly deeper.[8]

Nevertheless, this unassuming London side street had its compensations. From the windows on the very top floor, Dickens might have been able to see over the smoking 'chimbley pots' and roofs to the tree-tops of the Middlesex Hospital's back garden and the high triple roofscape of the Hospital itself, rearing above the neighbouring houses, watch the London pigeons, and seasonal arrivals like starlings and swifts. In that direction, too, the sun set. Lowering his gaze, or observing from a lower floor, he would have taken in the windows of the houses opposite, their street-level entries, and the pavement and roadway below, looking down to get a bird's-eye view of the tops of carts, waggons, cabs, and people.[9] Like Mr Pickwick, from his lodgings he could contemplate 'human nature in all the numerous phases it exhibits'.[10]

Norfolk Street itself was a short street of two rows of brick-built houses facing each other over a slender roadway. Several of the houses opposite had shops at ground level, but it is not known for certain whether any of them had Georgian bow windows, like the small run of shops that survives. That would certainly have made for a pretty street, but there are reasons for suspecting that it was not quite so. First, there is John Tallis, whose view up Norfolk Street we looked at earlier, who portrays a plain-looking street of modest flat-fronted Georgian houses, and what looks like a cobbled roadway, which would have been noisy.

The period in which these houses were built—the 1780s and 1790s—was one of plainness and simplicity in urban architecture: a Georgian variety of functional minimalism was in vogue. Most of

FIGURE 23. Close-up of Tallis's view of Norfolk Street. The road surface looks cobbled, just as the street to its east (now Goodge Place) remains today. Compare with the recent photograph (Figure 10).

these houses are likely to have been quite plain, and—except for their door-cases—unadorned: rather like the Workhouse, or the houses which still survive on the modest street now called Goodge Place, at the back of Dickens's home. This austerity was part of the architectural handwriting of the age. One of the houses opposite his, at No. 21 Norfolk Street, might have been slightly more interesting to look at than the rest, or more ornate inside, because it was the Horsfall household, probably built for the local builder/developer of that name. The houses London builders erected for themselves tended to be rather finer than those they built speculatively for unknown clients.

It's not easy to know whether John Tallis's views of subsidiary streets were intended to be taken as documentary truth. Perhaps understandably, his draughtsmanly interest tails off on small streets like this one. In looking up Norfolk Street, Tallis seems not to have noticed the bow-fronted shops of Mr Dodd and his neighbours, which were certainly there when the image was made, but he does show the Georgian shop frontages at each corner on Charles Street, with their multiple panes of glass and their angled entrances similar to the one which survives at 10 Norfolk Street today.

Tallis also indicates that the shop on the right corner with Charles Street was double the size of the one opposite, and he shows more uniformity on the nearer buildings on the right of Norfolk Street than on the left. Both characteristics accord well with a contemporary numbered street plan, so Tallis's view cannot simply be dismissed as schematic or imaginary. There is no vestige of most of these houses surviving now: the run of houses on the hospital side mostly disappeared in the early twentieth century to allow the hospital's expansion, and except for the four which survive today, the rest of those on Mr Dodd's side of the way were replaced by a single apartment building in the Edwardian era, so we have no guide to the original site boundaries on the ground now. Local rate-books show that in Dickens's day most of the houses in Norfolk Street were of a lower rateable value than Mr Dodd's, so they are likely to have been narrower, less imposing buildings, and their lack of size uniformity on the street plan suggests a variety of original builders, so quite possibly their appearances differed, too, just as Tallis seems to show.

Some of these houses may have had purpose-designed shop-fronts, which could have been quite elegant. A beautiful multiple-paned double shopfront survives further up Cleveland Street, which shows that—like Regency furniture—original frontages of that date were light and elegant, and simple in decoration.

Other houses in the street might originally have been intended as private residences, and this mix of purpose might have lent the street a slightly higgledy-piggledy look. In Norfolk Street, several of the ground levels were occupied by businesses and shops, perhaps not always those for which they were designed. This is a typical urban pattern of colonization in London, which can still be seen in places today: several examples survive in the older houses still standing on the northern arm of Cleveland Street. A favourite way of using the front room of a house for a shopfront or workshop was simply to extend the domestic window opening down to ground level, and insert a door. Some of the ground-floor rooms in Norfolk Street may have become open workshops, or may have had work-rooms at the rear, visible from the street. Dickens describes such a shop in *Pickwick Papers*: 'a newly-painted tenement which had been recently converted into something between a shop and a private-house', its shop sign inscribed 'above the window of what, in times bygone, had been the front parlour'.[12]

Except for the pawnbroker on the corner, who used some of his upper rooms for storing pledges, upper floors opposite were mostly occupied as housing (either by the ratepayer themselves or sub-let to lodgers) so they would probably have had window curtains and/or blinds, perhaps an occasional pot plant on a window sill. Servants might shake their dusters out of open windows, someone might sweep the front step and perhaps whiten it, sweep the street outside their house, sluice it down with water perhaps, clean the windows—all the small domestic touches which keep houses trim when they are lived in, and the cessation of which spells the appearance of neglect.[13]

Late at night the street might have presented more of a blank appearance, as indoor shutters were unfolded and closed against the weather and the night. But there were likely to have been interesting things to observe during that magical time as the light is fading, especially as the houses opposite No. 10 faced away from the sunset. Much later, the poet T. S. Eliot would characterize this hour as 6 p.m. in winter (the fag end of the day, he calls it) and he described that urban time before street lights are lit, when people might have lights on indoors before the closing of shutters and curtains: 'and then the lighting of the lamps'.[14] This is the time when a stroller, or an observer opposite, might be able to see into neighbours' windows—see pictures on the walls, furnishings. Norfolk Street not being very wide, the view into the houses opposite might have revealed people reading, sewing, talking, playing, arguing, working—multiple lives passing in their own domestic spaces, simultaneously.

People in Tottenham Street kept chickens in their backyards, so the neighbourhood might have been woken in the mornings at cock crow, and the noise of carts and waggons passing on the cobbles.[15]

The Workhouse bell clanged at 6.30 a.m., and on weekdays a variety of working sounds from the Workhouse and surrounding streets would gradually have risen. During the day, the child Dickens would have been able to watch daily events and characters in motion along the street: horses, coal and milk deliveries, building works, postmen, tradesmen, muffin-men, street sellers, street sweepers, funerals, rag-and-bone men, old-clothes-men, ballad-sellers: the sheer variety of London life as later recorded by Henry Mayhew would have passed along Norfolk Street at some time or another: it was not a quiet street.

From his upper window, young Dickens could have pondered the shop signs opposite, the lettering of shop names, and goods out on the pavement. A leather-cutter who dealt in huge hides, for example, occupied No. 17; a plumber and glazier at No. 24 with sheets of lead and glass to cut, form, and deliver; a coach trimmer at 27, mending or rejuvenating the upholstery of gentlemen's carriages (such as doctors' gigs); and at No. 28 was a cabinet maker who might be seen planing, sanding, and polishing the furniture he had created, or making repairs. This was a street mainly of artisans, any and all of whom would have been displaying goods outside, using the street as a storage space and occasional workshop, unloading a variety of curious materials and loading finished goods into barrows or delivery carts, all within the purview of the windows of No. 10.[16]

If something unusual caught the boy's interest—like a funeral or a street band, a muffin-man with his bell, a rag-and-bone man's call, the hubbub of an injured workman being rushed to the hospital by his workmates—he would not have been slow to go round to the side window to see if the spectacle was passing along Tottenham

Street. We know from the records of the Old Bailey that shops on Tottenham Court Road were often targeted by shoplifters, who would run down side streets like Tottenham Street to get away.[17] This description of a crowd chasing a thief from *Oliver Twist*, can be read as if from above, and reinhabits the view for us:

> 'Stop thief! Stop thief!' There is a magic in the sound. The tradesman leaves his counter; and the carman his waggon; the butcher throws down his tray; the baker his basket; the milk-man his pail; the errand-boy his parcels; the schoolboy his marbles; the paviour his pick-axe; the child his battledore. Away they run, pell-mell, helter-skelter, slap-dash: tearing, yelling, screaming: knocking down the passengers as they turn the corners: rousing up the dogs, and astonishing the fowls; and streets, squares, and courts, re-echo with the sound.[18]

The Tottenham Street side of Mr Dodd's house faced a row of modest houses and shops connecting Norfolk Street to busy Tottenham Court Road. More or less opposite the side window was a narrow alley in the direction of the Workhouse, and a small public house called the Lord Monson's Arms, which doubtless had its own interest at different times of day in terms of sweeping or swilling out, the delivery of barrels by the fine working horses and brawny men of the brewers' drays, the great iron-clad trapdoors in the pavement being lifted to take the great rolling barrels and for closure after deliveries, and all the other goings-on that a Victorian public house might generate, like scenes of conversation, sociability, laughter, raucous singing, drunkenness, ribaldry, arguments, perhaps hungry children hoping their parents might buy them some food before the money was drunk away, and sporadic late-night fights. When it was quiet, Mr Bumble and Monks, the gothic villain of *Oliver Twist*, might have sat to talk in just such a back-street public house.[19]

From that side of the house, too, the flank and roof of the Workhouse would have been visible during the day above the intervening houses; a more formidable presence after dark, whose curious sounds might punctuate the night when quietness reigned at last. The boy might have lain awake at night pondering these sounds, imagining the dark pavements and the interiors of the Hospital and the Workhouse. During the day, young Dickens doubtless observed other children on Norfolk Street, heard street cries, saw beggars and poor elderly, perhaps sad families on their way to or from the Workhouse. He would have grown to recognize the street in the variety of its comfort and poverty: not understanding everything, but puzzling and observing the business of life as it proceeded below.

While he might have been horrified by the ragged and hungry appearance of some of these poor people, Dickens's humane stance in later life came from education and example, from exposure to them, and from his parents' attitudes towards them. He was educated to feel Christian sorrow and pity for these pitiful folk in their predicament, and to recognize his own good fortune, despite his own family's difficulties. It is possible, too, that Mr Dodd had ways of showing kindness: being the first food shop that side of the Workhouse he was probably frequently importuned. As an adult, Dickens attended a local Unitarian chapel in Little Portland Street, a few blocks away from Norfolk Street, but we do not know which church he attended on Sundays as a child. It is most likely to have been Old Marylebone Church, where his father (and perhaps Mr Dodd) had been christened.[20] It is clear from his writings that Dickens's knowledge of the Bible, especially the New Testament, was profound and heartfelt.

Charles Dickens was a hyperactive adult, so when he wasn't unwell, he was probably much the same as a child. This is how Forster describes him:

> He was a very little and a very sickly boy...subject to attacks of violent spasm which disabled him for any active exertion. He was never a good little cricket-player. He was never a first-rate hand at marbles, or peg-top, or prisoner's base. But he had great pleasure in watching the other boys, officers' sons for the most part, at these games, reading while they played; and he had always the belief that this early sickness had brought to himself one inestimable advantage, in the circumstance of his weak health having strongly inclined him to reading. It will not appear, as my narrative moves on, that he owed much to his parents, or was other than in his first letter to Washington Irving he described himself to have been, a 'very small and not-over-particularly-taken-care-of boy;' but he has frequently been heard to say that his first desire for knowledge, and his earliest passion for reading, were awakened by his mother, who taught him the first rudiments not only of English, but also, a little later, of Latin. She taught him regularly every day for a long time, and taught him, he was convinced, thoroughly well.[21]

The interest in looking out of the window and journeying up and down to the basement kitchen most likely wore thin before too long.

Like most children, he probably disliked being cooped up indoors for long. In later life Dickens is said to have ridden or walked miles daily, a journeying habit rooted in a natural restlessness, which he likely suffered as a child: something difficult to deal with in confined lodgings, especially before the boy could entertain himself by reading.

During much of this stay in Norfolk Street, Mrs Dickens was pregnant and then nursing the new baby, and perhaps easily tired.[22] It could have been important to distract her little boy, to get him out of the house as much as possible. Aunt Mary might have been happy to take him to see various local relatives—the Charltons in Berners Street, Grandmother Dickens at Uncle William's shop in Oxford Street, or perhaps further afield.[23]

The servant might have been asked to take the boy out on errands to local shops, or perhaps for a romp on Primrose Hill or a trek to Hyde Park, or even to take him with her on visits to her own family. Very little seems to be known about the servant/nurse who worked for the Dickens family in Norfolk Street: she may have been one of the child carers Dickens later described as relishing his discomfort by telling him terrifying stories.[24] If so, she may also have relished terrifying him about the Workhouse, too, or—fearful herself—may have wanted to cross over the road to avoid its shadow (or the gruff gatekeeper and his ragged charges waiting by the gate) and may well have found other ways to teach the boy to feel the potency of the place.

Dressed to go out (perhaps not always quite so immaculately as he later described in the Soho Bazaar episode) and being brought out of the front door onto Norfolk Street, young Dickens would see the entire streetscape in a different way. Now he could see the familiar shops and houses opposite at their own level, and now too those on his own side of the way, as well as the entire view down to the cross-roads at Charles Street, where wider streets led in different directions from the front of the Hospital: out east and west to the coaching roads, and south to Oxford Street, Soho, and eventually the River.

Outside the house, he could compare Mr Dodd's shop window display with that of his arch competitor for local trade, Mr Stamp, the grocer and tea dealer right next door. One of Dickens's *Sketches by Boz* concerns the family of a London grocer on a holiday at Ramsgate, which describes a family of four who inherit some money, take on airs and graces, and are swindled by fraudsters, for which Mr Dodd or the Stamps next door might have been a model.[25] Then there was the discreet window of Mr and Mrs Bridger, makers of ladies' stays and gowns, and so on down to Charles Street.

In the mid-twentieth century, Mr Dodd's shop was occupied by an undertaker, who hung a painted board on the railings outside, advertising his services.[26] It is quite possible that the undertaker's notice was a distant replacement of hoardings originated by Mr Dodd, which would have been visible a good way down the street. Such boards—like other local shop signs—could have been among the first things upon which young Dickens tried out his alphabet: D-O-D-D, C-H-E-E-S-E in all the confusions of script and capital letters. The shop boards of Norfolk Street, and the street signs on Charles Street, might well have been where Dickens first learned to apply what his mother and aunt would have been teaching him upstairs.

From street-level the boy could try out the foot-scraper, or ponder the covered manholes in the pavement, down which he had seen the sooty coalman—shiny with coal tar—shoot the raw coal from huge sacks stiff with coal dust. He could peep down through the railings into the area below the shop, and into the bright kitchen window of Mr Dodd's basement, greet the cook, smell the savoury odours wafting up, or the domestic smell of boiling, or the scorched smell of ironing freshly starched laundry. As a small child, Dickens would surely have been profoundly impressed, even awed, had he happened to be playing by the front door when Mr Bumble the Beadle, or his equivalent, passed by on parish business: striding along Norfolk Street in full regalia, wielding his staff of office.[27]

Looking up the street (beyond the Workhouse) the long vista of Cleveland Street led north towards the green open fields and the northern heights of London: Hampstead, Holloway, and Highgate. From outside Mr Dodd's shop door, one could also peer around the corner towards the Regency Theatre on Tottenham Street to observe the Monson's Arms from a different angle, the shops and pie-houses, print-shops and timber-sellers, and in the distance the graveyard of Whitfield's Tabernacle (where body-snatchers had been caught) and the passing coaches, trundling wagons, and other traffic on the way to or from the turnpike at Tottenham Court.

Living on a corner has a special kind of potential, which is lacking in a mere component part of a long terrace of other houses. The similarity is noticeable between Mr Dodd's corner and the building on Wellington Street, Covent Garden, which Charles Dickens later chose for his editorial office of *All the Year Round* between 1859 and his death, with his own bachelor flat upstairs. That was also a corner shop facing west, with windows overlooking two streets, up towards Covent Garden Theatre and Long Acre, and down towards the Strand. It stood inside the parish of St Paul Covent Garden, and, curiously, the old name for one of the streets he overlooked there, too, was Charles Street.

Towards the later end of the period Charles Dickens first lived in Norfolk Street, when he was aged nearly 5, he might have been allowed out on short errands nearby without adult supervision, perhaps with his older sister Fanny. They might run down to pay the postman for a delivery, or a muffin-man, for example, or visit the bakery or the pie-shop round the corner on Tottenham Street, within sight of the side window, where—when the grown-ups were busy, and the servant occupied in the basement—the children might safely have run round to get a loaf, a hot pie for supper, or a treat of gingerbread.

Dickens and his older sister might occasionally have been allowed to play with other children known to the family, which did not involve going far afield, or they might have been thought sensible enough to run round together with a note or a special cake or pie to their great-aunt's home round the block in Berners Street. London children were much freer in the past than they are today, and parents far less fearful: short errands were a good way to allow a child to learn the important skill of becoming street-wise.[28] Despite the family's money problems, Dickens's mother was a sensible and intelligent woman, and her children probably were, too. It is quite possible that Dickens learned to navigate the local area in a simple way under the tutelage of Fanny, or the young servant, during this first stay in Norfolk Street.

Whether or not this was so, one cannot fail to wonder what little Dickens might have thought about the great Hospital and the

Workhouse, so close by. The Middlesex Hospital may have been less noticeable, as it was hidden behind the houses opposite; but the Workhouse was by far the largest building on the street, surrounded by smaller houses. Did the mystery of its interior provoke his curiosity? He would certainly have heard it spoken about, might have heard stories, seen sorry folk, and heard sorry tales. He would have become familiar with its bleak outside wall and gateway, seen the sculpture of the old man and may have tried to read his message— AVOID IDLENESS AND INTEMPERANCE—would have heard the Workhouse bell and other more curious sounds from within, might have witnessed wretched queues of people waiting to go in, or crocodiles of poor children forming up under their task-master, to be conducted to church on a Sunday.

My own childhood was passed in a district of London which housed a large convent surrounded by a high wall, which was always quiet. It is not easy to say what kind of influence this place had on the area—its great silent presence was akin to a black hole in the street plan, something we had to skirt round to get home from school. None of us had any real understanding of what went on inside. I always sprinted through its shadow if I had to pass by alone.[29] Our local workhouse infirmary was known as 'the Knacker's Yard', and other kids told me that when the workhouse chimney was smoking they were burning the bodies of those who had died in there. The Workhouse on Cleveland Street was a social black hole, but not a silent one. In the mornings, it too would have made a shadow on the street, and screams and moans, cries, shouts, the sounds of daily working, and of course the workhouse bell would surely have been audible in its vicinity. Coffins went through the gate. We do not know what stories local children heard or told each other about the Workhouse in Norfolk Street, what they believed about the fate of those who entered there, what hushed or fearful tones might have been used when speaking of it, or whether children learned to cross the road to avoid its malevolent shadow.

As well as deliveries, and arrivals and departures at the Workhouse gate, there might well have been moments which would have lent themselves to an observant eye. In an important early sequence in *Oliver Twist*, Dickens has a passing master-sweep halt to read the notice fixed on the Workhouse gate, offering the child for disposal with a five-pound premium:

It chanced one morning...that Mr. Gamfield, chimney-sweep, went his way down the High Street, deeply cogitating in his mind, his ways and means of paying certain arrears of rent, for which his landlord had become rather pressing. Mr. Gamfield's most sanguine estimate of his finances could not raise them within full five pounds of the desired amount; and, in a species of arithmetical desperation, he was alternately cudgelling his brains and his donkey, when, passing the workhouse, his eyes encountered the bill on the gate.

'Wo—o!' said Mr. Gamfield to the donkey.

The donkey was in a state of profound abstraction: wondering, probably, whether he was destined to be regaled with a cabbage-stalk or two, when he had disposed of the two sacks of soot with which the little cart was laden; so, without noticing the word of command, he jogged onward.

Mr. Gamfield growled a fierce imprecation on the donkey generally, but more particularly on his eyes; and, running after him, bestowed a blow on his head, which would inevitably have beaten in any skull but a donkey's. Then, catching hold of the bridle, he gave his jaw a sharp wrench, by way of gentle reminder that he was not his own master; and by these means turned him round. He then gave him another blow on the head, just to stun him till he came back again. Having completed these arrangements, he walked up to the gate, to read the bill.

The gentleman with the white waistcoat, was standing at the gate with his hands behind him, after having delivered himself of some profound sentiments in the board-room. Having witnessed the little dispute between Mr. Gamfield and the donkey, he smiled joyously when that person came up to read the bill, for he saw at once that Mr. Gamfield was exactly the sort of master Oliver Twist wanted. Mr. Gamfield smiled, too, as he perused the document; for five pounds was just the sum he had been wishing for; and, as to the boy with which it was encumbered, Mr. Gamfield, knowing what the dietary of the workhouse was, well knew he would be a nice small pattern: just the very thing for register stoves. So, he spelt the bill through again, from beginning to end; and then, touching his fur cap in token of humility, accosted the gentleman in the white waistcoat.

'This here boy, sir, wot the parish wants to 'prentis,' said Mr. Gamfield.

'Ay, my man,' said the gentleman in the white waistcoat, with a condescending smile. 'What of him?'

'If the parish vould like him to learn a right pleasant trade, in a good 'spectable chimbley-sweepin' bisness,' said Mr. Gamfield, 'I wants a 'prentis, and I am ready to take him.'[30]

Dickens shows this man's ill education in his efforts to read the notice, and his ingrained inhumanity in his treatment of his donkey. But worse yet is the complacent man in the white waistcoat, who has a duty to care for the children in his charge, and who approves this wretch as a suitable employer for little Oliver. These events take place in the street outside the workhouse in which Oliver Twist was born.

A late twentieth-century work on the topography of Dickens's life and fiction dismissed the two years Dickens spent in Norfolk Street as a child in the following terms:

> In 1816 John Dickens was transferred briefly to London, and Charles, aged four, entered the first of his many London homes, in Norfolk Street, off Fitzroy Square, St Pancras. We shall meet him there again in young manhood, but his first stay was not significant.[31]

Dickens's own discretion about his family's association with Norfolk Street seems to have contributed not only to the neglect of this locality in his biography, but also to the circulation of nonsense such as this, almost every element of which is inaccurate: the 'brief' transfer to London actually lasted two full years—January 1815 to January 1817— Dickens probably passed his third and fourth birthdays there; Norfolk Street is not situated 'off Fitzroy Square', and nor is it in St Pancras. How can anyone expect us to believe that this first stay—40 per cent of his life when he left there at almost 5 years old—was 'not significant'?

We have no way of knowing exactly how significant this first stay in Norfolk Street really was for Dickens, beyond our own sense that all childhood experience is formative, and that in every child's development the years between 3 and 5 are of deep importance. The years of childhood are so often and so evocatively featured in Dickens's works that it is perverse to think that this period in Norfolk Street might have been unimportant to him. Had Dickens spent these years anywhere else—in a mining village for example, or in a travelling showman's caravan, in a rural vicarage, or in the keeper's lodge of a zoological garden, or, indeed in a stately home—his biographers would not have been so very slow to speculate about the likely impact on his imagination and his later writing, or so swift to dismiss these years as 'insignificant'.

Dickens himself was highly conscious that he was the product of his own past, and equally aware of the contingencies of biography: how slight changes or chances can profoundly alter human trajectories. His silence about Norfolk Street bears an affinity to that which surrounds his social origins in the servant class, his fugitive grandfather Barrow, the Marshalsea Prison, and the blacking factory.[32] Each of these matters came to public knowledge only after his death, some of them long afterwards. Each of them, too, is now recognized as vital to his biography and to his development as a novelist.

Dickens's silences reveal that he was highly sensitive about his social origins: that he felt himself vulnerable to social snobbery, and to the family shame of financial failure and scandal. His cultivation of an oyster-like secrecy concerning these matters is informative, as it reveals that they were actually the reverse of insignificant to Dickens himself. Whether the reasons for his reticence about Norfolk Street were of similar origin, or if there might have been some other explanation for its almost complete obscurity in Forster and elsewhere is not known. Was this simply social embarrassment about being discovered to have lived over a cheesemonger's, a few doors away from a Workhouse?

CHAPTER 6

Calamity

SHEERNESS, CHATHAM, CAMDEN TOWN, MARSHALSEA, SOMERS TOWN

IT WOULD NOT be an overstatement to say that the interval between the two eras the Dickens family lived in Norfolk Street was one of very mixed fortunes. This chapter bridges the era of Dickens's life between these periods, so it glances at what happened to him between 1817 and 1829 fairly swiftly, for those unacquainted with the details. Biographers tend to cover this period, when he was aged between 5 and 17, in well-rehearsed ways, because very little first-hand evidence survives for most of Dickens's childhood and youth, and we are heavily dependent on Forster's rendering of the autobiographical fragment.[1]

Neither Cleveland Street nor its Workhouse make much of a showing in this chapter, because Dickens was not living in the near vicinity during these years. But I suggest how, through a series of encounters with other children—a servant, a chimney sweep, and the real Bob Fagin—the young Dickens might have heard about the inner workings of the workhouse system from the point of view of experienced child inmates. Behind these means of access to personal testimony lies his own experience of the family's imprisonment in the Marshalsea Debtors' Prison, in 1824.

At the beginning of 1817 Dickens's father was again posted out of London by his employer, the Navy Pay Office, this time to the naval town of Sheerness, on the Isle of Sheppey, in Kent. Shortly afterwards, the family moved again to the Medway estuary town of Chatham, nearby. The next few years in Chatham, between 1817 and 1822, are generally regarded as the happiest of Charles Dickens's childhood, being described by his biographer Edgar Johnson as 'the happy time'.[2] These were years when the family was mostly on a fairly even keel, and the boy Dickens read voraciously, explored, and play-acted. Above all, it was a time when he had regular schooling.

During their brief stay in Sheerness, the Dickens family's sitting room shared a party wall with the local theatre, and the family enjoyed hearing everything through the wall—presumably laughter and applause, even what was passing on stage—and joined in the singing of the national anthem at the end of the shows.[3] The gusto with which Dickens's father later recounted the story of this sitting room suggests a delightful level of enjoyment in the productions— and the absurdity of listening in for nothing. Dickens probably had his fifth birthday in this little house in Sheerness, and its situation doubtless added to his interest in play-acting. The theatre itself was due for demolition, having been leased until that Christmas to the theatrical family of the Jerrolds (friends of Dickens in later life), who had been presenting a wide repertoire, from Shakespeare plays to farces and comic songs. The plays the family heard through the wall could have been theirs.[4]

The family left Sheerness after only a few months. Until then, Dickens had been educated 'thoroughly well' by his mother, and understood some rudimentary Latin before he attended school in Chatham, so it is clear that she was an educated woman herself, and that she passed on a great deal to her eldest son.[5] His schoolmaster in Chatham was William Giles, an Oxford-educated Baptist minister. Although Dickens later described his education as 'irregular and rambling', the next few years were the best conventional education he had.[6] Giles appears to have had high hopes of this particular pupil, hopes which Dickens himself absorbed. Part of Dickens's subsequent disappointment in his parents was related to their lack of ambition for him when they became mired in their own financial difficulties. It looks as though he had acquired a modest expectation that he might attend a university, and that such ideas had been generated at this school.

Dickens is often thought of as essentially a London author, but it would also be true to say that Chatham, nearby Rochester, and the surrounding Kent countryside flow powerfully into several of his books, not least in the magnificently dramatic and brutal opening pages of *Great Expectations*, when the escaped convict Magwitch terrifies the young Pip into bringing him food, and a file to cut through his chains. The association of convicts with that part of the Kent coast derives from the Hulks, great old ships moored mid-stream, serving as holding prisons for convicts (most of them from London) destined for forced labour in the dockyards or for transportation to Australia. This punitive presence blended with the culture of the port in the days of the great sailing ships, the swaggering masculinity of the sailors, and the gender politics of the quayside, excitement of tales of travel, the mists and tides of the estuary, and the beauty of the local countryside: all these lie behind Dickens's memories of this period, which Dickens's biographer Michael Slater believes to have been profoundly nourishing to his imagination. Dickens's friend Forster regarded Chatham as 'the birthplace of his fancy'.[7] Chatham is also thought of as a positive time because family income improved again, and domestic arrangements seem to have been good for most of the time. The family was still growing, and the arrival of Mary Weller as the family's servant and mother's help looks to have been altogether a positive thing.[8] Dickens is said to have based the figure of Peggotty in *David Copperfield* upon her, and if Mary Weller really was as thoroughly lovable a person as Peggotty, then she alone would account for the happiness of Dickens's young days in Chatham.

The picture of golden memories with which we are presented, however, does not quite square with Dickens's later characterization of the Medway towns as 'Dullborough' or 'Mudfog', and with the bleakness and underlying sense of threat which imbues the Kentish parts of *Great Expectations*. Perhaps the lustre of the Chatham days was something Dickens appreciated only when he compared them with those which followed.

It was in Chatham that Dickens's Aunt Mary met and married Dr Lamerte, which was an early moment in the break-up of this happy home. I have always pondered if Dr Lamerte might have been an original for the charming but cold and domineering serial widower Mr Murdstone, in *David Copperfield*, as Dickens's aunt lived for only a short while after their marriage. His aunt's withdrawal from the family may have had an economic impact upon the household as well as an emotional one, because she may have helped financially and probably contributed to the nurture and the education of the children, too. Money difficulties were never far from the surface, even in this era of regular income. The family moved into smaller and cheaper accommodation, and thereafter things probably became even more constrained.

Dr Lamerte's son by a previous marriage became a lodger in her place, and his enthusiasm for amateur theatricals was of course infectious; but young Dickens suffered later from this fellowship, because it was Lamerte who later recruited him to work as a factory boy. Finances were already rocky when the family left Chatham for London in 1822, leaving young Dickens behind for a short while to finish his school term. Also left behind were debts, which eventually proved disastrous.

Mary Weller having married and remained in Chatham, the Dickens family brought with them back to London a young maid-of-all-work from the local workhouse in Chatham. The name of this young servant is not known, but she remained with the family for some time, and it is said that she was the model for the Marchioness in *The Old Curiosity Shop*. She was probably very young: working-class girls were often sent out into service at the age of 11 or 12, so she may not have been much older than Dickens himself, who at this stage was 10 years old. We don't know if this girl was unique among the family's servants, or whether the Dickens family had employed other workhouse children, nor if Mrs Dickens chose to do so from economy or benevolence: most likely both. As we shall see, it may have been from her that Dickens acquired some of his inside knowledge of workhouse life, and some recognition of his kinship and fellow feeling with the incarcerated poor.

Back in London, and coping again with a drop in pay, Mr and Mrs Dickens and their larger family had now to take accommodation in an area with far fewer pretensions to gentility than Norfolk Street. They found a small house in Bayham Street, Camden Town, which Forster describes as 'a mean small tenement, with a wretched little back-garden abutting on a squalid court'.[9] They now had six children, so the small house was probably very overcrowded.[10]

At the end of the school term, when Charles eventually joined them from Chatham, it was clear that his parents could no longer afford to continue his schooling. Things cannot have been easy for the whole family, being so short of money, and young Dickens's life at this time became somewhat aimless. His father, he told Forster,

appeared to have utterly lost at this time the idea of educating me at all, and to have utterly put from him the notion that I had any claim upon him, in that regard, whatever. So I degenerated into cleaning his boots of a morning, and my own; and making myself useful in the work of the little house; and looking after my younger brothers and sisters (we were now six in all); and going on such poor errands as arose out of our poor way of living.[11]

Many years later, Dickens wrote a delightful account called 'Gone Astray', about becoming lost in central London as a child, an experience which seems to date from this period.[12] He says he was taken one weekday morning to see the church at St Giles's—that dangerous district which both frightened and fascinated him. The excursion then extended further south to take in a view of the great stone lion, which in those days looked down from its lofty parapet on the grand old aristocratic palace, Northumberland House, which stood at the top of Whitehall, facing what would later become Trafalgar Square.[13]

The lion was one of the landmarks of Georgian London, known as the Percy Lion, after the great landed family of the Northumberlands. Lord Algernon Percy is mentioned in *Barnaby Rudge*, as he had commanded the London militias at the time of the Gordon Riots. Percy Street, which runs south of Goodge Street, took the family name, as did other mews and back streets in the area near Norfolk Street. Behind its wide frontage on the Strand, the great house's real front faced south, down a grand vista framed by high-walled formal gardens facing towards the wide bend in the River just above Scotland Yard, just to the west of where Dickens would shortly be employed at Hungerford Stairs. The site is now occupied by the broad carriageway of Northumberland Avenue.

Somehow, Dickens tells us, he and his adult guide became separated, and the boy suddenly realized to his own dismay that he was alone. Dickens was writing about this experience thirty or so years later, when he was in his early forties, and a father of ten children himself, when he probably had both a childhood recollection of becoming lost and a grown-up recognition of the panic the adult would also have experienced on making the same discovery. No blame is ascribed to the adult in the case, perhaps from Dickens's grown-up sense of the inevitability and inexplicability of such events. Something in Dickens's valedictory tone towards this lost guide suggests that it might have been his father, who, at the time Dickens was writing, had been dead just two years. The biblical resonances of the essay's title 'Gone Astray' would support the idea.[14] If true, the story serves to illuminate two oft-quoted comments about Dickens's education. According to Forster, when John Dickens was asked by a prospective employer where his son had been educated, he replied: 'Why, indeed, sir—ha! ha!—he may be said to have educated himself!' presenting an admirable recognition on the father's part of his son's independent process of development.[15] The description by another father—Tony Weller—of his son's education has often been taken as Dickens's own evaluation: 'I took a good deal o' pains with his eddication, Sir; let him run in the streets when he was wery young, and shift for his-self. It's the only way to make a boy sharp, Sir.'[16]

The lost boy was indeed surprisingly resourceful: as the adult Dickens describes it, he found his way along the entire length of the Strand from Charing Cross to Temple Bar, along the whole of Fleet Street to St Paul's, then via Cheapside to the Guildhall: quite a feat for a child at the age of 10 or thereabouts, unfamiliar with navigating central London alone. There, Dickens reports that he sat in a corner below the giant statues of Gog and Magog, which he already knew by repute as famous sights of the City, and had a rather Chaplinesque encounter with a dog. Altogether, it seems that the boy managed to have an interesting day, only faltering after it got dark, when he sought help from an official watchman, who got a message back to his distraught family.

Besides Dickens's perception of his own youthful streetwise common sense, the story serves to illustrate the effectiveness of the

FIGURE 24. The great statues of Gog & Magog at the Guildhall 1810.

London watch service before the days of Peel's Metropolitan Police, and the comparative safety of pre-Victorian London: the boy did not get kidnapped or run over, robbed, stripped, or worse, despite all we have heard about the criminal underworld of London, not least in Dickens's own works.

The Dickens family seems to have been on the slide towards the Marshalsea Prison even before their return to London. Indeed, debts they had left behind in Chatham contributed to John Dickens's imprisonment. It appears, too, that Dickens's father still owed money to Mr Dodd in Norfolk Street.[17] Before the catastrophe came to pass, Mrs Dickens tried her best to prevent it. She had been hampered from earning money outside the home by the family's genteel pretensions and by frequent pregnancies and escalating child-rearing duties, but now, with matters looking desperate, she determined to use what skills she had to try to save the family from catastrophe. Towards the end of 1823, she took a better house in Gower Street, and attempted to open a school. The idea was a good one: only a few years later, University College School would open its doors just over the road—and such was its success that it still thrives today.[18] Mrs Dickens's school might also have succeeded, given time and capital: but the family had neither. Dickens was later able to laugh at the predicament inside the family home with creditors shouting loudly from the street, and his mother's optimism despite the embarrassment of no takers at the school.[19] He is said to have been sent hither and yon on sorry journeys to sell and pawn belongings, including even the beloved books. But nothing could prevent his father being committed to the Marshalsea on 20 February 1824, and Mrs Dickens and the younger children shortly joined him there.[20]

The experience of living inside a Georgian debtors' prison is conveyed very effectively by Dickens in *Pickwick Papers*, *David Copperfield*, and *Little Dorrit*: the differing character of the two regimes operating within the one institution—one for the abject poor, hopeless of ever being able to earn their way out of debt, and likely to die there; the other for those who could obtain any comfort they desired if they could but find the wherewithal to procure it. Only Mr Dickens was technically the prisoner, so the walls were permeable to Dickens's mother and the rest of the household when necessary. Above all, the family could be together, even their servant girl could visit, and Charles—who lodged outside— could come in for breakfast and supper.

The family was surrounded by other prisoners, many of whom had very little hope of ever getting out, because the longer they were inside the prison, the less they could earn, the higher their legal costs, and the less likely it was that relatives or friends could raise the funds to save them. Between them, Mr Dickens (who became the chairman of the Marshalsea debtors' self-management committee) and Mrs Dickens seem to have known everybody in the place. A key nugget of information yielded by Forster from the family's prison experience is that Mrs Dickens had a knack of getting other prisoners to tell her their life stories. Forster quotes her son as saying: 'When I went to the Marshalsea of a night, I was always delighted to hear from my mother what she knew about the histories of the different debtors in the prison.'[21] This is about as close as we get to real information about Mrs Dickens, towards whom Dickens himself seems curiously ambivalent.[22] From it we can appreciate that she was quite as sociable as his father, and that Dickens's own love of characters and biographies, and his knack of observing and collecting them, probably derives from her relish in them. I suspect the germs of some of his stories derived initially from her.

While the family was in the Marshalsea, Dickens remained outside in lodgings at Camden Town, working during the day at Hungerford Stairs with the tidal Thames lapping round the foundations of the old warehouse:

The blacking-warehouse was the last house on the left-hand side of the way, at old Hungerford Stairs. It was a crazy, tumble-down old house, abutting of course on the river, and literally overrun with rats. Its wainscoted rooms, and its rotten floors and staircase, and the old gray rats swarming down in the cellars, and the sound of their squeaking and scuffling coming up the stairs at all times, and the dirt and decay of the place, rise up visibly before me, as if I were there again. The counting-house was on the first floor, looking over the coal-barges and the river. There was a recess in it, in which I was to sit and work. My work was to cover the pots of paste-blacking; first with a piece of oil-paper, and then with a piece of blue paper; to tie them round with a string; and then to clip the paper close and neat, all round, until it looked as smart as a pot of ointment from an apothecary's shop. When a certain number of grosses of pots had attained this pitch of perfection, I was to paste on each a printed label, and then go on again with more pots. Two or three other boys were kept at similar duty down-stairs on similar wages. One of them came up, in a ragged apron and a paper cap, on the first Monday morning, to show me the trick of using the string and tying the knot. His name was Bob Fagin; and I took the liberty of using his name, long afterwards, in *Oliver Twist*.[23]

Dickens walked daily to the factory and back from Camden Town. After he eventually complained of his loneliness and misery there, his parents somehow found him more congenial accommodation nearer the prison:

One Sunday night I remonstrated with my father on this head, so pathetically, and with so many tears, that his kind nature gave way. He began to think that it was not quite right. I do believe he had never thought so before, or thought about it. It was the first

FIGURE 25. Hungerford Stairs seen from the River. This interesting litho-graph by G. Harley and D. Dighton was published by Rowney in Rathbone Place, Marylebone, in 1822, in the year before Dickens was sent to work in the blacking factory, which occupied the house on the right. Dickens is known to have played with other boys on coal barges like the one shown in the fore-ground. His older work-mate Bob Fagin lived nearby with a relative who was a waterman on the River. The spire in the distance belongs to St Martin's-in-the-Fields. The stairs and the streets nearby disappeared for the construction of Charing Cross Station and Hungerford Bridge.

remonstrance I had ever made about my lot, and perhaps it opened up a little more than I intended. A back-attic was found for me at the house of an insolvent-court agent, who lived in Lant Street in the borough, where Bob Sawyer lodged many years afterwards. A bed and bedding were sent over for me, and made up on the floor. The little window had a pleasant prospect of a timber-yard; and when I took possession of my new abode I thought it was a Paradise.[24]

It is worth observing how easily Dickens slips in the fact that he utilized his own lodgings as the model for his fictional character Bob Sawyer: how knowingly he transmuted what he knew directly into his fictions, and how unembarrassed he is about it. This is a process not at all confined to Lant Street, and it seems to be very widely accepted by Dickens aficionados that Dickens used places he knew in his books. It is clear from his own words that the transcription is more or less direct.

This is part of the puzzle of Norfolk Street. In *Pickwick Papers*, Dickens mentions the following places by name, all of which we know he inhabited: Gower Street, The Polygon, Somers Town, Little College Street, Camden Town, the Marshalsea Prison, and Lant Street. He also mentions the public house The Fox under the Hill near the bottom of Hungerford Stairs. But the only reference to Norfolk Street that I have been able to find is in his story Mrs Lirriper's Lodgings, which is supposed to be about Norfolk Street, Strand. None of his biographers have so far looked at the real Norfolk Street from this point of view.

Forster continues with the story:

From this time he used to breakfast 'at home,'—in other words, in the Marshalsea; going to it as early as the gates were open, and for the most part much earlier. They had no want of bodily comforts there. His father's income [i.e. his Navy salary] still going on, was amply sufficient for that; and in every respect indeed but elbow-room, I have heard him say, the family lived more comfortably in prison than they had done for a long time out of it. They were waited on still by the maid-of-all-work from Bayham Street, the orphan girl of the Chatham workhouse, from whose sharp little worldly and also kindly ways he took his first impression of the Marchioness in the *Old Curiosity Shop*. She also had a lodging in the neighbourhood, that she might be early on the scene of her duties; and when Charles met her, as he would do occasionally, in his lounging-place by London Bridge, he would occupy the time before the gates opened by telling her quite astonishing fictions about the wharves and the tower. 'But I hope I believed them myself,' he would say. Besides breakfast, he had supper also in the prison, and got to his lodging generally at nine o'clock. The gates closed always at ten.[25]

This is one of the earliest moments in which Dickens mentions an awareness that he could spin stories out of the air and create astonishment. Dickens's relationship with this girl (who would probably have been about 13 or so by now)—she to whom these tales were told—spans Chatham, Bayham Street, the blacking factory, and the Marshalsea. We don't know when she and Dickens had opportunities to talk at length other than during the period when the family was in the Marshalsea, and it seems from Dickens's account that their relationship deepened in that period. As Forster reports things, these conversations were largely one way: Dickens casts himself as the hero-storyteller, astonishing her. But nothing is said about what this young woman might have conveyed to him.

In *Pickwick Papers*, and in other places, Dickens posits situations in which people sit together in groups and tell each other stories, as a social activity. So I wonder about the reciprocity in the case of the girl on the bridge; I wonder if there wasn't also some storytelling on her part. It seems to me quite likely that at some point she might have relayed quite a bit of her own biographical narrative concerning life in the Chatham workhouse, and that its details were heard and absorbed by Dickens, almost as if he had experienced them himself.[26] It may be that things she conveyed to him came to mean more to Dickens when he was in the moils of drudgery in the blacking factory, especially if some of the other boys there were parish apprentices, as well they might have been. One can imagine him binding and knotting the jars, mulling things over in some deep part of his mind, possibly allowing him to appreciate that, however bad his own experience, others suffered worse. At least the family was together in the Marshalsea.

Dickens was known at the blacking factory as the 'little gentleman', and generally kept himself somewhat socially aloof. But he occasionally played with a couple of the boys on the coal barges by the River. On one occasion, when he had been unwell during the day, Bob Fagin insisted on seeing him safely home:

> I got better, and quite easy towards evening; but Bob (who was much bigger and older than I) did not like the idea of my going home alone, and took me under his protection. I was too proud to let him know about the prison, and, after making several efforts to get rid of him, to all of which Bob Fagin in his goodness was deaf, shook hands with him on the steps of a house near Southwark Bridge on the Surrey side, making believe that I lived there. As a finishing piece of reality in case of his looking back, I knocked at the door, I recollect, and asked, when the woman opened it, if that was Mr. Robert Fagin's house.[27]

A cluster of associations links Dickens's experience in the blacking factory with the workhouse, Thames bridges, and a loyal female figure. These associations seem to come to a kind of fruition in *Oliver Twist*, when the information imparted by a poor girl on London Bridge is a matter of life and death, and associated with a different Fagin.

A single exposure to a child with inside knowledge of workhouse life would have been sufficient for Dickens's identification with the plight of the workhouse child, and his sure grasp of the institutional atmosphere of the workhouse regime. There were probably other such encounters, including other boys—as I have already suggested—in the blacking factory. It may actually be that Bob Fagin, who was himself an orphan, had spent time in the Cleveland Street Workhouse before being claimed by his brother-in-law, who worked on the river barges by Hungerford Stairs.

There is another instance in which Dickens relates having met and conversed with a workhouse child. In one of his early *Sketches*, Dickens describes a childhood encounter with a climbing boy: a young chimney sweep. Dickens indicates that they were both about the same age. His lack of fear of the other boy—completely black from head to foot from soot, and standing in his own home—if true, is interesting. The encounter has a quite intimate atmosphere, as though no one else was present:

> We remember, in our young days, a little sweep about our own age, with curly hair and white teeth, whom we devoutly and sincerely believed to be the lost son and heir of some illustrious personage—an impression which was resolved into an unchangeable conviction on our infant mind, by the subject of our speculations informing us, one day, in reply to our question, propounded a few moments before his ascent to the summit of the kitchen chimney, 'that he believed he'd been born in the vurkis, but he'd never know'd his father.' We felt certain, from that time forth, that he would one day be owned by a lord: and we never heard the church-bells ring, or saw a flag hoisted in the neighbourhood, without thinking that the happy event had at last occurred,

and that his long-lost parent had arrived in a coach and six, to take him home to Grosvenor-square.[28]

The passage demonstrates young Dickens's curiosity and empathy with the other boy, and (as in the wand story from the Soho Bazaar) the strength and persistence of his desire for resolution to painful human predicaments, for fictional happy endings. Yet, at the same time, in his own adult knowledge, Dickens smiles knowingly at his own hopeless innocence in such hopes. The long afterlife of Dickens's childlike investment of hope in the other boy's biography re-emerged in the story of *Oliver Twist*—not a sweep, but a child almost disposed of as one: an innocent child unfit for the maltreatment to which he is subject, and deserving of something more honourable from those responsible for his fate. When such a point of view is adopted, one can also see that Oliver stands also for Dickens himself.

Dickens acknowledges in the *Sketch* just quoted that his hope for the boy's eventual recognition was rooted in a much-repeated London story of the period, an urban legend of child-theft and rediscovery. It concerned a rich lady's recognition of her own stolen child, who, having been forced to work as a sweep, had descended the chimney into her empty bedroom, and was found by her, exhaustedly asleep in his soot on her pristine bed. The coincidence in this story, which Dickens retells in the same *Sketch*, and which is well illustrated in the magazine in which it appeared, prefigures that in *Oliver Twist*, where after the burglary Oliver collapses on the doorstep of a house which turns out to belong to his own long-lost great-aunt/adoptive grandmother.

Long walks from his lodgings to the factory and back took young Dickens daily through the middle of London. Michael Allen's recent discoveries amongst old records of litigation concerning the blacking business indicate that—dating from Hungerford Stairs and the factory's move to Chandos Street—Dickens was probably a factory boy for a year or more, perhaps until the autumn of 1824, when he was twelve and a half.[29] The work for Lamerte therefore seems to have continued even after Dickens's father was freed from prison under insolvency legislation, when the family left the Marshalsea at the end of May 1824.

Dickens's drudgery ended suddenly and unexpectedly, when his father quarrelled with Lamerte, freed his son from the blacking business, and at last sent him back to school.[30] The dispute seems to have centred upon the way young Dickens had been set to work with Bob Fagin in the shop window in Chandos Street, often gathering a crowd of onlookers by their dexterity and speed in tying the pots, and doubtless serving as a compelling advertisement for Lamerte's business. One wonders if it was on this same occasion that Dickens was witnessed at work by Mr Dilke, whose recollection later provoked the writing of the autobiographical fragment, and whether Mr Dilke's half-crown did not shame John Dickens into perceiving at last what had happened to his own son. Working in the window at Chandos Street may have reminded Mr Dickens of the fate of the debtors on the 'poor' side of the Marshalsea, who took it in turns to expose themselves behind a grille which opened onto the street so as to beg for alms from passers-by, although it also partook of the nature of the showmanship for which his son was later so well known.

Although Dickens denied it, he seems to have been decidedly resentful of his mother's attempt to smooth over this argument with Lamerte:

> My mother set herself to accommodate the quarrel, and did so next day. She brought home a request for me to return next morning, and a high character of me, which I am very sure I deserved. My father said I should go back no more, and should go to school. I do not write resentfully or angrily; for I know how all these things have worked together to make me what I am; but I never afterwards forgot, I never shall forget, I never can forget, that my mother was warm for my being sent back.[31]

For Dickens, this looks to have been something of a parting of the ways (emotionally speaking) from his mother. That reiterated three-fold inability to forget, so long into his adulthood, is eloquent indeed. Dickens probably had no notion what his earnings of six or seven shillings a week may have meant to her housekeeping, or what her hopes might have been for him in the world of business, or what it meant to her that a dispute should exist between her husband and her own relations. We know that a decade or so later there was such a serious rift between John Dickens and other members of his wife's side of the family (the old problem of not repaying loans, it seems) that Charles Dickens wrote letters apologizing for his inability to issue invitations to his own wedding.[32] Perhaps Dickens really resented his mother's concern for that other motherless boy, Lamerte, the stepson of her own dead sister, Dickens's Aunt Mary.

Oliver Twist's aunt, Rose Maylie, welcomes Oliver into her family as the son of her own dead sister, but that same sister's older stepson is the vile Monks, the evil genius of the book's convoluted plot.

When Dickens composed the 'autobiographical fragment' from which Forster later worked, his sense of anger was still fierce: so much so, that it appears he was unable to consider that he might actually have gained anything from the blacking factory. His own subsequent success as an entrepreneur, writer, and publisher in the Strand/Covent Garden area however suggests that for all its agony, the experience may actually have been more formative in a positive way than he could bring himself to admit, it having taught him a number of things he might otherwise never have learned so early in life: an appreciation of business practice, manual dexterity and speed, self-discipline, application; an understanding of the importance and value of money and of hard work in getting it; managing on a meagre income (budgeting and paying one's way); preserving one's own inner dignity even in the midst of social mortification; learning to recognize and address the humanity of social 'inferiors'; fitting in to other domestic establishments; recognizing that working lives are often forced and irksome, that terms of employment can be demeaning, and that bare survival is uncongenial; understanding that the cowl doesn't make the monk and the applicability of that insight to others as to himself; and being able to transform the negativity of feeling demeaned and undervalued into an inner generating force for personal development. For Dickens the whole experience seems to have been thoroughly negative; he was still smarting from it nearly a quarter of a century later. He believed he had been robbed of his childhood.

Dickens had also become immersed in the busyness and the variety of London life, traversing central London daily by foot, alone in the early morning and at night, experiencing its excitements and dangers. Walking and traversing London remained important to him for the rest of his life, and oftentimes seemed almost as necessary to his writing as breathing. All these things, including his private suffering, would later prove of importance in the formation of the great writer he became. For now, the Dickens family wanted to put memories of this painful time firmly behind them:

> From that hour until this at which I write, no word of that part of my childhood which I have now gladly brought to a close has passed my lips to any human being. I have no idea how long it lasted; whether for a year, or much more, or less. From that hour until this my father and my mother have been stricken dumb upon it. I have never heard the least allusion to it, however far off and remote, from either of them. I have never, until I now impart it to this paper, in any burst of confidence with any one, my own wife not excepted, raised the curtain I then dropped, thank God.[33]

Young Dickens may not have been aware of having learned much when he went back to school, but the other boys there seem to have had a sense that he was more mature than they.[34] The family was now settled in the poor district of Somers Town, which lay north-east of their usual stamping ground of Marylebone, between the eastern flank of the Prince Regent's Park and the meandering course of the River Fleet by the ancient church of St Pancras. The small house his parents rented in Johnson Street backed onto open fields south of Camden Town.[35] The area is built over now, and it is not at all easy to imagine the semi-rural place it was at the time Dickens was living there between the ages of 13 and 16, when cows grazed in the pastures behind his home. Sadly, not a single building dating from the time of his family's stay—between 1825 and 1828—survives there.

The district was ruthlessly cut about on both sides by the arrival of the great London railway termini after the 1830s: the Euston line came in first, on the Regent's Park side, and then the vast swathe of tracks followed to serve the great stations of St Pancras and King's Cross, to the east of Somers Town. It is very likely that Dickens was thinking of this district when he later wrote about the impact of railway development on existing urban settlements in his essay 'An Unsettled Neighbourhood'.[36]

A splendid cartoon by George Cruikshank called *London Going out of Town*, shows a shower of bricks and phalanxes of animated hods and chimney pots invading the countryside to the north of London, sad hedges being felled, and haystacks gathering up their skirts and running further away.[37]

Dickens's generation witnessed and experienced the process Cruikshank satirized. He knew London before the process had really gathered pace and saw it swiftly change: he knew the Marylebone

Road when it still had its old tea gardens and statuaries, its ancient inns and cowkeepers; the turnpike on Tottenham Court Road, and Somers Town before the railways. In his lifetime, the age-old farms and fields and footpaths around the northern edge of London were gradually swallowed up in streets, roads, and railways. In the process, areas of that hinterland became scrubby, seedy, and unhappy: north of King's Cross, for example, Dickens famously described 'a tract of suburban Sahara': 'where tiles and bricks were burnt, bones were boiled, carpets were beat, rubbish was shot, dogs were fought, and dust was heaped'.[38]

The small house on Johnson Street had something in common with the one on Norfolk Street in so far as each occupied—constituted, even—significant boundaries. While Mr Dodd's house formed part of the east–west border between Marylebone and St Pancras, the back garden wall at Johnson Street formed part of the northern boundary of the Duke of Bedford's estate: there is said to have been a boundary stone embedded in the back garden wall to that effect.[39] While the Dickens family was living there, this old estate boundary was also the north–south border between London itself, and the next village.

The position of the house gave it wide views over the intervening meadows, but some things rendered it less than bucolic: the St Pancras parish workhouse was within view east across the fields, and the houses were vulnerable to predation by gangs of boys, who came over the back walls.[40] There were stories of body-snatchers frequenting the large burial ground around old St Pancras Church. Indeed, while the family had been living away, in another burial ground a couple of fields to the north, an extraordinary event had occurred which doubtless became part of local folklore:

> On Saturday se'enight about four o'clock, a party of resurrection men scaled the walls of St Martin's [in the Fields] burying ground, situated in the fields at the back of Camden Town, for the purpose, as it is supposed, of stealing the body of a grenadier nearly seven feet high, who had died in the poor house of that parish . . . The sexton, to guard the ground, had, more ingeniously than lawfully, put together a number of gun barrels, so as to form them into a magazine that they might be discharged together. After burying the bodies of the paupers, he made it a practice to direct the muzzle of this formidable engine towards the mound of earth which was the general receptacle for the dead parochial poor. [The following day, he] found spades, shovels, pickaxes, and other resurrection paraphernalia. Among other things he found a man's hat, through one side of which a bullet had evidently passed [leaving no mark of its exit] and concluded that the bullet had lodged in the head of the owner and killed him, and that he had been carried off by his associates.[41]

So even though the pastures gave the impression of rural peace during the day, the feeling of vulnerability and marauding criminality at night on this northernmost edge of London cannot have been very welcome. The intervening fields were soon, however, to be engulfed by bricks and mortar: as a local newspaper report had it 'assisting London in its progress towards York'.[42]

John Dickens's debts had been cleared with help from a legacy left by his mother, who had died while her son was in the Marshalsea Prison. Now, Mr Dickens was about to be pensioned off from the Navy, and was developing an alternative career as a freelance journalist, an idea his son would later follow. It was a precarious means of earning a living, but for the next two years, there was evidently sufficient to pay for Dickens to attend the 'Wellington Classical and Commercial Academy', a boys' school just across the pastures of Rhodes's Farm to the west of Johnson Street, at Mornington Crescent.

When Forster was writing the biography soon after Dickens's death, he was able to make contact with a number of Dickens's fellow pupils at the school. These were surviving contemporaries who remembered Dickens as a young teenager. They provide useful corroboration (and modification) of Dickens's own recollections. One of them had not known that the great novelist was the same boy with whom he had attended school, until he read an essay in *Household Words*, called 'Our School', from which he recognized the fact. He had written to Dickens before his death: 'I was first impressed with the idea that the writer described scenes and persons with which I was once familiar, and that he must necessarily be the veritable Charles Dickens of "our school,"—the school of Jones!'[43]

The Wellington Academy was wrongly believed to be a 'superior' school, according to these ex-pupils. One of them said: 'it was most shamefully mismanaged, and the boys made but very little progress.

The proprietor, Mr. Jones, was a Welshman; a most ignorant fellow, and a mere tyrant; whose chief employment was to scourge the boys.'[44]

One cannot help thinking that the loathsome schoolmaster in *Nicholas Nickleby* probably owes a lot to this ignorant bully. But there was also a much more sympathetic usher, who knew everything and did most of the teaching. Despite general agreement about the intimidating headmaster, all Forster's correspondents seemed to recollect a lot of mischief and fun. According to Forster, Dickens himself recollected:

> linnets, and even canaries were kept by the boys in desks, draw-ers, hat-boxes, and other strange refuges for birds; but...white mice were the favourite stock, and...the boys trained the mice much better than the master trained the boys. He recalled in particular one white mouse who lived in the cover of a Latin dictionary, ran up ladders, drew Roman chariots, shouldered muskets, turned wheels...who might have achieved greater things but for having had the misfortune to mistake his way in a triumphal procession to the Capitol, when he fell into a deep inkstand and was dyed black and drowned.[45]

One of Dickens's fellow students commented that Dickens's recollections of the school were true to life, but that all the names had been 'feigned'; we shall discuss this later when looking at an analogous process: the use to which Dickens put local names from Norfolk Street.[46] Another fellow pupil judged Dickens's account to be 'very mythical in many respects, and more especially in the compliment he pays in it to himself. I do not remember that Dickens distinguished himself in any way, or carried off any prizes.' The mythic qualities of reality are part of the strength of storytelling, and one cannot know what to believe here. Dickens clearly felt rewarded, but the other observer seems sceptical. The same man denied there had been any Latin teaching at the school, whereas others recollected the Latin master, so his testimony may not be altogether reliable. All these schoolfriends remembered Dickens as the life and soul of everything, a 'handsome, curly-headed lad, full of animation and animal spirits'. The boys were avid readers, especially of cheap pamphlet fiction, the *Penny Magazine* and the *Saturday Magazine*.

They also recalled taking great pleasure in stage plays: 'We were very strong in theatricals. We mounted small theatres, and got up very gorgeous scenery...Dickens was always a leader at these plays, which were occasionally presented with much solemnity before an audience of boys and in the presence of the ushers.' Play-acting spilled out onto the street, too, and whereas in the blacking factory period Dickens had feigned affluence to deceive the anxious Bob Fagin, here he felt confident enough to feign poverty for fun. In Drummond Street (near another Charles Street) just north of Euston Square, another friend recalled:

> I quite remember Dickens on one occasion heading us in Drummond Street in pretending to be poor boys, and asking the passers-by for charity,—especially old ladies, one of whom told us she 'had no money for beggar-boys.' On these adventures, when the old ladies were quite staggered by the impudence of the demand, Dickens would explode with laughter and take to his heels.[47]

But financial difficulties were actually never far off. In 1827 the family endured the humiliation of an eviction from their small home in Johnson Street, for the non-payment of poor-rates, the local taxes which paid for policing, street-lighting, and the care of the poor. Before stabilizing again, and moving back, the family lodged for a time in 'The Polygon', an unusual near-circular block of flats, nearby. The Polygon had literary associations with writers of an earlier generation, such as William Godwin and Mary Wollstonecraft, and probably carried its seediness well in a district overcrowded with immigrants and refugees.[48] Dickens used the place later as the home of Mr Skimpole in *Bleak House*.

Dickens's father was now working full time as a freelance journalist, and Dickens himself was submitting small news stories to the press by 1825–6 (when he was 13–14 years of age) for the glorious payment of a penny-a-line.[49] 'Depend on it', one of his schoolfriends said, 'he was quite a self-made man, and his wonderful knowledge and command of the English language must have been acquired by long and patient study after leaving his last school.'[50]

Now adult work was found for Dickens. Great-aunt Charlton knew that his parents were on the lookout for an opening for him. One of her lodgers in Berners Street was a solicitor at Gray's Inn, Edward Blackmore. He liked the look of Dickens, thought him a bright lad, and took him on as an office junior. In any legal office at this stage Dickens would have been a lowly figure, being still very young and ignorant of the law and its doings, and neither particularly well educated nor well connected. As far as we know, he was not actually apprenticed to either partner at Ellis and Blackmore's, the fees for which would have been beyond his parents' reach—his work was clerical in nature, associated with paperwork and keeping the office ticking over: he was not on track to become a lawyer, but to join that large underclass who serviced them, and the courts.

The job of an office junior might be to find or file documents, shift old legal rolls, trunks, and boxes, to slip out on urgent errands, perhaps to purchase legal stationery or supplies, carry confidential messages, briefs, and other documents from office to chambers or to court. He would be at the beck and call of others, might be set to learn accuracy in copying documents, might be asked to serve as a kind of receptionist-cum-gatekeeper in the outer office to defend the chief in his inner sanctum from importunate clients. He would have to learn who was to be ushered in, who excluded, would have to learn the lingo, learn to fib—would have to learn fast. Older clerks, more settled in their ways, might tease or even mock Dickens for being green and tender. He for his part would observe with fine discernment how the world worked, how human stories could be buried in sheaves of paper, indeed how paper could impact on lives: a wise child on the threshold of adult life in London.[51]

A little cashbook survives from 1828, with entries in Dickens's 16-year-old handwriting, which shows him by then in a position of trust and responsibility: keeping account of petty cash for the entire office. The small pages record payments to porters for the delivery or receipt of legal documents, payments for repairs and maintenance, and other small amounts for ordinary letters and parcels.

Many of the entries are marked up to be assigned to ongoing cases. There are also entries recording the acquisition of parchment, string, and, yes: red tape.[52] Dickens's clerk's wages of 15 shillings a week (the same amount as Scrooge paid Bob Cratchit) may have helped make a real difference to the family finances, allowing his parents to contemplate better accommodation. His older sister Fanny was teaching music now, too, so at last both the older children were net contributors to the family's economy. Early in 1829, when Dickens was just 17, the household left Somers Town and moved back to Norfolk Street.

CHAPTER 7

Young Dickens

RETURN TO NORFOLK STREET, YOUNG PROFESSIONAL, FIRST ESSAYS

D ICKENS MIGHT WELL have walked down Cleveland Street since the family arrived back in London. The chances are high that he'd taken that familiar way south from Camden Town or Somers Town: down past the Workhouse and the old family home perhaps to get to Aunt Charlton's, or possibly, in earlier difficult times he didn't want to think about, to bring things discreetly to the corner pawnbroker.[1] The Dickens family returns to Norfolk Street in this chapter, and we are able to observe the process of development undergone by the young Dickens from his initial employment as a junior legal clerk to his new work as a freelance journalist, which took place during this second period he was living there, above Mr Dodd's shop once more, between 1829 and 1831. Young Dickens was becoming a young man of the world in London.

Walking south, down Cleveland and Norfolk Streets, and crossing over Charles Street at a diagonal towards Berners Street, Dickens had probably already noticed changes since the family had been living away. Apart from Mr Dodd and a couple of others, almost every shop in Norfolk Street had changed hands in the family's absence. Twelve years is a long time to a teenager, and in his walks Dickens would have noticed the many small signs of prosperity or its opposite, which had altered in the interval. The leathercutter had gone, and in place of his hides, great rolls of oilcloth were stacked up outside. Mr Dodd's old competitor next door at No. 9 had disappeared too—replaced by a furniture broker, whose second-hand stock overflowed onto the pavement, blew about on hooks by the door, and festooned his railings. Mr Bridger's widow at No. 8 was valiantly running the gown-shop alone. Mulloy the solicitor at No. 5 had sold out to a tailor. The Staffordshire chinaware shop was still in Cleveland Street, perhaps with a figurine of the recent murder victim Maria Marten in amongst the dishes and figures in the window, but the sculptors on the corner of Howland Street had gone.[2] The area was changing, becoming less interesting, less arty perhaps: tailors, straw hat-makers, wire-workers, and other poorer trades were moving in, and some of the houses seemed rather full. Small indicators, like the state of paintwork or the cleanliness of windows, were slight, but noticeable.

Until the family actually returned to Mr Dodd's to live, though, the atmosphere inside the house—the smell of the front hall, the way the light fell on the stairs, the dimensions of the rooms, the views from upstairs—were childhood memories, which had probably not yet been overlain. There was probably a strange sensation of déjà vu.

Dickens was almost a man now—in February 1829 he was 17—already out at work and earning his living. To this smart young man these old rooms would have felt smaller, now he was grown. Aunt Mary—who had slept there—was already several years dead, and so much else had happened in the interval.[3] His sister Letitia had been born here. When they were last here Mr Dodd's debts were the problem, not his father's. The Dickens family had been to the Marshalsea and back since then, and he had survived the blacking factory ... and the Wellington Academy. His little sister Harriet had since arrived and departed, and they no longer owned most of the furniture or the precious books that had found their niches in these strangely familiar rooms before.[4]

But there must have been things—like the handrail on the stairs, the fireplace, the water closet, the corner cupboards, and the dark kitchen below stairs—which remained just as they had been. It was probably a strange return, enough to make Dickens feel curiously old, despite his youth.

And when he gazed down, did the street feel smaller too? Did he notice that the treetops in the Middlesex Hospital garden were taller than they had been when he'd had to climb on a chair to see them? And did he notice what changes twelve years had wrought upon the shops and houses within the purview of the familiar windows? The public houses were still where they had been, and so was the pawnshop, looking much the same. The windows opposite might have looked less so, other than Miss Horsfall's, who was still there, too, twelve years older.

Mostly the houses probably seemed very much the same, if a little dustier. But a freshly painted shop board on No. 20 over the way announced an arrival on the street: Daniel Weller, a man who dealt in boots and shoes, and cared for them.[5] There was a new butcher and a new fishmonger; and another coffee-shop had opened across the street. The choreography of straggling geraniums or herbs on window sills might differ, but the place hadn't altered that much: the chimneys opposite were still smoking away, and the view was much the same—perhaps a little worse for wear, but still the same old street.

In many ways it was probably good to be back. The place was much closer to the heart of London than was Somers Town or the Polygon, and there was a congenial bustle around Charles Street and Tottenham Court Road, a feeling of variety and liveliness in Norfolk Street, which was probably lacking in the shabbier ladder of streets the family had just left behind. The extended family was closer to hand, which may have been an important consideration.[6]

Young Dickens could enjoy the news Mr Dodd passed on to his parents, as they picked over what had come to pass in the street during the family's absence. Old Mr Dugard had died, but his Chancery case endured, and had passed down to Miss Dugard, still at No. 32.[7] Old Miser Nollekens in Mortimer Street was dead, too. The theatre in Tottenham Street had changed its name again, and playbills were up in the shop windows, but there were some shady characters living round there now. Tottenham Mews had been completely rebuilt since it was burned down in a fire so fierce that the heat had cracked the Workhouse windows... and speaking of fires, there'd been a terrible one—just down from the Hospital, at the top of Wells Street—nearly the whole block had gone up, a hundred families homeless, everything lost.[8]

At this stage, Dickens was not yet a writer, so he did not sit down to write a sketch or a passage for a chapter which utilized the experience of returning after long absence to lodge above Mr Dodd's shop. But later on, in his early *Sketches*, he did carefully analyse the way shops change over quite long periods of time, and the small indicators which reveal their owners' (mis)fortunes.[9] The experience of Pip in *Great Expectations*, returning to visit Miss Havisham, has a similar quality, perhaps, to this sense of time passing, and the visible indicators of life-cycles in houses as in persons. Returning to Dullborough town was no doubt a fine description of an adult experience in the Rochester area, but it may well have been informed by the sensations Dickens encountered returning to Norfolk Street in 1829.[10]

Norfolk Street emerges repeatedly in historical records as a locale in cases of insolvency: there was at least one bankruptcy in each of a dozen of the thirty-four houses in the street between 1815 and 1840.[11] But what such records do not tell are the variety of causes of impoverishment, and the efforts made by those on a downward trajectory to put up a good front, and to avoid their fate, especially in a street where a busy workhouse served as a standing rebuke to economic failure. Dickens's interest in these secret struggles for survival might well have been influenced by lives he witnessed in this street. The consumptive shop girl, for example, in his *Sketch* on shops, was quite possibly someone whose decline he had observed over time in one of the buildings opposite during the time he was living there.

Dickens's interest in what passed behind shutters and curtains, his interest in household secrets, is a crucial element in his story-making. It may have been influenced by a tale by one of his favourite authors, whose student protagonist is fascinated by the Devil's ability to render roofs and walls permeable: to witness whatever he wished to observe.[12] But it may also have something to do with his lengthy double exposure—as child and as near-adult—to this well-populated street where several houses opposite were in multiple occupation, and whose rooms and occupants were probably visible to the observant eye … and where a great hospital loomed behind the houses in one direction, and a workhouse and its graveyard in the other.[13]

Probably the most straightforward description of what Dickens might have seen pass by on the street is his portrayal of the pauper funeral Oliver witnesses, conducted along the streets with no conveyance, at a smart walking pace by Mr Bumble and Mr Sowerberry. Four men from the workhouse served as bearers, carrying the feather-light coffin of a woman who had died of want, and they were followed by her poor husband and old mother, forced to hurry along after, so as not to keep the clergyman waiting. Needless to say, they are forced to wait in the rain (while the parish employees wait in the warm), the churchman being late himself.[14] As a child and as an adult, Dickens had probably witnessed many such pauper funerals hurry past his home, bringing the bodies of poor people who could afford no better, from the main parish in Covent Garden to burial in the Workhouse ground. These sorts of funerals proverbially took place in the early part of the day, and were referred to within living memory by Londoners as the 'nine o'clock trot'.

Unless Dickens had gained access to a building with windows that overlooked the walled graveyard at the back of the Workhouse, however, he had probably not seen what really passed for a funeral in that place. The description of the callous churchman hastily putting on his surplice as he crossed the churchyard, and his perfunctory service, is known to have come from elsewhere.[15]

As a child Dickens might have shrunk from these sad processions with horror; but as a young man, he probably understood so much more about the humiliation and hurt behind such scenes. The walking rebuke they presented to the society which disregarded them was probably indelibly imprinted in his memory from Norfolk Street.

Exactly when young Dickens gave up working as a legal clerk isn't known, but at some point at about the period we have now reached, he decided against it as a way of life. He had walked daily to Gray's Inn for two years now, and perhaps became just as 'precious warm' as Mr Lowten, the lawyer's clerk in *Pickwick Papers*, who walks to Gray's Inn from the Polygon. Dickens's working experience informs his later depictions of Bob Cratchit in *A Christmas Carol*, and the kindly Wemmick, clerk for the sharp and clever criminal lawyer Jaggers in *Great Expectations*, both of whom are presented as having reserves of humanity their work does not employ. Both have lives beyond the office—in each case, lives which contribute to the plot, and the charm, of the story.

Dickens had become keenly aware of the pathos of the clerk's life. The impoverishment he had observed among older clerks presented no hopeful future whatever for himself. Mr Jinks in *Pickwick Papers*, clerk in a magistrate's court, is described as a 'pale, sharp-nosed, half-fed, shabbily-clothed clerk, of middle-age', who retires 'within himself—that being the only retirement he had, except the sofa-bedstead in the small parlour which was occupied by his landlady's family in the day-time'.[16] Dickens's naturalist's eye examines the niches in the rainforest of London where such organisms thrived, survived, or perished.[17] Jinks services the mighty bombast of the magistrate—is constantly at his beck and call—yet outside the court through poverty has the most precarious of domestic arrangements as a lodger in other people's accommodation. Jinks is not developed as a character, nor is his human predicament explored any further than this brief description, but the sorry sofa bed and his tentative occupancy of it is memorable, nevertheless.

From his later accounts of clerks' lives it's clear that being a clerk had been a kind of servitude Dickens found thoroughly irksome. The subordinate status and the sheer boredom of being an employee of low status, the under-use of his capacities and undervaluation of his abilities appear to have given Dickens the determination to improve himself as a means of escape. One possible route his ideas took was to consider entering the law himself, but although he held on to the possibility for several years, mercifully, Dickens found other ways of making his living: it would not have suited him.

Dickens's lawyers, in *Pickwick* and elsewhere, suggest that he came to regard much of the legal system as a conspiracy: efficiently extracting as much cash as possible from anyone unfortunate enough to fall into their hands. Clerks are shown aping their masters in superciliousness and contempt, especially towards clients impoverished by the law itself. In this, Dickens joined an existing tradition: another novelist ascribed a particularly hellish demon to assist the work of attorneys, bailiffs, pleaders, counsel, and judges, while Fleet

Street caricaturists pictured a conversation (observed by a lawyer's clerk, concealing his laughter behind his hand) between a naïve country Farmer and his predatory well-dressed lawyer:

> Farmer: 'When do you think the Cause will be finished, you know I've sold my farm and I really am reduced to my last guinea, which makes me very unhappy.'
> Attorney: 'Why, if that's the case I really believe it's very near finished. But you ought to be very happy when you consider I have reduced your opponent to the last farthing.'[18]

The pity of these kinds of goings-on is dealt with in *Pickwick* mostly in a light and comedic fashion, but the truth of what Dickens had observed nevertheless shows through: a promising case concerns not its justice, but its potential for fees. Decent lawyers appear in the novels too, but the young Dickens generally presents his legal professionals and the system they stand for as altogether without principle.

After Ellis and Blackmore Dickens tried a brief spell as a clerk to an attorney, but he eventually found the law insupportable as a prospective career choice for himself. Fortunately there were other routes out of clerkship, and exposure to the legal labyrinth of London for a couple of years had been valuable in helping Dickens perceive that his future rightly lay elsewhere. It had been extremely useful to him. Like the blacking factory and the Wellington Academy, his exposure to the legal life of London provided him plenty of material.[19]

Dickens's father had learned shorthand, and was supporting the family as a freelance newspaperman. He seems to have acquired knowledge of the skill and the business of journalism from his own brother-in-law, Mrs Dickens's brother John Barrow, who in 1828 had established the best parliamentary reporting journal of the day, *The Mirror of Parliament*. Despite the insecurity of journalism, its variety and interest—and especially the freedom of the working life his uncle and his father were carving out for themselves—appealed to young Dickens. It was not long before the disaffected young clerk determined to learn shorthand himself. He had kept his day job for the time being, studying in whatever spare time he could find. Long afterwards, when he came to write *David Copperfield* (whose hero undertakes a similar course of self-education), Dickens described with some humour the difficulties involved in mastering this skill:

> I bought an approved scheme of the noble art and mystery of stenography (which cost me ten and sixpence); and plunged into a sea of perplexity that brought me, in a few weeks, to the confines of distraction. The changes that were rung upon dots, which in such a position meant such a thing, and in such another position something else, entirely different; the wonderful vagaries that were played by circles; the unaccountable consequences that resulted from marks like flies' legs; the tremendous effects of a curve in a wrong place; not only troubled my waking hours, but reappeared before me in my sleep.[20]

The technique involved learning to think phonetically, and the signs for every sound or combination of sounds. Transcribing speech into the sign language of shorthand was a matter of getting 'up to speed', so that an accurate record might be kept at the normal speed of speech. He had then to be able to complete the procedure by deciphering correctly what had been transcribed. Much of this effort was probably done at home in Norfolk Street, using his siblings to dictate to him.

Copperfield makes wry fun out of the difficulty of the entire process, but in fact, young Dickens seems to have applied himself so well to the task that it wasn't long before he decided to try earning a living by it, and within a comparatively short time, he had so mastered it as to become recognized as pre-eminent, even by other reporters. It was while he was living above Mr Dodd's shop in Norfolk Street that Dickens passed his seventeenth, eighteenth, and nineteenth birthdays, and first entered the Reporters' Gallery in the Houses of Parliament. His life was changed from this address.

Father and son belonged to an era which greeted with interest and satisfaction the publication in 1830 of an anonymous work entitled *The Pursuit of Knowledge Under Difficulties*, which featured nearly a hundred short biographies of men lacking social advantages or university education who had nevertheless made a success of their lives: figures such as Shakespeare, Benjamin Franklin, Benjamin West, and Richard Arkwright.[21] The book exemplified the value of self-discipline and self-education, and asserted the dignity and importance of the class of men below the gentry and aristocracy, always the objects of social snobbery.[22] The book was a runaway bestseller, since it answered the longing of many an under-educated person for recognition of their merit, in spite of their social predicament, and served as an inspirational self-help guide to ways out of

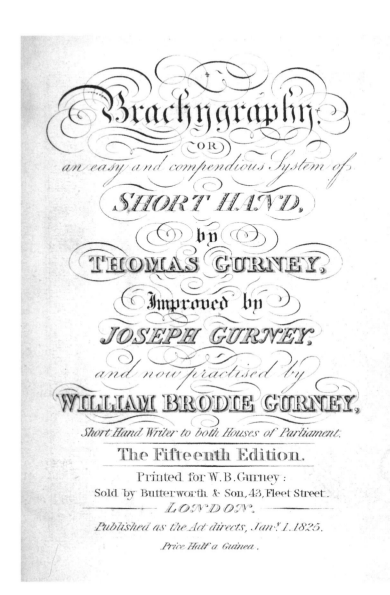

FIGURE 26. Thomas Gurney's *Brachygraphy*: the edition that Dickens bought to teach himself shorthand. Title page and shorthand versions of the opening verses of Genesis, and the Lord's Prayer. Published in London by Butterworth, 1825.

184

(6)

GENESIS, Chapter I.

2 3 4 5 6 7 8 9 10 11 12 13 14 15 16 17 18 19 20 21 22 23 24 25 26 27 28 29 30 31

The Apoſtles Creed.

The Lords Prayer.

FIGURE 27. Young Dickens, *c*.1830. Stipple engraving from a miniature painted by Dickens's aunt, Janet Barrow, at about the time the 18-year-old Dickens was living in Norfolk Street. She was living in Marylebone at the time. The engraver is unknown.

the trap which—despite industrialization—feudal society continued to impose.

In a society that was rife with social snobbery, and socially still quite rigid and closed to the working classes and those below them, the book stood for a movement which was coming of age just as Dickens was coming of age himself, to expand the notion of social worth and human potential. Dickens was later a passionate campaigner for wider educational facilities, public libraries, educational institutes, and ragged schools. In 1843 he addressed the inaugural meeting of the Manchester Athenaeum, alongside Benjamin

Disraeli, on the contrast between the 'path jagged of flints and stones' laid down by brutal ignorance for the homeless to walk upon, and the boon of literacy by which one could join in company:

> watching the stars with Ferguson the shepherd's boy, walking the streets with Crabbe, a poor barber here in Lancashire with Arkwright, a tallow-chandler's son with Franklin, shoemaking with Bloomfield in his garret, following the plough with Burns, and, high above the noise of loom and hammer, whispering courage in the ears of workers I could this day name in Sheffield and in Manchester.[23]

The time spent in study, perfecting his shorthand and getting up speed, had helped propel the transformation of the factory boy into a young writer. Within a decade of starting out as a junior clerk, Dickens was the well-known author of *Sketches by Boz*, *Pickwick*, and *Oliver Twist*.

A remarkable object dating from this era of Dickens's life is his calling card. Only one example is as yet known to be in existence. It carries the legend 'Mr Charles Dickens, Short Hand Writer, 10 Norfolk Street, Fitzroy Square'.[24]

The calling card is neat, diminutive, and elegant: so fragile and ephemeral that its importance might be easy to overlook. But, like the old workhouse, and Mr Dodd's house on the corner, it is a most extraordinary survival. Having a calling card was part of the process

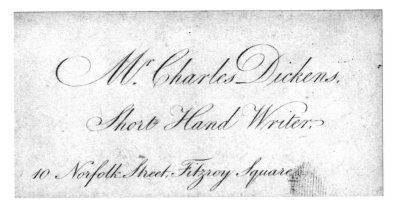

FIGURE 28. Charles Dickens's calling card, demonstrating his professional status while he was living in Norfolk Street for the second time, *c*.1830.

of becoming a professional, just as it is today. This card may have brought Dickens work, or contacts that brought him work. It was almost a travelling part of himself: a statement of professional status, an object which served to solicit employment, and which has travelled through time to us. Where might Dickens have been when he reached into his pocket-book to take it out, and hand it over...and to whom? Research may yet reveal the story of its survival, but for now it is enough for us to recognize that it constitutes a vital piece of incontrovertible evidence that young Mr Dickens lived in Norfolk Street, and of his adulthood at the time.

The card is important because it gives us a clear view of how Dickens wanted to present himself to others as he began to operate as a professional shorthand writer. This is really helpful, because the Norfolk Street years (1829–31) come at the end of a period of his life difficult to chart in any detail. Only three letters survive for the entire period up to 1831, none of them from this address. The lettering on the card is calligraphic rather than typographic in inspiration, resembling the personal quality of handwriting rather than the impersonality of type. Its modest flourishes suggest and demonstrate Dickens's love of elegance, a sort of controlled flamboyance: slightly flowery, but perfectly legible. The lettering leans forward, optimistically, as if it has great expectations! The 'Mr.' gives this young man a grown-up feel, while the 'Fitzroy Square' appended to the Norfolk Street address, would have looked socially good to anyone who did not know the area too well.[25] To us, it reveals his social aspirations. The central statement, 'Short Hand Writer', shows his pride in his own accomplishment. The card demonstrates Dickens's self-respect: his recognition of his own achievement, his trust in his own competence, in the value of his own mental and manual labour, and his satisfaction in the financial rewards of independence.

Dickens would not have spent precious earnings to pay to have something as important as this printed had he believed it would become obsolete quickly, so the card shows, too, that at the time he had it printed—which is likely to have been in 1829 or 1830—Dickens felt Norfolk Street was a secure address from which to advertise his talents: it was home.

The chronology of the key decade in Dickens's life between the ages of 15 and 25 (shown in Table 5, page 312) demonstrates that his determination to acquire and perfect his shorthand skills materially changed his life and prospects. Dickens's decision to extricate himself from the world of the legal clerk set the course for the possibility of his later writing.[26]

A number of his biographers ascribe the impetus for self-improvement to Dickens's meeting with Maria Beadnell in May 1830 and their subsequent futile courtship, but the chronology demonstrates it pre-dated that. The pivotal era appears to anticipate the key change from clerk to reporter, employee to freelance, between Somers Town and Norfolk Street. In relating David Copperfield's passion for the vacuous Dora, Dickens presents his efforts as biographers have generally accepted, but in real life Dickens applied for his ticket at the Reading Room of the British Museum before he met Miss Beadnell. Aspiring to marry was doubtless an effective stimulus when he flagged, but it was a product rather than the cause of his determination to improve himself.

Dickens seems to have made the transition from clerk to independent professional shorthand writer around the time of the family's move to Norfolk Street, and he applied for his Reader's ticket at the British Museum from there too. The alacrity with which he applied for his ticket suggests that he had been waiting some time for that day to arrive. The entry in the great ledger still preserved in the Museum for 8 February 1830, the day after his eighteenth birthday, reads:

> Dickens (Chas.) 10 Norfolk Street Fitzroy Square. C.W. Charlton
> 16 Berner St W. Ward 48 Berner St.[27]

The two names which follow Dickens's address here are those of the sureties or referees all new Readers were required to furnish: in his case Uncle Charlton, and a neighbour of his in Berners Street, William Tilleard Ward, a doctor who specialized in human deformity, especially of the spine.[28] Dickens renewed his ticket nine months later in October 1830, and again after a further nine months had elapsed in May 1831, in each instance from Norfolk Street. John Dickens followed his son into the Reading Room in the midsummer of 1832, attending along with George Hogarth, his son's future father-in-law, and a friend from Lincoln's Inn, James Bacon, who later served as approving Counsel to Dickens's contract with Chapman & Hall for *Nicholas Nickleby*.[29] John Dickens's referees were Henry Bacon of the Temple, and his own brother-in-law, John Barrow.[30]

The kind of journalism in which Dickens and his father were apparently occupied at that time generally appeared anonymously or pseudonymously—either without bylines, or with (often false) initials—and hence almost impossible to find, or attribute. Young Dickens seems to have gone about with his father at the outset, visiting public legal venues, such as police courts and inquests, to pick up stories. Jobbing newspaper hacks were paid a penny or a penny-half-penny a line, but it was the skill of finding lines that newspapers would pay for which was the key to success: looking for hot news or unusual stories, finding the angle of interest in mundane stories, writing persuasively, getting material written in advance of other journalists, finding niches to supply within the print industry of Fleet Street, or elsewhere.[31] It may be that for a time, neither of them felt sufficiently confident to follow verbatim stories alone, that they were taking shifts with each other, and assembling stories together later.

It was helpful to both of them that Uncle John Barrow had ploughed his own furrow ahead of them in the world of the press: he had worked as a shorthand writer at Doctors' Commons, an ecclesiastical court dealing with matrimonial law and wills, and had then made his name as a shorthand journalist covering the scandalous divorce trial of Queen Caroline and King George IV for *The Times*, in 1820. Barrow was also a good source of information: he understood relationships within Fleet Street, could help with introductions (i.e. networking), and (as we have already seen for John Dickens at the British Museum) he could and did provide character references. He later employed Charles Dickens on his own journal, *The Mirror of Parliament.*

It was a definite advantage to a journalist to be able to tap into a field of expertise. It is known, for example, that in 1826 Dickens's father, under the initial letter 'Z', published a series of nine articles on marine insurance in a newspaper called *The British Press*, in which he recommended the probity of Lloyd's of London. These articles presumably utilized existing knowledge from his naval employment. The underwriters at Lloyd's allowed John Dickens a grant of 10 guineas for the articles, after he appealed to their good offices when the newspaper for which he had written them failed, owing him payment. The exchange of letters detailing this interchange, and the bad luck behind it, was only discovered in the 1950s, and helps us appreciate that not all of John Dickens's financial difficulties were self-generated. Freelance journalism is an unreliable business.[32]

It was natural too that Dickens should develop an interest in law reporting. This kind of work was a treadmill, no doubt, like all daily work, but much depended on the energies and initiative of the individual, and that doubtless made it much more congenial to

Dickens than being a clerk. John Britton, later a literary supporter of Dickens, referred to his own years as a junior in a solicitor's office as a kind of 'slavery'.[33] But as a freelance, unless Dickens churned out material, he had no pay. In order to sell work, both Dickens and his father would have had to cultivate a style of reporting as close to existing newspapers' styles as possible, so it is likely that most of their material will never be identified.[34]

In 1830, while he was living in Norfolk Street, Dickens followed his uncle, and began work at Doctors' Commons, where Uncle Charlton worked as a clerk.[35] Dickens worked from the Reporters' Box as a freelance shorthand writer for the proctors there, recording cases verbatim when required. He said afterwards that 'it wasn't a very good living (though not a *very* bad one), and was wearily uncertain'. Dickens had desk space in adjacent Bell Yard, for quiet work transcribing and writing. His income at the time was both low and irregular. This is the period of his life in which the Dickens scholar John Drew suspects Dickens might have been composing verses for advertising shoe-blacking, for the princely sum of three shillings and sixpence each set of verses.[36]

Doctors' Commons was situated in a warren of streets between St Paul's Cathedral and the River, within easy reach of the Old Bailey and the lesser courts Dickens already knew from his clerking days. It was also conveniently placed for the newspaper world of Fleet Street, and the many small publishers around the western fringes of the City, in Paternoster Row and Cheapside. Among these was an enterprising printer-publisher, Jack Fairburn, whose songbooks, jest-books, cheap gothic novels, 'crim-con' divorces and horrid murder case reports, news chapbooks, and twelfth-night entertainments were displayed in his shop window on Ludgate Broadway, '*OPPOSITE THE OLD BAILEY*', a lane or two towards Fleet Street from Bell Yard.[37]

In among the unique Dexter Collection of rare Dickens materials held in the British Library is a sixpenny chapbook published by Fairburn, entitled *Burking the Italian Boy: Fairburn's Edition of the Trial of John Bishop, Thomas Williams, and James May for the Wilful Murder of the Italian Boy*. It is inscribed on its outer wrapper with a handwritten note from Dexter himself:

> F.W. Pailthorpe gave me this pamphlet
> stating that it was 'reported' by
> Charles Dickens & that he had
> this information from an authoritative
> source. The description of the prisoners
> (pp: 21–22) bears evidence of C.D's hand.
>   John F Dexter.

This little chapbook may be among the earliest things Dickens wrote, and as we shall see, the Italian Boy had a sad connection to Norfolk Street. Pailthorpe was a late Victorian illustrator of Dickens who had known George Cruikshank in his later years. Cruikshank and his father and brother, and possibly his nephew, had all worked for Jack Fairburn.[38] This chapbook looks to have been a hasty production, designed to cash in on the great wave of fear known as 'burkophobia', which gripped the metropolis late in 1831, when it was discovered that the crimes of Burke and Hare

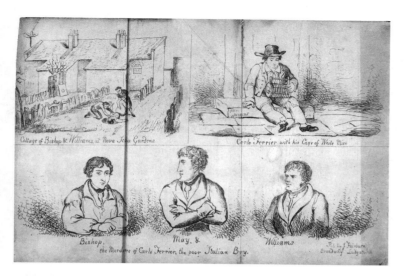

Cottage of Bishop & Williams at Nova Scotia Gardens

Carlo Ferrier with his Cage of White Mice

Bishop,
May, &
Williams
the Murderers of Carlo Ferrier, the poor Italian Boy.

Pub. by J. Fairburn
Broadway Ludgate Hill.

FIGURE 29. The murderers of the poor Italian Boy. Fold-out frontispiece from *The Italian Boy* chapbook, published by Jack Fairburn, London 1831. The images show signs of haste and are the work of more than one hand.

had been replicated in London. In Edinburgh in 1828, Burke and Hare had murdered sixteen people, mostly lone street folk seeking shelter.[39] The motive for that ghastly series of killings had been the money raised from the anatomist Dr Knox, who had purchased the corpses for dissection, and who had asked no questions as to how they had been obtained.[40]

When the new discovery was made in November 1831, 'burko-phobia' broke out afresh, now with a metropolitan focus. The poor were so fearful that even regular burglars were shopped as possible body-snatchers.[41] Three men, seasoned body-snatchers, had delivered the sacked-up body of a young teenager to the new Medical School at King's College Hospital, at the City end of the Strand. Suspicious about the cause of death—the anatomist had asked them to come back later for their money, pretending he had only a large bank-note—the police were waiting.[42]

It turned out that the victim was an Italian boy, Carlo Ferrari, who had made his living on London's streets showing a little revolving cage of performing white mice. He'd been seen begging outside a public house near Nova Scotia Gardens, Bethnal Green on the dark afternoon of 3 November, and there had fallen prey to two of the most despicable ruffians in London, Bishop and Williams, who plied him with drink (perhaps laced with opium) and, under cover of darkness, drowned him in a well in their garden. It was a cunning means of murder, which left no obvious marks. The men had already sold corpses, which despite their freshness had not raised suspicion. The major problem with burking was the destruction of evidence in the dissecting room, but fortunately in this case that was circumvented by the anatomist's quick thinking. The third brute, May, had helped transport the corpse, and extracted the boy's teeth after death for sale to a dentist, but had apparently not been party to this murder.

Whether Dickens wrote the report on the trial of the 'London Burkers' for Fairburn will probably never be known for certain. But it seems to be possible, both because of Pailthorpe's statement to Dexter, which is likely to have been reliable, and because of the date of the events, which fell in a parliamentary recess, when Dickens would have been short of regular work. A number of other threads connect Dickens to the story, and perhaps link the Cruikshank family of artists to its illustrated frontispiece.[43]

If Pailthorpe's informant was Cruikshank himself, it may be that the chapbook is the earliest item on which his family and Dickens worked together, unwittingly and without collaboration.[44] Near the end of *Oliver Twist*, when Fagin is in the dock at the Old Bailey, Dickens has him fix his attention for a few moments on a young artist sketching his likeness from the public gallery, perhaps nodding to Cruikshankian efforts at documentary recording for Jack Fairburn in that very courtroom. If this idea is correct, this reference complements the manner in which Cruikshank had pictured likenesses of Dickens himself in the illustrations to *Sketches by Boz*, before the real identity of 'Boz' had become publicly known. By picturing an anonymous artist in the gallery at the Old Bailey during Fagin's trial, Dickens may have been making a reciprocating nod towards the relationship and identities of the author and the illustrator within *Oliver Twist*.[45]

The collector J. F. Dexter evidently had a distinct sense that Dickens's voice could be heard in parts of prose in Fairburn's chapbook, which appears to me justified. It says 'TAKEN IN SHORT HAND' on the title page, with the words given separately, just as they appear on Dickens's calling card.[46] The manner in which the testimony is reported and edited is simple and clear, the case is presented to the reader in a thoroughly competent, straightforward way. This partly reflects the skill with which the prosecution lawyers built their case, but the chapbook's summaries are both pertinent and succinct, the whole production well crafted in a journalistic sense, too.

One of those giving evidence in the case was a member of the 'New Police' (recently instituted by Robert Peel), who sounds like a seasoned detective: his evidence is given to the reader without flinch. Another witness, a boy of only six and a half, was first examined as to the nature of an oath. The report reads: 'The child, with infantile simplicity, said that he knew it to be a very bad thing to tell a lie; that

FIGURE 30. *Early coaches*, an original Cruikshank etching from *Sketches by Boz*, showing Charles Dickens (in the top hat by the counter) incognito, in 1836.

it was a great sin; and that he who would swear falsely would go to h--l, to be burnt with brimstone and sulphur.'

It's the space and weight given in the report to the process of clarifying the boy's views, the language of the boy's statement, and the sentiment in that 'infantile simplicity' which feel to me like Dickens. This moment seems also to find an ironic late echo twenty years afterwards in *Bleak House*, when Jo the crossing sweeper expresses uncertainty about the afterlife in the Coroners' court: 'Can't exactly say what'll be done to him arter he's dead if he tells a lie to the gentlemen here'—and is dismissed from the stand.[47]

There are other moments, sometimes turns of phrase, spellings, and sentence constructions we know Dickens used, the confident use of 'we' meaning oneself; and moreover a sense of both analysis and power in the writing, which even at this early stage in his writing career (the chapbook appeared two years before the first of his *Sketches* was published) could indeed be his voice. There is a single snatch of quoted dialogue so telling that it could not be improved upon. One of the guilty men is reported as having said to the other: 'It was the blood that sold us.'

It is difficult to draw any stylistic conclusions from the edited transcription of other people's words taken down in shorthand. But while the Jury was out, the process of verbatim reporting was suspended, and the Fairburn correspondent described the tense atmosphere in the court in his own voice. The change of voice is signified in the chapbook in a different typeface. Some extracts are given here, so the reader can catch their flavour:

The interval…was a period of intense anxiety to every one in court; and, as is usual on such occasions, there were various conjectures hazarded as to what would be the verdict as to all the prisoners. That a verdict of 'Guilty' would be returned against two of the prisoners, namely Bishop and Williams, none who heard the evidence, and the summing up of the learned Judge, could entertain any rational doubt... [concerning the third defendant, May] the general opinion, as far as we could judge from what was passing around us, was—that the circumstantial proof not being in his case so strong as it was in the case of his fellow-prisoners, the Jury would acquit him; but still there were many who thought the proof of a participation in the murder clear and perfect as to all the parties.

The most deathlike silence now prevailed throughout the court, interrupted only by a slight buz in the reintroduction of the prisoners.

Bishop advanced to the bar with a heavy step, and with rather a slight bend of the body; his arms hung closely down, and it seemed a kind of relief to him, when he took his place, to rest his hand on the board before him. His appearance, when he got in front, was that of a man who had been for some time labouring under the most intense mental agony, which had brought on a kind of lethargic stupor. His eye was sunk and glassy; his nose drawn and pinched; the jaw fallen, and of course the mouth open; but occasionally the mouth closed, the lips became compressed, and the shoulders and chest raised, as if he was struggling to repress some violent emotion. After a few efforts of this kind, he became apparently calm, and frequently glanced his eye towards the Bench and the Jury box; but this was done without once raising his head. His face had that pallid blueish appearance which so often accompanies and betokens great mental suffering.

Williams came forward with a short, quick step; and his whole manner was, we should say, the reverse of that of his companion in guilt. His face had undergone very little change; but in the eye and in his manner there was a feverish anxiety which we did not observe during the trial. When he came in front, and laid his hand on the bar, the rapid movement of his fingers on the board—the frequent shifting of the hand, sometimes letting it hang down for an instant by his side, then replacing it on the board, and then resting his side against the front of the dock, shewed the perturbed state of his feelings. Once or twice he gave a glance round the Bench and the Bar, but after that he seldom took his eye from the Jury box.

The spellings of 'buz' and 'shewed' are typical of Dickens, and the insightful attention to posture, gesture, facial expression, and movements of the singular eye as a means of accessing/conveying mental state are all suggestive of his early style. The closest parallel however, is the 'deathlike' silence, which is a description Dickens actually uses in *Oliver Twist* for the hiatus in court at the exact same moment the verdict is about to be given in Fagin's trial:

As he saw all this in one bewildered glance, the death-like still-ness came again, and looking back, he saw that the jurymen had turned towards the judge.[48]

Interestingly, when extracts from the Fairburn chapbook were tried in the text search facility of the British Library's online newspaper collection, it emerged that several passages closely resemble coverage of the trial in the weekly newspaper *The York Herald*, which appeared a week after the trial. Internal evidence suggests that Fairburn's chapbook was probably written and rushed into print straight after the death sentences were handed down at the end of the trial on Friday, 2 December 1831, so as to be ready for sale to the crowds attending the execution at Newgate on the following Monday morning. The pamphlet mentions that the criminals had been sentenced the previous day, but does not cover the double execution, whereas the York newspaper report appeared the following Saturday, and covers the entire trial and execution. Further research will be required to discover if anything more can be found to clarify the source of the report: if Dickens had associations with York at that time, if he (and/or his father) might have done other work for the *York Herald* as freelance London correspondents, or if the paper simply noticed the quality of the text in Fairburn's chapbook, and pirated it.[49]

Dickens knew and loved Fairburn's output of comic songs, toasts ('May the wing of friendship never moult a feather') and glees, from little books which he may have seen and acquired from Mr Dodd's shop.[50] Among Fairburn's chapbook output are others which Dickens could well have known, such as the dramatic report of the wrecking of a pleasure steamer on the coast of North Wales, with terrible loss of life. Fairburn's *Narrative of the Total Loss of the Rothesay Castle Steam Vessel* on 17 August 1831 has a colour fold-out frontispiece showing a spectacular aerial view of the great deck of the ship dramatically tilted towards the viewer, with individuals discernible in the water or in desperate positions on the deck, awash, about to be shot into the waves, with a storm at its height, and all in tragic sight of land.[51] The chapbook sold for sixpence. Reading the text, I wondered if John Dickens might perhaps have had a hand in it, as it seems to be an informative and dextrous compilation of reports he might have been able to access at Lloyd's and elsewhere, with parliamentary material, perhaps obtained via the *Mirror of Parliament*. The 'melancholy catalogue of mortality' listing those known to be lost, and the detailed descriptions of the still unidentified drowned bodies, including those of young children, with carefully catalogued identifiers like height, hair colour, and details of initials on linen, and calling cards, for each body washed ashore on the Welsh coast, makes for very poignant reading. In later life in *David Copperfield* Charles Dickens wrote a dramatic description of a shipwreck (in which Steerforth is drowned), and many years afterwards, he made a special journey to the desolate rocky coast of Anglesey, after the wrecking of the *Royal Charter* steamship in the great hurricane of 1859. The journey resulted in one of his finest essays, 'Shipwreck'.[52] The latter, in particular, is so very similar to this early chapbook in content, that it prompts thoughts about some of Fairburn's output, and its influence upon—or creation by—John Dickens and son.

Fairburn's 'Extreme Cruelty to Children, MURDER!' reported the details of an inquest on the bodies of two young girls, who had been apprenticed out 'on-liking' from two London workhouses, St Martin's and Cripplegate, and who had been starved and maltreated to death in 1829 by their employer, Esther Hibner, in a domestic manufactory close to Somers Town.[53] In this instance, I would not suggest Dickens reported on the case, but it was widely reported and

is likely to have been familiar to him, since the manner in which
Oliver is so starved as to be grateful for animal scraps to eat at
Sowerberry's perhaps recalls details from the trial. Hibner's trial
revived popular memories of a much older case, that of Elizabeth
Brownrigg, hanged for a similar murder in the 1760s.[54] Brownrigg
was infamous as an archetype of female cruelty from chapbooks
and ballads, and her fate at the gallows awaited the guilty employer
in this case, in 1829.[55] Jack Fairburn's chapbook has a dramatic fold-
out frontispiece, showing the entire Coroner's jury viewing with
horror the emaciated body of one of the girls who died from the
maltreatment, Margaret Howse, or Hawse.[56]

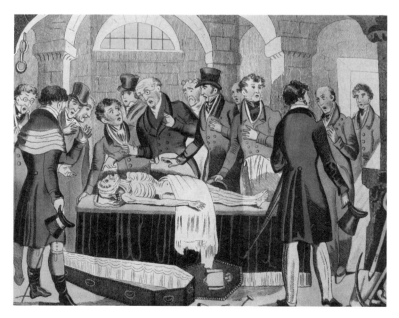

FIGURE 31. *The Coroner's Jury.* The extraordinary frontispiece to 'Extreme
Cruelty' published by Jack Fairburn, London, 1829, reporting the dreadful
facts of the Esther Hibner case. Artists unknown.

The chapbook catalogues a sequence of vicious maltreatment by the girls' employers, and fatal neglect on the part of the parish authorities. As in the case of the factory boy Robert Blincoe from St Pancras Workhouse, whose appalling experiences have already been mentioned above, there was no real oversight of the fate of these children once they were apprenticed out. At their worst, workhouse apprenticeships like these can be seen to have been almost an official form of child trafficking. The brutish treatment meted out to these girls, and the desperate fear among the other friendless apprentices at the factory, who were cowed into silence by the sadistic brutality they had witnessed being inflicted, is the real-life background to the collusion in *Oliver Twist* of the workhouse management personified by the man in the white waistcoat, and the sadistic employer—Gamfield, the donkey-beating master sweep—on the doorstep of the workhouse. Although Dickens is often accused of melodrama, he is seldom described as a master of understatement. Yet his use of Gamfield's treatment of the donkey as an analogue for institutional inhumanity towards the child, is masterly.[57]

Deaths like those of Francis Colpitts and Margaret Howse, and especially the murder of the Italian Boy, revealed a murderous level of predation upon poor children in London, which had probably not been contemplated before. Dickens's friend Leigh Hunt was still thinking about it several years later, when he published this passage in the *London Journal* in 1834:

I had only just heard of the murder of the poor wanderer, Carlo Ferrari, and having walked out in the hope of removing from my mind the painful feeling such an atrocity awakened, I happened to overtake a lad with an organ and a little box of white mice. I now found any attempt to forget the murder fruitless, and now minutely observed the youth before me. [He sees he is Italian and follows] ... he stopped opposite to a print shop, and having scanned the contents of the window, he suddenly fixed his attention on a drawing: a gleam of pleasure lightened up his face [the boy had seen a picture of the Madonna and Child] 'And they have murdered thy countryman,' thought I, 'and he was a stranger'.[58]

There is good reason to believe that the Italian Boy's case held especial resonance for Dickens. A cluster of curious affinities suggests why this might have been so. His possible authorship (or co-authorship with his father?) of the Fairburn chapbook is one. Another is that the Italian Boy's body was buried in the pauper burial ground right behind the Cleveland Street Workhouse. Like so many other poor people from the parish of St Paul, his coffin had been borne out of central London and carried past the front door of 10 Norfolk Street.

Later, from the rear windows of the Workhouse the pauper inmates might have witnessed the sorry process of exhumation, when the boy's body was judicially dug up again for a fresh official identification, and buried a second time. The woman who identified the Italian Boy's body in the burial ground behind the Workhouse had last seen him alive in Oxford Street, and another witness had seen Bishop's children playing with white mice in a revolving cage. Both Oxford Street and white mice would have had echoes for Dickens—the latter with those hidden in his own desk at the Wellington Academy.[59]

In 1836, nearly five years after the Italian Boy's case, Dickens visited Newgate Prison for a *Sketch* he was writing, a visit which doubtless also influenced his conception of the end of *Oliver Twist*. The first criminals he mentions having encountered there were Bishop and Williams:

> Following our conductor by a door opposite to that at which we had entered, we arrived at a small room, without any other furniture than a little desk, with a book for visitors' autographs: and a shelf on which were a few boxes for papers, and casts of the heads and faces of the two notorious murderers, Bishop and Williams—the former, in particular, exhibiting a style of head, and set of features which would have afforded sufficient moral grounds for his instant execution at any time, even had there been no other evidence against him.

The Parish of St Paul Covent Garden had been the prosecutor in the murder case at the Old Bailey, because before his death the Italian Boy had been living in that parish: his lodgings had been in a well-known rookery in Charles Street, near Covent Garden: a dead-end at the southern end of Bow Street. Later, in the mid-1830s, this slum was cleared and a new street was cut through southwards to the Strand and Waterloo Bridge. The new thoroughfare was called Wellington Street North, and Dickens later occupied two premises there: first for the offices of *Household Words*, and another for *All the Year Round*. The latter occupied a corner, overlooking the site of the old slum.[60]

It's clear from the 'autobiographical fragment' that as a child in the blacking factory Dickens had felt abandoned, and that his later observations on that period of his life reflect his subsequent memories of his feelings as a boy. Objectively, while his parents were in the

FIGURE 32. Covent Garden Market. A lovely watercolour by George Scharf, 1825. It shows the busy market as Dickens would have known it when he was a child worker in the nearby blacking factory, only the previous year. He often wandered through the market alone, experiencing the profusion and liveliness of the place. There would have been other times, too, when it was silent and empty of stalls, a wide open space. The pent roof and clock tower of Inigo Jones's great Church of St Paul Covent Garden rears above the stalls on the right. The Italian Boy's lodgings had been close by.

Marshalsea he was indeed an abandoned child. But the Italian Boy's case (and most likely others to which Dickens was exposed in the press of the day, and in the courts he attended as a reporter) compounded these early memories with an overlay of adult knowledge of what might have happened to him, had he been less lucky. Garments from people other than the Italian Boy were found buried at Nova Scotia Gardens. Before their execution, Bishop and Williams are rumoured to have confessed to sixty murders, not just the one for which they were finally caught.[61]

It is known that in the 1840s Dickens visited a charitable school for Italian boys established in Clerkenwell on more than one occasion. 'I was among the Italian Boys from 12 to 2 this morning,' Forster quotes him writing in a letter.[62] It would appear that Dickens had taken the original Italian Boy's predicament very much to heart.

Dickens once commented to Forster on chance and mischance in altering lives, when he told him about an opportunity he had missed, through illness, to audition as an actor at Covent Garden Theatre: 'See how near I may have been, to another sort of life.' The sentiment could surely have applied to the Italian Boy; and to a different sort of death.[63]

·CHAPTER 8·

Workhouse

ST PAUL'S PARISH, FARMING THE INFANT
POOR, PAUL PRY, PARLIAMENT

T HE SAME YEARS were important for the Workhouse, too. In several parishes with which Dickens was familiar— St Paul Covent Garden, St Giles and St George Bloomsbury, and in St Marylebone—there were active moves afoot to bring greater democratic oversight to the management of the local government.

Parish 'Select Vestries' were unelected, self-perpetuating parish management committees, and were widely regarded as corrupt. St Martin's in the Fields (which surrounded Covent Garden parish) was a particular focus of parishioner disaffection.[1] Reform was 'in the air', and the political agitation of the day was in many places focused as much towards unrepresentative local government as it was towards the unrepresentative national Parliament.[2] To give an idea of the nature of the local democratic deficit, the population of the parish of St Paul Covent Garden was over 5,000, while the number of property owners who had a right to vote for parish representatives was only 73.[3]

There had been rumours buzzing around the parish of St Paul Covent Garden for some time, when on April Fools' Day 1828 rumours became allegations: of gross feasting on the part of the Select Vestry, and of corruption involving hush-money from brothel owners. Printed caricatures showing the gentlemen of the Select Vestry feasting at public expense were put up on display in print-shop windows in Piccadilly and elsewhere, spreading the story far and wide, well beyond the parish. Displayed legibly on the carica-ture was an itemized hospitality bill: dinners at 9 guineas a head, prodigious amounts of alcohol, champagne, rose-water, et cetera, and the added costs of coaches, and broken glasses. The faces of

FIGURE 33. *Select Vestry Comforts*, showing the gluttony of the Select Vestry of the parish of St Paul Covent Garden. Added manuscript annotations in the border suggest that the artist's likenesses closely identified several of those involved. Etched by Thomas Jones, published by Fores of Piccadilly, 1828.

the diners were portrayed so well as to render them individually identifiable.[4]

The Parish Beadle was shown wielding his staff of office to keep intruders out while the 'Select' were 'busy', and a wall-notice announced their power to impose any poor-rate they chose. The gluttony is depicted as having followed upon an inspection of the parish's Infant Poor Establishment, the austere exterior of which features in a painting on the wall in the same caricature.

Since 1767 a special Act of Parliament known as Hanway's Act, designed to prevent devastating levels of infant mortality among parish children in the metropolis, required every London parish to establish a 'branch' workhouse in the countryside at least three miles outside London, in which to rear their infant poor.[5] Parish children were sent out to these places—also known as 'baby farms'—after weaning, and reared until they were old enough to return to the workhouse in town, from which they would be assigned to employers. Periodic 'inspections' of these baby farms were part of parish management of the metropolitan poor. Dickens mentions that Mr Bumble was always sent a day ahead to warn of a likely inspection, and that the children always looked 'neat and clean, when they went; and what more would the people have!'[6]

Branch workhouses were unique to London. The fictional work-house in *Oliver Twist* has been supposed to be located about seventy miles north of London from two things: a milestone Oliver sees when he runs away, and his entry to London in the book via Barnet, which stands on the Great North Road.[7] But the fact that baby Oliver is sent after weaning for rearing at a branch workhouse, before being brought back to the main workhouse and apprenticed out, reveals that Dickens was actually thinking of a metropolitan setting. The presence of a branch workhouse in *Oliver Twist* is fundamental to an understanding that Dickens's seventy miles are completely fictional: Oliver's days on the road are part of the allegorical journey of the book's original subtitle, 'The Parish Boy's Progress'.[8]

The baby farm in *Oliver Twist* is placed 'three miles off' from the workhouse itself, which under Hanway's Act was the regulation minimum distance for a branch workhouse. It is not known if the image of the St Paul Covent Garden Infant Poor Establishment labelled 'British Pauper Children Asylum' which appears in the caricature 'Select Vestry Comforts' bore any real resemblance to the actual place, though that is certainly possible since the artist was on target with so much else in the caricature. It may simply have been designed to appear as a farm building so as to refer to its baby-farming activity, which Londoners would have known would be in the fields. The place is shown as a barn-like building on a hill, surrounded by a wall, and with a large millstone leaning against it, the deeper meaning of which is explained by Dickens, when Mr Bumble describes Oliver as a 'porochial 'prentis, who is at present a dead-weight; a mill-stone, as I may say, round the porochial throat'.[9]

Pauper children from the parish Workhouse of St Paul Covent Garden in Cleveland Street were actually sent out after weaning to the parish's branch workhouse which stood in the old hill village of Hendon, north of London, over whose fields the battle of Barnet was fought.[10] The mistress of the institution in Dickens's time was a Miss Merriman; in the book this figure is named as Mrs Mann.[11] Old manorial field maps show that at the heart of Hendon village was a milestone showing the distance to Charing Cross: known and labelled as the 'seven mile stone'.[12] In placing Oliver seventy miles away in the book, Dickens may simply have inserted a zero: he may have disguised the place very well indeed by adding nothing.

For Dickens, seven miles was an easy walk—up to Hampstead, and through North End (which he knew well) and Golders Green to Hendon village. Hendon churchyard, which had a magnificent view, was a favourite haunt of his.[13] Dickens's passion for active excursions was not that of everyone, however, and the distance does help explain the cost of the coaches hired to carry the Select Vestry of St Paul Covent Garden out to Hendon and back in the caricature, and Mr Bumble's need for a drink of the parochial gin-and-water upon his arrival. Hendon was clearly on Dickens's mind, too, as he was writing the novel, because during Bill Sikes's flight after murdering Nancy, the killer thinks of the village as 'a good place, not far off, and out of most people's way'. But when Sikes gets there, even 'the very children at the doors' look at him with suspicion.[14] Dickens would probably have known that some of the child population of Hendon in 1837 would have been what he ironically described as 'juvenile offenders against the poor laws', from Cleveland Street.[15]

Wincing with discomfort from the bad publicity caused by the caricature, the chastened Covent Garden parish authorities demonstrated their new probity by establishing a subcommittee to advise on the 'revision' of the administration of poor relief in the parish: the sting redounded on the poor. The recommendations of this committee were applied in 1830–1, while Charles Dickens was living in Norfolk Street. If news got out around the neighbourhood, the keen young journalist would have heard it.

Part of this 'revision' of the Workhouse in Cleveland Street reflected a broader shift in attitudes towards poverty. Rising population, and the number of widowed and deserted families from the Napoleonic Wars, as well as urbanization and the piecemeal eviction of the rural poor during the enclosure and clearance of estates, had swelled the population of London alarmingly. Metropolitan parishes especially were stretched to alleviate the levels of homelessness and want within their boundaries, especially during winter. Many politicians were persuaded by the ideas of Thomas Malthus that poor relief merely encouraged the poor to breed. Unmarried mothers and their offspring should receive the brunt of the blame for rising poor-rates, not errant fathers. Indeed, some influential figures went so far as to accuse all institutions which assisted childbirth among the poor (such as the lying-in charities) or those offering charitable care to the orphan poor (such as the Foundling Hospital) of encouraging immorality: they were to be regarded as altogether pernicious.[16]

Opponents of these harsh and uncharitable opinions raised kinder voices, urging solicitude towards the less fortunate. A correspondent in the *London Journal*, for example, cited especially the plight of ballad singers, whose desperate state had brought them to this last stage of existence before applying to the parish. The writer ascribed their pitiful vocal efforts to hunger: 'I hear the notes falling like drops of lead'. Children who joined their voices to those of street singers are described in such a way as to remind one of the photographs of children saved by Dr Barnardo from the streets of late Victorian London, or the gangs of street children in Third World cities today:

> half a dozen of the poorest squalid little creatures; and yet they sang, or attempted to sing, with all their might, though their cheeks were pinched by famine, and their uncovered little toes were smarting with the cold mud of the street.[17]

Readers will surely have no difficulty in knowing where Dickens stood on these matters, and what his views would have been concerning the extensive industry called 'farming' the poor. Private companies were positioning to offer themselves as contractors in warehousing the poor more cheaply than parishes might manage themselves. One such company sent advertising handbills to a number of London parishes in 1830 offering to 'farm' their female poor for only four shillings a week each, including washing and medical attendance, lying-in women at no extra cost. Remember, Dickens had been paid six shillings a week at the blacking factory, and had often been hungry. The company's private workhouse in Lant Street, Borough, was advertised as capacious, clean, and airy, and the thin diet laid out as a Bill of Fare: on Mondays, Wednesdays, and Fridays, merely gruel and bread, on other days, a little meat or soup.[18] That such painfully meagre (malnutrition level) alternatives to existing workhouse provision could be proffered to local authorities without shame indicates the punitive attitudes towards the poor these contractors were hoping to meet and satisfy. Many London parishes, including St Paul Covent Garden, did use these places as reservoirs for their own recalcitrant poor, and Poor Law authorities perhaps gained courage from such starvation dietaries to shrink their own.[19]

Attitudes were polarizing at the time: sympathy for the lot of the poor was giving way in powerful places to a level of harshness and unconcern previously unknown. At the time, a wave of political agitation was running in favour of much greater democracy, both nationally and locally, and huge numbers of people were mobilizing in support of parliamentary reform. But in many quarters this movement fed old fears of the Gordon Riots of 1780 or of the French Revolution, and many supporters of reform recognized the need to extend the franchise so as to prevent revolutionary fervour. So while the idea of greater democracy had wide support, part of the push for change had a hard edge of parsimony and retrenchment on the part of property owners, of pulling up the ladder. The economics of poor relief were bearing heavily upon the classes just above the very poor, who were voteless, and disgruntlement was widespread. The government eventually did slightly extend the franchise, in the Reform Act of 1832, which was widely hailed as great victory on its passage; but the voting qualification had been very carefully set at a property valuation of £10 sterling, which still excluded the vast majority of the population. Then came the New Poor Law.

Most localities in this era went through only one major upheaval in parish poor provision, when the 1834 New Poor Law was put into force, bringing in 'unions' of parishes, punitive workhouses, the enforced break-up of families, and rigorous 'tests' for poor relief. But in some places the political will to alter the administration of poor relief pre-dated the drafting of the new law, and retrenchment was introduced well in advance of its passage through Parliament. These parishes had a second period of change when adopting the New Poor Law after 1834. St Paul Covent Garden was one of them.

Under the New Poor Law's process of reorganization and the amalgamation of parishes into 'unions' for reasons of greater economy, the Cleveland Street Workhouse was designated as the main workhouse for a new union of parishes in the Strand district, and its name was therefore changed to the Strand Union Workhouse. The appointed day for the adoption of the New Poor Law in the Strand Poor Law Union was 24 June 1836. Dickens began writing *Oliver Twist* within a year of its operation.[20]

To allow his hero to grow up from birth in a workhouse, and to become a parish apprentice and trainee thief within the time-frame of the novel's serialization during 1837–8, Dickens set the story back in time. So although when it was written, the book was a bold attack on the spirit of the just-being-implemented New Poor Law, the fictional workhouse at the opening of the story was one where rigorous parsimony was already in force ahead of the Act itself: where the spirit of the new legislation was at work before the fact, yet where there were still signs of the Old Poor Law in operation. Some writers on Dickens have thought he was deliberately vague and confusing about the timescale of the book, but in fact when we look at the Cleveland Street Workhouse we can see that it fitted the bill well. Covent Garden was one of those parishes where change had arrived in two stages, and where the second stage was the New Poor Law, which served simply to reinforce the first.[21]

The Covent Garden Vestry's *Report* on the implementation of the first phase of reforms at Cleveland Street in 1830–1 reads almost like a source-book for the opening chapters of *Oliver Twist*. The parish subcommittee had evidently grappled with the fundamental problem of what a workhouse was really for—sanctuary or punishment—and had come down in favour of the latter. There was no notion of sympathy for, or even recognition of seasonal unemployment, or of the deep dips of mass unemployment caused by recessions or trade cycles, or of the sheer helplessness of babies, children, the sick, the disabled, the elderly, or the dying. The divide for them was straightforward: between deserving and undeserving poor. Neither would be provided with anything more than bare subsistence. The Workhouse was to provide the absolute minimum: to shelter and sustain those 'who are ready to perish'. The Workhouse should be:

> a suitable Asylum for the aged, the imbecile, the unfortunate who are without friends to supply their wants, and whose means are wholly inadequate to their support, while their bodily or mental powers are too far spent to enable them to procure the sustenance, clothing or the shelter which nature requires. While to those whose mental or physical powers remain in sufficient vigour to enable them to secure by their labour the means of support, but who from idle, disorderly, or thriftless habits, have reduced themselves to merited indigence and disgrace, your Workhouse should be for such a place of wholesome restriction and discipline . . . [as to] convince such individuals of the propriety of providing the means of their own support by their own industry elsewhere.[22]

First, the Workhouse master and matron were replaced with a younger couple 'without any objectionable incumbrance', that is, having no responsibility for children or aged parents themselves. The committee then tackled the matter of gendering the institutional space, cutting off all communication between the men's and the women's sides of the building, thereby separating married couples, and disallowing meetings even at meals. The committee recognized at the outset that the architecture at Cleveland Street did not suit the asymmetry of its population: 'the number of female poor, is nearly double that of males.' Separation involved some building work and the locking of doors in strategic places, for the assignment of separate stairways, dining areas, and workrooms. The turning of keys firmly in the Workhouse locks is almost audible.

The committee's report then concentrated on the curtailment of the Workhouse diet, listing in the 'new-modelled diet table' gruel every day for breakfast, and an allowance of bread (no mention of butter, or dripping) with a portion of boiled meat on Sundays, Tuesdays, and Thursdays, with soup on each day following, made from the broth in which the meat had been boiled. On Saturday neither meat nor soup, but a small portion of cheese, and with butter available instead only for the young. Tea, sugar, porter (ale), mutton or mutton broth, were permitted only on a doctors' prescription.

The dietary looks to have been only marginally better than the pauper-farmers' advert, and its indulgences reveal the true niggardliness of the regime: boiled mutton once in six weeks; pork and baked plum pudding once a year on Christmas Day with a pint of porter, and 'cross buns one to each on Good Friday'. Unless expressly prescribed by the Medical Attendant, and entered by him in the ledger devoted to that purpose, it was specifically emphasized twice that there was to be: *'no addition to the above allowance in any case'*, and *'on no account any additional allowance to be given'*. If Dickens had seen this document, the idea of the terrible workhouse transgression of asking for more would have jumped off the page.

The Workhouse in Cleveland Street was cleaned and whitewashed, the separation of the sexes accomplished, and the new Workhouse dietary introduced. New regulations had been devised and enforced to ensure that while 'reasonable comfort' was available to the deserving and helpless poor, the Workhouse was rendered 'undesirable to all who could support themselves by their own labour elsewhere'. Punishments were devised for 'refractory' and 'obstinate' paupers, which included being sent to the refractory ward (otherwise known as the 'black hole'), half-diet, being 'sent away', and if necessary, being taken before the local magistrate for further punishment. Being 'sent away' for adults probably meant being sent to one of the existing privately run pauper 'farms', several of which by 1832 had as many as 500 'undesirables' as inmates.[23]

Children (except in cases of misconduct) were permitted to walk out and enjoy a half-holiday every Saturday 'under the superintendence of the School Master', but adults were to have only one half-day in six weeks. Visitors were permitted only once a month, on the third Wednesday in every month, 'between the hours and

10 and 12 in the forenoon'. There was no discussion as to how working people might visit relatives or friends on such a mid-week work day: one gains the impression that this morning had been deliberately chosen to curtail the possibility of visits. By locking the wards during the day, the subcommittee had been able to save money on coal. After daily prayers ('the consolations of religion') at 7.30 and gruel, the inmates were to be kept at work in the workrooms until 5 p.m. in winter and 6 p.m. in summer. For two hours every morning, boys were to be taught reading and writing; girls scouring, washing, ironing, mending, and cooking. All the bed-sacking, and all the linen of the house (including the paupers' uniforms and burial shrouds), were to be produced in-house.

The committee reported that at no time had they lost sight of 'the great object of Economy'. By the 'rigid enforcement' of the new parish regulations, they proudly announced that they had saved nearly £200 per quarter, especially by 'cutting off the tea and sugar, which under the former practice had been allowed to all above 70 years of age'.

We do not know how open or closed the Workhouse was in terms of news on the street, but because Mr Dodd dealt in both tea and sugar, the grocer's shop is likely to have been a route of news about the dietary and other changes afoot if visitors came to obtain supplies for inmates, or if employees came to purchase little luxuries for themselves.[24]

Charles Dickens was still living in Norfolk Street while this first tranche of institutional change was being implemented inside the Workhouse on the next block. He said years afterwards that he was 'not eighteen' at the time he became a Parliamentary Reporter, which dates this important transformation in his working life to the same period at which we are looking, while he was in Norfolk Street: 1830 or early 1831.[25] He was probably working on his uncle's *Mirror of Parliament*, initially trying to get up to speed to become a professional salaried newspaper staffer, which indeed he eventually succeeded in doing.[26]. But a lack of firm evidence has led some biographers to be vague about the date of his entry to the Reporters' Gallery in the old Houses of Parliament, and some ascribe it to the more certain time of his work on the newspaper *The True Sun*, from March 1832 onwards. Either way, he would have witnessed the tail end of the stormy passage through Parliament of the Great Reform Bill, and would have been without work during parliamentary recesses, which were many during the political upheavals of that time.[27]

In the late spring or early summer of 1831, Dickens's father again fell into financial difficulties, and for a period ended up 'going to ground'—living alone in hiding—presumably to prevent being rearrested and imprisoned again for debt. There is good evidence for a similar episode in 1834, when John Dickens was arrested and held again in Cursitor Street (near Chancery Lane), and was freed by his son's efforts.[28] It is possible that a similar train of events had occurred in 1831. It looks as though the family fled Norfolk Street in a hurry, probably to evade creditors, apparently changing address several times. The fearful possibility of returning to the Marshalsea must have been serious.[29] But Dickens renewed his own Reader's Ticket at the British Museum from 10 Norfolk Street in May 1831, so the evidence for that year is difficult to read, unless he had gone back, or continued to use that address for reasons of stability.[30]

Family tradition says that in 1831 (perhaps later in the year) Dickens also shared rooms in Buckingham Street, Strand, with J. E. Roney, a reporter on the *Morning Chronicle*. Buckingham Street (which still runs south from the Strand, near Charing Cross) would have been very convenient for the journalism and parliamentary work in which Dickens was increasingly involved. The story goes that Dickens gave David Copperfield his rooms there: in a letter written years later, Dickens himself invited his friend's recognition of the use he had made of them in the novel.[31] This may have been a significant time for him: Dickens looks to have been earning enough independent income to rent his own living space, at least for a while: his first period living away from his parents since the blacking factory. Once again, he was down between the Strand and the River: he would have been able to see the site of the old blacking factory at Hungerford Stairs from the river end of Buckingham Street, so his pervasive sense of the Marshalsea period together with the cluster of associations of the Strand, Norfolk Street, and the blacking factory are likely to have been reinforced.[32]

Although Dickens was no longer living beside the Workhouse, the part of eastern Marylebone he knew so well remained a stamping ground for him, because even after his parents and the rest of the family had vacated the rooms above Mr Dodd's shop, they remained strongly attached to the area. Documentation is thin, but apart from places to which they had to flee to evade creditors (near the Strand or out at Hampstead) the family's known addresses over the next few years are all in Marylebone. During John Dickens's debt crisis in 1831, the family was scattered, but by the late spring of 1832 the whole family was back together, living in Margaret Street (just south of the Middlesex Hospital); then for the rest of that year, in Fitzroy Street, just behind the Workhouse. In January 1833, they settled in Bentinck Street, off Marylebone Lane, where Dickens's 21st birthday was celebrated 'with quadrilles'.[33]

To be a Gallery Reporter in Parliament was something Dickens had intensely wanted to do, worked hard to achieve, and something at which he became superbly accomplished. Among its eighty or ninety reporters he is said to have occupied 'the very highest rank, not merely for accuracy in reporting but for marvellous quickness in transcribing'.[34] Dickens is likely to have entered upon the job with high hopes in 1831, but it is certain that he was wearied of it by the time he left in 1836. Forster puts it well: 'his observation while there had not led him to form any high opinion of the House of Commons or its heroes... he omitted no opportunity of declaring his contempt at every part of his life.'[35]

It was Dickens's destiny to witness the ascendancy in Parliament of similar attitudes to those we have just seen triumph in the management of the Workhouse in Cleveland Street. In 1831 the government appointed a Royal Commission to examine the workings of the Old Poor Law. The Commission's harsh recommendations were enshrined in the New Poor Law of 1834.[36]

The central feature of the New Poor Law regime would be the 'Workhouse Test' (devised by Edwin Chadwick) which provided that the workhouse would become the only kind of help offered to anyone seeking assistance, and that the standard of relief there should be worse than the standard of living of the poorest labourer outside. It was this philosophy that Dickens characterized as having been devised by someone whose 'blood is ice, whose heart is iron'.[37] People could be offered the House; if they refused it, they could suffer at their own choice outside; if they accepted it, they accepted the regime on offer. Large workhouses were to be established by unions of parishes, not as humane refuges for the sick and elderly, but as deterrent institutions designed to be inhospitable to the 'able-bodied'. No unemployment pay, district nursing, or other help was to be available even in times of high unemployment, dearth, or temporary desperation, and a key element of the regime was to prevent procreation. Dickens would have been well aware of the Royal Commission and its recommendations, which were published by order of Parliament in 1834. All this was in the air around Westminster during Dickens's time there.

Dickens was in the Reporters' Gallery recording in shorthand and re-transcribing word for word into longhand what politicians had said during some of the debates on the Great Reform Bill in 1831 and 1832 so he is likely also to have heard and reported upon the debates concerning another important piece of legislation, the Anatomy Bill, which went through both Houses of Parliament at that time.[38] The battle over the Reform Bill extending the franchise and abolishing 'rotten boroughs' attracted extensive coverage in all the newspapers of the day, while the Anatomy Bill received almost none: partly because it was crowded out, but also because for political reasons it passed through most of its parliamentary stages late at night.

The Anatomy Bill was a measure designed to prevent body-snatching and murder for dissection. An earlier bill with the same intention had been thrown out by the House of Lords at the time of the first wave of burkophobia in 1828–9.[39] That version had been nicknamed the 'Midnight Bill', because it, too, had made its passage at night.[40] The new Bill was more deftly drafted, and had been ready for introduction to the Commons when news of the Italian Boy's murder hit the headlines.

Under existing law, the only legal source of corpses for dissection in anatomy schools had hitherto been the gallows: the bodies of murderers were handed over after execution. But there were insufficient corpses available from judicial sources to supply the schools, so since at least the mid-eighteenth century body-snatchers had been paid to obtain them from graveyards. Their job was dangerous, public opposition was fierce, and danger money was payable. Eventually, the level of remuneration commanded by body-snatchers reached such a high level that some wretches (Burke and Hare, Bishop and Williams, and probably others never caught) came to regard the money as an incentive to murder.

The Anatomy Bill was designed to completely undermine this market and render body-snatchers and burkers redundant by the provision of a new free source of corpses. The first draft of the Bill had been explicit in naming who the new constituency for the slab would be: the workhouse poor. Effectively, the proposal was to make a direct transfer of what for many centuries had been a punishment for murder, to poverty.

The first Bill had earned itself the opposition of charitably minded MPs and Lords, and it failed. The new version, whose progress Dickens would have witnessed, was instead carefully evasive. It appeared innocuous by conveying the positive impression that its intention was to allow executors to donate bodies for dissection. In fact, the intention was identical: it simply granted to those legally 'in possession' of the dead, the power to dispose of them, and workhouses and other institutions in which the poor died were technically deemed to be 'in possession'.[41] The Bill made its way successfully through both Houses by a deliberate policy of downplaying its significance, known as 'taisez-vous' (or 'shut-up') where even staunch supporters were warned to keep quiet.

But the politicians did not have it all their own way: the intention of the legislation was vilified in a caricature by 'Paul Pry', in which the new sources of corpses for anatomy were shown in detail. Its central vignette shows deals being done between institutional employees and body-snatchers in a busy marketplace between a cluster of buildings labelled 'WORKHOUSE', 'HOSPITAL', 'JAIL' and 'KING'S BENCH', which last may have promoted a close personal appreciation of the legislation on Dickens's part, perhaps a recognition of kinship with workhouse inmates.[42] Dickens may be commenting upon such deals when he has Mr Bumble help himself to snuff from the undertaker Mr Sowerberry's proffered snuffbox, which takes the form of a patent coffin—a symbol of secure burial for those with money to pay for it—but also a reminder of the threat of dissection—during a conversation about profit-making from pauper coffins.[43]

The Anatomy Act, which became law in the summer of 1832, perfectly complemented the wishes of those who were planning to bring in the new 'deterrent' workhouse system. In fact the Anatomy Act can be thought of as an advance clause of the New Poor Law, because it yoked together the terrible fear of dissection, which had been cultivated by legislation for centuries, and death in the workhouse.[44] A pauper's funeral now meant not just a workhouse shroud, a thin deal coffin, and a hurried burial in a pit behind the workhouse: it meant being treated like the worst of murderers. The same 'Paul Pry' caricature portrays the contrast between a safe vault for the rich and a poor man's grave then, and now. The image is of traditional churchyard rest versus a dunghill ('desected [dissected/desecrated] remains may be shot here') with a dog/fox and a pig rooting about amid human remains, watched by a carrion crow; or, sold in joints at a street butcher's stall.

The atmosphere of this dark time stayed with Dickens. Twenty years later, in a powerful editorial in *Household Words*, he described five bundles of rags he had witnessed lying against the workhouse wall in Whitechapel. He and his friend Albert Smith (with whom he had just had a convivial meal) did not realize at first that these heaps were human beings shut out of the workhouse:

Crouched against the wall of the Workhouse in the dark street, on the muddy pavement-stones, with the rain raining upon them, were five bundles of rags. They were motionless, and had no resemblance to the human form...five dead bodies taken out of graves, tied neck and heels, and covered with rags—would have looked like those five bundles upon which the rain rained down in the public street.

Dickens nipped inside the gate adeptly when it was opened, and sent in his card to the workhouse Master. The workhouse was full.[45] Returning outside, Dickens woke the poor souls by the wall to give each money to find food and lodging. The association between these poor human heaps, the workhouse wall, and body-snatched corpses is eloquent indeed, and would have been grasped by his readers. Dickens asked rhetorically: 'Stop and guess! What is to be the end of a state of Society that leaves us here!', and in his own voice, concludes in exasperation:

I know that the unreasonable disciples of a reasonable school, demented disciples who push arithmetic and political economy beyond all bounds of sense (not to speak of such a weakness as humanity), and hold them to be all-sufficient for every case, can easily prove that such things ought to be, and that no man has any business to mind them. Without disparaging those indispensable sciences in their sanity, I utterly renounce and abominate them in their insanity; and I address people with a respect for the spirit of the New Testament, who do mind such things, and who think them infamous in our streets.[46]

There was bitter popular opposition to the proposed anatomy legislation, as there was to the New Poor Law, but the constituency of its victims was voteless, and politically insignificant. The new anatomy legislation disarmed charitable opposition by releasing the rest of society from fears of being body-snatched themselves, and by confining dissection to an institutionalized group, isolated and socially spurned. It was the clearest illustration of the scapegoating of the poor that the era could provide, and the clearest indication that entering a workhouse was to become a kind of social death. In 1831 dissection was a deliberate aggravation of the death penalty, a fate worse than death, inflicted upon Bishop and Williams for their bestial murder of the Italian Boy. In 1832, by Royal Assent, it was imposed on the institutionalized poor.

Through the Reform crisis in 1832, Dickens worked for several months as a Parliamentary Reporter on a radical newspaper called the *True Sun*. That December, a report of an inquest in London's East End appeared in the paper, which appears to have been written by a penny-a-liner attending there 'on spec' for a good story. The inquest concerned the body of young woman, Polly Chapman, or 'Handsome Poll', who, being unable to pay her rent, had drowned herself after having been turned out of her lodging. The Coroner was asked by a churchwarden if he might legally give up the body to the London Hospital, as it was not claimed by any relatives, and the Coroner agreed as an example to prevent suicide among 'unfortunate women'. The report continues:

Several of the latter class of females, who had conducted themselves with great decorum during the proceedings, here begged
with tears and the greatest earnestness, to be allowed to pay a
mark of respect to their unfortunate companion, by burying her
in consecrated ground, for which purpose they had already
raised £3.0.0 by subscription, and given to an undertaker. They
described her as of the best and most inoffensive disposition, and
incapable of injuring anyone.

The coroner, however, replied that it was necessary to make
an example. The spirit of the Anatomy Bill would not be acted
up to if the body was not given up. Any resurrectionist might
claim the body as a friend, and afterwards sell it. A Juror said he
thought the London hospital had bodies enough from the
poor-houses; and that the poor creatures present had shown
much good feeling, and ought to have the corpse. Mr Wilson, the
Overseer, wished to take the sense of the Jury on the subject.
After such discussion, it was decided that the body should be sent
to the hospital. The announcement of this decision was received
with the most bitter lamentations by the females, who appeared
much attached to the deceased.[47]

Although Parliament was in a long recess at this time (August 1832
to January 1833) it's unlikely this report was by Dickens: the
inquest was heard in East London some way from his usual
territory, and furthermore Dickens was busy working as a poll
clerk for a politician in Lambeth in December 1832, which gave
him paid work for some weeks.[48] But he may well have read this
piece, which is likely to have been written by someone he knew.
The sensibility of the reporting is quite Dickensian, in so far as it
is written with such skill that one can read it as an objective record
and nevertheless sense the reporter's views on the matter, and thereby

sympathize with the lamentations of Polly Chapman's unfortunate friends.[49]

Two vignettes in the 'Paul Pry' caricature anticipate similar moments; in one a weeping old woman is told: 'The Body of your Daughter—you ain't going to Gammon me—I'm not to be done out of my dues—we sold her'; in the other, a fat overseer answers the expostulations of a poor man: 'Your Friends, eh? Do you suppose we are to keep a parcel of rascals in our House to be Buried like their betters?—No no, they are cut up long before.' As Dickens has Mr Bumble comment to Mrs Sowerberry: 'What have paupers to do with soul or spirit? It's quite enough that we let 'em have live bodies.'[50]

Although the report concerning Polly Chapman was probably from another hand, it may be worth saying that it demonstrates that the *True Sun* allowed its journalists a measure of licence to express their own views critical of prevailing policies, which was completely lacking in the direct transcriptions Dickens had been producing for the *Mirror of Parliament*, and which he may regretfully have had to relinquish when he went to work on salary at the *Morning Chronicle*, whose proprietor was a staunch supporter of the New Poor Law.[51] Dickens is known to have had many arguments with that newspaper's Editor about the politics of the Poor Law.[52] The necessary suppression of his own humanitarian sympathies in his journalism at the *Morning Chronicle* may eventually have helped prompt Dickens to write his *Sketches*. What was proscribed in one place grew to flourish in another: his ideas and commentary were fashioned into freelance essays; observations on the streets and in police courts, pickpockets, a hospital patient, low life, London characters and institutions, and in the process, Dickens was making the transition from description to fiction.[53]

233

The successful passage of the Anatomy Act demonstrates that the political alliances that created and passed the punitive legislation of the early 1830s repudiating the poor were effective inside both the unreformed and the 'reformed' Parliament. As a Gallery Reporter Dickens would have been closely aware of the process by which the Reform Act and the Anatomy Act (both 1832) and subsequently the New Poor Law (1834) made their parliamentary passage.

Through the onerous manual and mental work involved in processing their privileged words, Dickens had a good grasp of the thought-processes of those who held power. After he had left the Gallery, Dickens said that he had been there 'a great deal too often for our own personal peace and comfort'. His antipathy suggests that he may have felt implicated or sullied by the association.

The punitive new system introduced by Parliament in 1834 failed to differentiate between the work-shy and the disabled, the sick and the well, the feckless and the old, infirm or the infant child: all were treated alike, and all blameworthy. When he chose the term 'parcel of rascals' in the caricature, 'Paul Pry' characterized the attitude with precision.

Dickens's anger at the brutalization of the workhouse system eventually emerged in the biting satire of the opening chapters of

Oliver Twist. Simply by showing the birth and institutional rearing of such a child, he addressed head-on the cultural failure of imagination he had witnessed among Parliamentarians as to what it might be like to be born in a workhouse, 'to be cuffed and buffeted through the world—despised by all, and pitied by none'.[55] The sheer brutality of the system is exposed by the story. Through no fault of his own (other than breathing) Oliver is neglected, exploited, threatened with being devoured, maligned, threatened with being hanged, drawn, and quartered; he is starved, caned, and flogged before an audience of paupers, solitarily confined in the dark for days, kicked and cursed, sent to work in an undertaker's, fed on animal scraps, taunted, and forced to sleep with coffins.

The book opens with Oliver's birth: his mother Agnes, we learn, had been on her way to his father's grave when she herself is found moribund on the street, and taken to the workhouse to die. Her poor corpse is preyed upon after her death by the woman who lays out the body, who steals her locket. Although at the book's end a monument is erected to her memory, it does not mark a grave. Dickens makes clear that her identity was unknown, which is why Oliver is given a completely fictitious name by Mr Bumble, who goes to some effort to discover his mother's origin:

> 'And notwithstanding a offered reward of ten pound, which was afterwards increased to twenty pound. Notwithstanding the most superlative, and, I may say, supernat'ral exertions on the part of this parish,' said Bumble, 'we have never been able to discover who is his father, or what was his mother's settlement, name, or condition.'[56]

Oliver Twist began publication in 1837, the New Poor Law had been law since only 1834, and the Anatomy Act since 1832. Contemporary readers would have understood that the body of Oliver's mother was unclaimed. The disappearance of her corpse is explicitly stated in the book's final paragraph: Dickens emphasizes the absence of her body: 'There is no coffin in that tomb.' It is part of the subtext of the novel that the poor young woman who dies in its opening pages was being dissected while her son was being starved.

It is a measure of Dickens's genius that he does not name the New Poor Law in *Oliver Twist* and he neither names nor mentions the anatomy legislation either, although the first time we meet Bill Sikes he threatens to burke Fagin. Having kicked his dog across the room, Sikes turns to make the threat:

> 'I wonder they don't murder you; *I* would if I was them. If I'd been your 'prentice I'd have done it long ago; and—no, I couldn't have sold you arterwards, though; for you're fit for nothing but keeping as a curiosity of ugliness in a glass bottle, and I suppose they don't blow them large enough.'[57]

This is Dickens letting us know just what kind of hands Oliver has fallen into, and its brutal equivalence to the New Poor Law workhouse system, which, while he was writing, was being implemented in Cleveland Street. Dickens discreetly emphasizes the innocence of Oliver's mother—'poor lamb' says the workhouse nurse—and the profoundly unchristian behaviour of the authorities in charge of her child: ' "They'll never do anything with him, without stripes and bruises," says the same gentleman in the white waistcoat as would have consigned him to Gamfield the sweep.' Stripes and bruises—meaning lashes and blows—were inflicted as part of the sufferings of Christ.

In the Strand parishes the operation of the New Poor Law took a couple of years to plan and prepare, so although rumours were doubtless circulating and fears rising, it was not until after the day appointed for its implementation, 24 June 1836, that the impact began to be felt. The application of the new law was swift and harsh. Surviving documents show that although Divine Service was scheduled in the workhouse twice every Sunday, at 9 a.m. and 3 p.m., families were cast asunder as soon as the Act was adopted. Rules were laid down before 24 June that year to the effect that 'all relief to non-resident poor is prohibited', and within a month, even churchmen were learning the limits of their influence. When he remonstrated on behalf of a poor parishioner, Ann Nugent, the Reverend Richard Burgess of Cadogan Place received a polite rejection letter from the new 'Guardians of the Poor', who found a ready defence by taking refuge in the proscribed limits of their own powers: 'had any deviation from the rule been allowable the circumstances of the case so forcibly stated by you would have justified such deviation'.[58]

By August 1836 the work of the Board of Guardians had been simplified by the drafting of a standard refusal letter for the Clerk to utilize for respectable correspondents who, like the

Revd Burgess, had taken it upon themselves to remonstrate about the inhumanity of the new law in particular cases: 'Some very strong cases of non-resident paupers have come before the Board and have ended in the same result.'

These cases most probably concerned elderly parishioners living with their own families, whom the little help the parish had given had previously helped keep them together. The New Poor Law insisted on no out-relief, so the elderly had no choice but to enter the workhouse, or the family was deprived of any help if they chose to keep them at home. If nursing the elderly occupied a wage-earner, or diminished home earnings, poor families who might try to keep their elderly at home could become impoverished by the effort.

The Strand parishes which formed the Strand Poor Law Union covered between them a considerable area of the heart of London: St Paul Covent Garden, St Clement Danes, St Mary-le-Strand, the Liberty of the Rolls, the Precinct of the Savoy, St Anne, Soho (up to 1868) and (after 1868) St Martin's-in-the-Fields. The Strand Poor Law Union would remain in existence right through the rest of the nineteenth century, until the Great War. Families hitherto entitled to receive parish help to survive at home if the breadwinner was sick, were now broken up, and whatever belongings they had were sold to recompense the parish for their board and lodging. Soon after the New Poor Law was applied in the district, for example, John Powell was sent to Cleveland Street, while his wife Elizabeth was ordered to the old St Clement Danes Workhouse in Portugal Street; Daniel James went to Cleveland Street while Ann James went to Hendon; of the Jackson family, Thomas was sent to Cleveland Street, Mary to Portugal Street, and their children Henry and Mary to Hendon.

All the children from St Clement Danes Workhouse were ordered to be ready at first light on 24 June 1836 for transportation to Hendon, but it transpired that it was found 'inconvenient' on that day. There seems to have been considerable local opposition to the changes, as repairs were ordered on 30 June to 'all the broken glass', and the Police Office at Bow Street was requested to keep extra constables in the vicinity.

The guiding hand of the Poor Law Commission was felt immediately upon the local administration. The Workhouse Master was told if necessary he might disobey the Overseers, who were, he was told, 'unknown to the Law'.[59] It seems they were too kind for the efficient implementation of the Act, and had been deliberately written out of the operation of the new law in its drafting. Correspondence with the Commission's Secretary, Edwin Chadwick—covering everything from seeking guidance concerning small gratuities for pauper nurses (refused) and the appointment of Porters, or gatemen—rapidly became grovellingly deferential.

The old gatekeepers, it seems, were too elderly, so they were sacked. The new ones were ex-policemen, who were required to be more vigorous as they were empowered to keep the peace at the workhouse gates, and when necessary to take offending parties into custody. The tone of voice in letters from the Poor Law Commission, stressing the danger of 'disorder and laxity of discipline' was peremptory: 'even individual Guardians acting other than collectively at the Board have no ... authority', and rapidly infected the voice of the new Guardians: 'immediately inform me by what authority you have allowed some of the Pauper Inmates of the Cleveland Street Workhouse to have a holiday today ... no holidays are allowed under the new system.'[60]

Tradesmen felt the impact of the new regime too. A new weighing machine was purchased to ensure the parish was receiving goods as agreed per contract. Goods and services for the new Union of parishes were tendered for, and new rates agreed, many of them lower than before. The contract for parish coffins, for example, was awarded to John Dix, four feet and upwards at a shilling per foot, under four feet, sixpence per foot, shrouds included, less than the price paid in the 1790s.[61] Dix later solicited a Guardians' letter recommending him as official undertaker to the Inspector of Anatomy, so we can be sure that bodies from Cleveland Street were going to the medical students of the hospital across the way.[62]

Ratepayers would also have been made aware of the new regime, because rate-collectors were awarded sixpence in the pound for every amount collected under £20, fourpence if the amount was over £20, which ensured they focused on the bulk of smaller ratepayers. By July 1836, Cleveland Street was almost military in discipline: the Board Room must be ready prepared for a meeting of the Board of Guardians, staff were to be lined up at 6 p.m. in the Hall ready for inspection.

Inmates had been set to work making extra mattresses for Hendon, and new hammers were purchased for stone-breaking. Uniforms of brown Yorkshire cloth, with special buttons marked 'STRAND UNION', were instituted for all men and boys, and blue check dresses and aprons for all women and girls. The only exception to this uniformity of dress was for unmarried pregnant or lying-in women, who, during the entire period of their stay in the workhouse, were forced to wear 'the yellow gown'. In bastardy cases, infants went to Hendon, and the mothers refused relief.[63] A ban was enforced on paupers attending another hospital, or being allowed out of the

FIGURE 34. *The Empty Tomb*, from the first edition of *Oliver Twist*. Oliver stands beside Rose Maylie, to contemplate the church memorial commemorating Oliver's dead mother. Etched by George Cruikshank, 1838.

house on any other pretext without the permission of the Board of Guardians sitting as a body; no pauper women might be sent to help at Hendon who had children there, and so it went on.[64]

Dickens probably used the Strand Union Workhouse as his model not only because he already knew the workhouse well from having lived nearby, but also because it was an exemplary institution. The extent to which the authorities of the Cleveland Street Workhouse willingly adopted the dictates of the new law, and rendered it a model institution from the point of view of the new Poor Law Commissioners is revealed by a comment from Charles Mott, one of its own Commissioners, that the Strand Union: 'for correctness and management and strict adherence to the rules cannot be surpassed by any Union in England'.[65] Many other parishes in the London region did not embrace the new law so enthusiastically, in some cases remaining fiercely parochially independent until at least the 1850s. The Marylebone Workhouse, which was on the New Road west of Marylebone High Street (its site is currently occupied by the University of Westminster) was quite unlike the Strand in its refusal to collaborate with the new regime.[66]

Dickens is strictly accurate for Cleveland Street in some of the details he uses in *Oliver Twist*, not only in small domestic matters such as the iron bedstead in which Oliver's mother dies, and the brown cloth of the workhouse uniform Oliver wears, but in real events. For example, Oliver narrowly avoids being sent out to become a chimney sweeper's climbing boy, but two boys from Cleveland Street, Thomas Jackson and John Woodward, were actually sent out 'on liking' to chimney sweeps in August 1836, and in fact master sweeps seem to have been quite frequent applicants as employers of pauper children from the Cleveland Street

Workhouse.[67] It is evident, too, that as in Oliver's case, exile and harsh employment were being used at Cleveland Street as forms of punishment for children like Oliver, who were labelled as 'refractory'. In September 1836, the Guardians unanimously required the Workhouse Master to furnish: 'names and ages of those boys and girls whose conduct is disorderly or refractory preparatory... for sending them to the Manufacturing districts to be employed in the factories under the sanction of the Poor Law Commissioners.'

We can see from this decision that the Strand Guardians were an ideal target for Dickens to use in the book, as they were identifying themselves so closely with the New Poor Law regime. Factory discipline seems to have been favoured under Edwin Chadwick at the Poor Law Commission, rather than the naval discipline of the Sea Service (Royal/Merchant Navy) from the Port of London, to which boys from other London parishes were more likely to be sent.[68]

Dickens is equally accurate in other matters. He has Mrs Mann banter with Mr Bumble:

'by coach, sir? I thought it was always usual to send them paupers in carts.'

'That's when they're ill, Mrs. Mann,' said the beadle. 'We put the sick paupers into open carts in the rainy weather, to prevent their taking cold.'[69]

which conversation is explained by a letter of August 1836, preserved in the Strand Guardians' minutes, addressed to their counterparts at Kingston-on-Thames, concerning the 'very irregular manner' in which a sick woman, Margaret Wilkin, an inmate at Kingston Workhouse, but originally a parishioner of Clement Danes, had been carried to town in an open cart, and put down at the Elephant and Castle, despite being ill. Normally arrangements were made in advance, but in this case it seems no warning had been given, no arrangements made. How Margaret Wilkin eventually arrived at Cleveland Street is not explained by the letter, but the poor woman was evidently very poorly: 'If death should ensue' they were told, 'your office would be clearly liable to be indicted for the offence.'[70]

No newspaper source has yet been found from which Dickens might have obtained this story, which suggests that Dickens may have known someone inside the institution, who was acting as his informant.[71] So far, it is not clear who this person might have been, unless it was a disaffected employee from the old regime, which is possible after the sackings of the old workhouse master, matron, and gatemen. There is another possible source of information: one of the new guardians themselves. This idea is not as far-fetched as it may seem, as one of them, Valentine Stevens, worked as a law bookseller in Dickens's old stamping ground at Bell Yard, Doctors' Commons, and another, George Cuttriss, ran the Piazza Coffee House in Covent Garden, which we know Dickens frequented, and where the Guardians had their Christmas dinner in 1836.[72]

Dickens's knowledge of accurate details from inside the Workhouse on Cleveland Street might also have been gained via Mr Dodd, who probably knew everyone on the street, or from the local publican of the 'King and Queen', which stands right opposite the Workhouse, who might have heard a lot of things while he was polishing tankards. It may be that Dickens kept quiet about his association with the street in order to protect someone still living there, and if this is the case, the publican is likely to be a possibility.[73]

Reading through the surviving documents, it is easy to see that while there might be written rules and regulations, and while these might or might not be rigidly enforced, no serious money had been spent to improve the facilities in the Workhouse to cope with the influx of desperate poor from the new conglomeration of parishes of the Strand Poor Law Union, or for the rearrangement of pre-existing human relationships which were now to be forced to fit the rigid boundaries and constrained charity of the new parish unions.

The records are very incomplete. From a long list of ledgers concerning the internal management of the House, including the Workhouse Master's punishment books, the Gateman's Day Books, and the Parish Doctor's ledgers, all of which regulations specified must be kept by the various officers of the Strand Union, none remains. Yet from the New Poor Law Guardians' minutes, some of which do survive, we can discern indicators of strain, such as a comment about the noxious effluvia from the men's latrines in the Workhouse yard fronting onto Cleveland Street, and the 'choaked' privies at Hendon. From these it is possible to read between the lines of the Clerk's formal script to think about the real lives of the people who were being herded out of central London into these places, and indeed, those who were stuck outside. By the last year of William IV's reign, the New Poor Law had been implemented in the Strand Poor Law Union, and the stink was noticeable in Cleveland Street.

Works

CONTEMPORARIES, *SKETCHES*, SPECTRES,
OLIVER TWIST, NAMES, ECHOES

C HARLES DICKENS WAS already the author of an impressive number of clever *Sketches* published pseudonymously in the press in 1836, when the New Poor Law was being implemented in Cleveland Street in 1836, He had moved away to live on the borders of the City at Furnival's Inn, where just around the corner lay both Field Lane, where he would locate Fagin's den, and Bleeding Heart Yard, which he would use later in *Little Dorrit*.[1] Important events occurred that same year: his *Sketches* were collected into two volumes, under his pen name 'BOZ', and Dickens married Catherine, the daughter of his father's friend George Hogarth.[2] Then, the soaring popularity of his *Sketches* brought young Dickens the commission from Chapman and Hall to write *The Posthumous Papers of the Pickwick Club*, to be published in parts over the next couple of years.[3] Michael Slater is surely right to describe 1836 as Dickens's 'break-through year'.[4] 'No writer ever attained general popularity so instantly as "Boz"', said *The Spectator* in December 1836: 'and certainly no-one has made such industrious use of his advantages...he is seized by the multitudinous hands of the public, and meets with a spontaneous and universal welcome.'[5]

'Boz' was appointed Editor of *Bentley's Miscellany* in early November 1836, before he had finished with Mr Pickwick, and he resigned from his job at the *Morning Chronicle* the following day. Almost immediately, he began *Oliver Twist*.[6] The book's dramatic opening with the naked baby coming into the world was published less than a month after Dickens's own first child was born at Furnival's Inn.[7]

There had been another family upheaval when John Dickens was arrested for debt in November 1834, but not long afterwards, Dickens's parents were back in Marylebone again.[8] In 1836 they were in Edward Street (today part of Wigmore Street) and in March 1837 Dickens himself returned to live in the area, when he took lodgings for his own small family in Upper Norton Street (now Bolsover Street) between leaving Furnival's Inn and moving into Doughty Street.

He returned again more permanently in 1839, when he took a large house at 1 Devonshire Terrace, at the top end of Marylebone Lane, close to the two churches of St Marylebone, old and new. Dickens settled his growing family there for over a decade until 1851, during which time he wrote all the major works of his middle years: *The Old Curiosity Shop, Barnaby Rudge, American Notes, Martin Chuzzlewit, A Christmas Carol, The Chimes, The Cricket on the Hearth,*

The Battle of Life, *The Haunted Man*, *Dombey and Son*, and *David Copperfield*. From this address, too, Dickens launched the *Daily News*, and *Household Words*.[9] All the Marylebone addresses I have mentioned are within a short walk of Mr Dodd's corner shop and the Cleveland Street Workhouse, and if one walked as briskly as Dickens is said to have done, the journey time would be briefer still.

Once one starts looking, it becomes noticeable that it would not have been easy for Dickens to keep too far away from the area for long because so many of his friends, and families of friends, lived there. Maclise, for example, lived in Pitt Street near the Middlesex Hospital, and then in Charlotte Street, and George Cattermole moved his home from the northern end of Cleveland Street down into Berners Street between 1826 and 1846.[10] Samuel Lover lived in Charles Street, by the Middlesex Hospital.[11] The Landseers, Augustus Egg, Frith, G. A. Sala, and John Hullah all had roots in Marylebone.[12]

Dickens came back for other reasons, too. Years afterwards, he mentioned in a letter to an actor, William Mitchell, that he had admired his performance in a play called *The Revolt of the Workhouse* at the theatre in Tottenham Street in 1834, when Dickens was living in Furnival's Inn.[13] The play was by Gilbert A'Beckett, a lawyer, prolific journalist, and playwright, who specialized in humorous periodical writing and theatrical burlesque.[14] It was a Cockney send-up of a recent ballet called *La Revolte au Sérail*, the opening night of which had been only nineteen days earlier at

Covent Garden. Instead of a revolution in an exotic eastern harem, A'Beckett's version was set inside a London workhouse.[15] Dickens had been planning a series of sketches—and perhaps a novel—on parish subjects since the time of his first published sketch in 1833, so no doubt he was intrigued by the play's title.[16] A'Beckett and Dickens moved in similar circles, and it is not at all surprising that both men should have been thinking of a workhouse theme in 1834, while the New Poor Law was progressing through Parliament.[17]

When the text of A'Beckett's play was published in 1835, it had a frontispiece by Cruikshank, and opened with the verse from Dr Johnson's *London*:

> All crimes are safe but hated Poverty,
> This, only this, the rigid law pursues,
> This, only this, provokes the snarling muse.

A'Beckett's preface proceeded to analyse different sorts of poor, one of which—since we are thinking about *Oliver Twist*—is perhaps significant:

> a little urchin, whose parents (having been beggars) are dead; or else such as having run away from their masters, follow this strolling life. The first thing they learn is how to cant and the only thing they practise...is to creep in at windows or cellar-doors.

Another is a sturdy big-boned knave, who carries a short truncheon, and whose profession is to be 'idle and vagabondical'. The master of the workhouse in the play calls himself the Workhouse King, and makes the female paupers kneel to him; the vain Beadle loves the lace that glitters in his hat, and his staff of office, and says:

That public justice may be well protected
'Tis right her officers should be respected.

The workhouse tea, made with half an ounce of tea-leaves for the
entire workhouse ward, is the root of the trouble:

I'd say without compunction—
'Twas but a cup of neat Grand Junction

FIGURE 35. *Heaven and Earth*, an extraordinary complex and arresting image,
created in 1830 by the artist Robert Seymour, the original illustrator of *Pickwick
Papers*, who committed suicide in 1836, just as the popularity of *Pickwick* was
mounting. Many details in this caricature suggest Seymour's work may have
influenced the young Dickens: his depiction of the soured relations between
haves and have-nots, and his portrayal of seriously hard times: poverty, jobbery,
parochial tightfistedness, unemployment, and hunger among the poor, while
others were feasting. The central figure of the Parish Beadle could well have
been a model for Mr Bumble, and his cockney idiom for Mr Weller's diction.

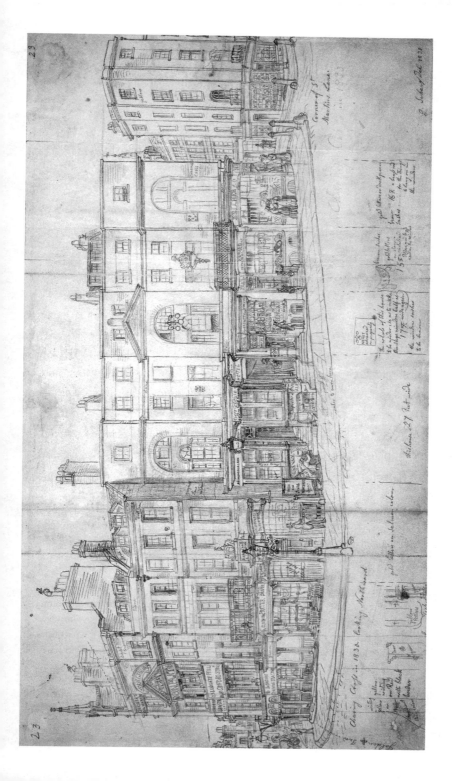

—meaning that it tastes like canal water. A revolt ensues and the workhouse clerk is soused in the laundry washtub. But A'Beckett's revolt is a comedy with a happy ending. After a facetious battle, the female paupers win the day, and the police and the workhouse master sue for peace. The terms agreed are the provision of bread less than four days old, sugar for the inmates' tea, and cheese 'in any quantity the ladies please'. The show ends with a rousing chorus in which the workhouse inmates sing:

> Let workhouse struggles end
> And let the Beadle be the paupers' friend.

What Dickens made of this almost pantomimic entertainment is anyone's guess. He seems to have enjoyed the efforts of the actor Mitchell who cross-dressed to play Moll Chubb, one of the female leads. But since Dickens probably had a good idea about the full seriousness of what was in the parliamentary pipeline, he cannot have been as sanguine as A'Beckett about the likely outcome of conflicts inside such institutions in real life. Whether he was aware of the full details of what revisions had already been made in 1830/1

FIGURE 36. (*Overleaf*) Old shops at Charing Cross, which faced the top end of Whitehall. A fine view sketched by George Scharf in 1830. This entire row was demolished soon after the drawing was made, for the construction of the south-eastern quadrant of Trafalgar Square. The stables of the famous coaching-inn, The Golden Cross, occupied the land behind these shops; its entrance was at their western end. Scharf records the variety of shops and watering-holes for which the area was well known, and the interest of their windows. The central shop is a silversmith and pawnbroker. Below, Scharf's marginal notes record the three golden balls and the legend of the shop's signboard: 'Money advanced on property'.

in the workhouse around the corner from the theatre we cannot be certain, although he was undoubtedly accurate in several significant respects when he came to write *Oliver Twist.*

Closer to his own turn of mind than the Gilbert A'Beckett play may have been the opening of a triple-decker novel (also of 1834) called *The Pauper Boy* by 'Rosalia St Clair' (a pseudonym) which opened with a death, and features a brutal workhouse master who is exposed and loses his job, but is reinstated because he has influence among the workhouse guardians. The book deteriorates into a religio-romantic novel, but its interesting start is noteworthy for a number of reasons, not least because the book is narrated by the solitary workhouse child at its centre, who is given a small ebony crucifix by his old workhouse nurse, which, she tells him, 'may one day be the means of discovering your kindred'.[18] The boy is sent out as a parish apprentice, to a Charing Cross pawnbroker and his wife, who emerge as sympathetic figures in the story, which allows the narrator to observe that 'many a tale of broken-hearts and ruined prospects might be drawn from the records of a pawnbroker's repository'.[19] This woman dies before imparting the whole story. The boy is accused of a crime he did not commit, and meets a sympathetic woman who helps him by the stairs descending to the River by Westminster Bridge. He is later imprisoned with various low-life characters.

Dickens's own series of *Sketches* on parish characters and parish matters had begun appearing in various newspapers and magazines in the early months of 1835, and continued through 1836. The *Sketches* are highly significant in Dickens's development as a novelist, in a way not dissimilar to the manner in which, twenty years later, *Scenes of Clerical Life* allowed George Eliot to find her voice in fiction. Part of their charm for readers when they first appeared was that, while the *Sketches* were topical, they were also geographically vague: clearly London-based, but no one knew either who 'Boz' was, or exactly where his observations were being made. Part of the frisson of excitement was that Boz's way of seeing, perhaps, served to encourage ordinary Londoners to see their own neighbours and neighbourhoods with a new acuity.

There is a possibility, now that Dickens's association with the Norfolk Street locality is better understood, that originals for some of these tales may become traceable. So far, in only one case has a fictional character been found in one of Dickens's *Sketches* who seems to relate to a real person: someone who lodged with Mr Dodd in Norfolk Street.

The *Sketch* Dickens entitled 'The Dancing Academy' is significant, since it prefigures the case of Bardell versus Pickwick—a breach-of-promise case—which occupies a central place in *Pickwick Papers*. Dickens presumably came across plenty of such stories at Doctors' Commons, an ecclesiastical court dealing with such matters. 'The Dancing Academy' features the family of a dancing master with the unlikely name of Signor Billsmethi, and his luckless rather green bachelor pupil Mr Augustus Cooper, who is first charmed and then frightened into paying a large sum of money to his dancing master's daughter under threat of such a case, even though the level of his involvement in any kind of courtship had been non-existent. In the story Dickens frankly denies that it has anything to do with the area of Marylebone in which we know he lived. The manner in which he does so, however, gives the impression of protesting too much. This is how he introduces the dancing academy:

Of all the dancing academies that ever were established, there never was one more popular in its immediate vicinity than Signor Billsmethi's, of the 'King's Theatre.' It wasn't in Spring Gardens, or Newman-street, or Berner's-street, or Gower-street, or Charlotte-street, or Percy-street, or any other of the numerous streets which have been devoted time out of mind to professional people, dispensaries, and boarding-houses; it was not in the West-end at all, it rather approximated to the eastern portion of London, being situated in the populous and improving neighbourhood of Gray's-inn-lane. It wasn't a dear dancing academy—four and sixpence a quarter is decidedly cheap upon the whole. It was very select, the number of pupils being strictly limited to seventy-five; and a quarter's payment in advance being rigidly exacted. There was public tuition and private tuition—an assembly-room and a parlour. Signor Billsmethi's family were always thrown in with the parlour, and included in parlour price; that is to say, a private pupil had Signor Billsmethi's parlour to dance in, and Signor Billsmethi's family to dance with; and when he had been sufficiently broken in, in the parlour, he began to run in couples in the Assembly-room.

This *Sketch* offers a rare instance in which Dickens names streets he would have known well from living in and around Norfolk Street: Berners and Newman Streets, particularly, but also Charlotte Street (the southern end of Fitzroy Street, behind the Workhouse) and Percy Street, parallel to Tottenham Street, south of Goodge Street. To map the area they indicated would have given a good idea where to find people who knew 'Boz', if one didn't already know him. The 'King's Theatre' was a play on the 'Queen's Theatre', the name given to the old 'Regency Theatre' in Tottenham Street in the 1830s. The denials about the school's location first led me to examine the dancing academies which did exist in the area, and to discover that there was a surprising number. That area north of Soho was well known as a musical and artistic district: it seems that fair-sized rooms that suited artists as studios and exhibition spaces because of their lowish rents could also serve for the tuition of dancing. A search for dancing schools near Gray's Inn yielded only one in Hatton Garden. Blanks were everywhere concerning Signor Billsmethi, until the following entry in the *London Gazette* made me sit up. It concerned a man who became an insolvent debtor in 1840:

> William Menzies, formerly of 10, Fludyer-street, Westminster, then of No.9 Charlotte-street, Bloomsbury then of No.10, Norfolk Street, Middlesex Hospital, then of No.47, Charlotte-street, Fitzroy-square, then of No.45, Regent-square, and late of No.9, Wakefield-street, Regent-square, Gray's-Inn-Road, Music and Dancing-Master, and whilst residing at No.45, Regent-square aforesaid, his wife a Schoolmistress.[20]

Bill Menzies is not that far from Billsmethi, but it's the biography that is so noticeable. Menzies had moved from a small house in Westminster to Norfolk Street, to the top end of Gray's Inn Road—a shabby-genteel area north of the Foundling Hospital, actually not that far from Doughty Street.[21] It looks as though this man and his family had been lodgers in Mr Dodd's house, and ran a dancing school there, perhaps at the same time the Dickens family was living there for the second time. The noise of the music and footwork (especially of beginners) was probably not delightful to Mr Dodd, and probably not very beneficial for the structure of the corner house. The grandiose terminology for its modest living rooms—

'parlour' and 'assembly room'—is laughable, and Dickens's addition of 'Signor' may suggest the assumed continental airs and graces of the man. We have no further knowledge from the *London Gazette*, of course, concerning the breach-of-promise thread of the story, which may have been grafted from elsewhere, or if true may perhaps have provided needed extra income (on more than one occasion?) for this sorry family on its way down towards the debtors' prison. Dickens may have kept in touch with Mr Dodd, and heard the sequel.[22]

It used to be thought that Dickens kept no working notebook until late in life, but this surely cannot be taken to mean (as it seems to have been by some) that he kept no working notes.[23] As a journalist he would have had to take notes, and as a reporter in Parliament, the reams of words he would have had to take down in shorthand, and then transcribe into fair copy for the printers must have required a lot of paper. Whether or not these notes took the form of a memorandum book, like the one that survives from the last decade of his life, seems not to be known.[23] That Dickens drew strongly upon his own memory for places, faces, posture, tones of voice, and so on surely cannot be doubted, but I would hazard a guess that he kept notes throughout his working life. Someone recorded seeing him perched on a barrel in a bar, taking shorthand notes of men in conversation.[24] A comment in a letter to Macrone, the first publisher of *Sketches by Boz*, supports this idea:

I find in some memoranda I have by me, the following Head-
ings. 'The Cook's Shop'—'Bedlam'—'The Prisoner's Van'—
'The Streets—Noon and Night'—'Banking-Houses'—'Fancy
Lounges'—'Covent Garden'—'Hospitals'—and 'Lodging-
Houses'—So we shall not want subjects at all events.[25]

In the small memorandum book that survives from the 1860s, we find
Dickens making careful notes of ideas, things he'd seen or heard,
turns of phrase he liked or recordings of moments he had witnessed
which had made him laugh, scenes and sketches which existed in his
imagination, but which he never wrote up.[26] There are also long lists
of names, and ways of playing with names, cutting them in half, looking for congenial syllables, trying permutations of suffixes and so on;
such terminations as -straw -ridge - bridge -brook - bring - ring - ing
are listed. Elsewhere, his working notes for *David Copperfield* show how
the evolution of the name that we take for granted from his title was
actually arrived at: 'Flower—Brook—Well—boy—field—Well-
bury—Copperboy—Flowerbury—Topflower—Magbury—Cop-
perstone—Copperfield'—then underneath again, as if he was sure
of it, 'Copperfield'.[27] How good it would have been to get sight of his
running notes and memoranda for *Oliver Twist*.

Local names and street names in the Norfolk Street vicinity are
very suggestive. Just across Charles Street from the bottom end of
Norfolk Street, for example, in Berners Mews, were the premises of
two tradesmen named Goodge and Marney. This same mews was
close to the old home in Mortimer Street of the famous local miser,
the sculptor Nollekens; the district was known for another miser, too,
proud of his own dire parsimony and known as 'The Celebrated
Marylebone Miser'.[28] Marylebone itself, incidentally, was sometimes

mis-spelled (and often pronounced) Marleybone, and Marley was also a local name (another cheesemonger in nearby Titchfield Street, and there was another Marley shop board on Oxford Street), so it seems possible that Dickens played with the consonances of Marney and Marley before settling on the name of the Ghost in *A Christmas Carol*.[29] The permutations of the name of the entire parish are many: Samuel Pepys called it Marrowbone, others, Maribone, and—taken with Mr Menzies's sham title—we need not ponder long as to where Signora Marra Boni comes from in Dickens's *Sketch*, 'The Vocal Dressmaker', especially as a female 'Professor of singing' occupied a house opposite Mr Dodd's.[30] Sowerby was the name of a publican in Goodge Street—not far perhaps from Oliver's employer, Sowerberry the undertaker. A baker in Tottenham Street was Jonah Dennis, a surname Dickens used in *Barnaby Rudge*, and a tailor called Rudderforth lived and worked at 36 Cleveland Street, whose name led me to look again at a passage in *David Copperfield*:

> 'And how's your friend, sir?' said Mr. Peggotty to me.
> 'Steerforth?' said I.
> 'That's the name!' cried Mr. Peggotty, turning to Ham. 'I knowed it was something in our way.'
> 'You said it was Rudderford,' observed Ham, laughing.
> 'Well?' retorted Mr. Peggotty. 'And ye steer with a rudder, don't ye? It ain't fur off. How is he, sir?'[31]

Corney, the name of the woman whom Mr Bumble courts and marries in *Oliver Twist*, was also the name of a glover and hosier at 178 Oxford Street, and there was a Mrs Malie commemorated in the local churchyard, whose name may have served for the kindly woman upon whose doorstep Oliver collapses.[32] This is not to say that

Dickens did not utilize other sources for names: he mentions the trade and street directories of London in several of his novels, and in the surviving 'Memorandum Book', Dickens noted the source of one of the lists he quarried, it was derived from the Privy Council Education Lists. Local street names crop up, too: Mr Micawber in *David Copperfield* adopts the name Mortimer when he is sued for debt, there's Newman used as a first name for Newman Noggs, Charlotte in the undertaker's in *Oliver Twist*, and sweet Betsey Ogle, perhaps from Ogle Street and Ogle Mews, at the back of the pub opposite the Workhouse, as well as the working of the eyes.

In his later essay of 1853, 'Where We Stopped Growing', Dickens tells the story of the White Woman of Berners Street, who has often been taken for the original of Miss Havisham in *Great Expectations*.

> Another very different person who stopped our growth, we associate with Berners Street, Oxford Street; whether she was constantly on parade in that street only, or was ever to be seen elsewhere, we are unable to say. The White Woman is her name. She is dressed entirely in white, with a ghastly white plaiting round her head and face, inside her white bonnet. She even carries (we hope) a white umbrella. With white boots, we know she picks her way through the winter dirt. She is a conceited old creature, cold and formal in manner, and evidently went simpering mad on personal grounds alone—no doubt because a wealthy Quaker wouldn't marry her. This is her bridal dress. She

is always walking up here, on her way to church to marry the false Quaker. We observe in her mincing step and fishy eye that she intends to lead him a sharp life. We stopped growing when we got at the conclusion that the Quaker had had a happy escape of the White Woman.[33]

The essay is significant for this book, because in it we find Dickens admitting in 1853 to a childhood/youth association with the part of London at which we have been looking closely, although he is 'unable to say' if the White Woman was ever seen further north, in Norfolk Street for instance. He passes rather dramatically from past to present tense, and from Berners Street to 'here', as if he still lived in the near vicinity. Is Dickens saying that he had seen this woman pass up Norfolk Street, or possibly reach Devonshire Terrace? His arch prose, especially the 'we hope' in brackets, and the 'no doubt', lead one to think this is more of a tale he is enjoying in the telling, or a knowing elaboration of a local urban legend, than a witnessed reality. The curiosity of this story is compounded by two others, from different sources. Neither concerns Berners Street. The first is from nearby Oxford Street itself, and not in Dickens's time:

Amid all its bustle and business, Oxford Street has nevertheless had a touch of 'the romantic,' if a peculiar eccentricity, brought about by disappointment in love affairs, can be called a romance. At all events, we read how a certain Miss Mary Lucrine, a maiden of small fortune, who resided in this street, and who died in 1778, having met with a disappointment in matrimony in early life, vowed that she would 'never see the light of the sun!' Accordingly the windows of her apartments were closely shut up for years, and she kept her resolution to her dying day.[34]

The Victorian book from which this account came provides no source for its information, so if we accept the date it offers we must conclude either that there were two such disappointed women in adjoining streets, and that one stayed indoors in the eighteenth century and the other walked out when Dickens was growing, or, that both stories attach to the same person.

The third tale is the account of an inquest of a real woman, a 'wealthy and eccentric lady', discovered by the Dickens scholar Harry Stone.[35] Her death was reported in a news item Dickens himself published in a news supplement to *Household Words* in 1850 ('Where We Stopped Growing' appeared in 1853, *Great Expectations* in 1860). She had been badly traumatized twice as a young woman: first, her father was robbed and murdered in Regent's Park; then, she had lost her reason when her mother rejected her suitor, and he blew his brains out while sitting beside her on the sofa. This lady lived as a recluse in Marylebone, three blocks west of Dickens's home at Devonshire Terrace. She never went out, and dressed in white. How Dickens came to know of her story we are not told; she does not come up on database searches of other contemporary newspapers, but she certainly was a real person as she appears as Miss Joachim, 27 York Buildings, New Road, in the 1846 *Kelly's Post Office Directory*.

The Dickens scholar Harry Stone has also uncovered a wonderful character based on the White Woman of Berners Street called Miss Mildew, of much the same ilk, who was played in drag onstage in 1831 at the Adelphi by Dickens's favourite actor, Charles Mathews. There's a good chance Dickens saw the performance, because he went anywhere to see Mathews, and in April 1831 he was freelancing and possibly living in the vicinity of the Strand, having just left Norfolk Street. Stone makes a splendid argument for Dickens's weaving of Miss Havisham from the White Woman, Miss Joachim, and Miss Mildew.

Miss Mildew visits somewhere called the Great Expectoration Office to seek an expected fortune, which never arrives, which suggests she may have been a model for Dickens's character Miss Flite in *Bleak House* (1852–3). The office Miss Mildew visits, and the one Miss Flite visits in the Chancery Court bear an affinity to both the Circumlocution Office (in *Little Dorrit*, 1855–7) and the Legal Loophole Office in one of Jack Fairburn's *Quizzical Gazettes*.

The interweaving of story and locality is curious, made still more so by the added finding that the extinct peerage of Haversham was associated with two old houses on different sides of Soho Square, and that a livery stable in Newman Street was run by a man called George Habbijam, an unusual old English name that would have appealed to Dickens, especially in Mrs Gamp mode.[36]

Livery stables usually occupied mews premises, behind main streets, and were often accessible only through arches through street premises. Very often the interior walls of these arches featured large signboards with the names of the stable keepers or the tradesmen occupying the mews. I imagine Goodge and Marney had just such a sign in Berners Mews, Habbijam too, in his access-way to Newman Yard, behind Newman Street. And I wonder if Dickens was familiar with the sign of Bardell, another local livery stable keeper in Gresse Street, just off Percy Street?[37]

Several of the *Sketches*, it seems to me, resonate with the possibility of deriving from experiences in Norfolk Street and its vicinity, such as Dickens's careful observations concerning the life-cycles of shops. Norfolk Street was full of shops, and we know that Dickens has seen their alteration between the two periods in which the family lived there, perhaps while they were there, and afterwards. There are, for example, a couple of shops in Norfolk Street which over time were divided into half-shops, which is something he describes; and of course he lived right next door to a broker, which is the subject of another *Sketch*.

Most particularly, I sense that the first appearance of Sam Weller in *Pickwick*—in which he makes philosophical observations on the relationship between the personality of the footwear he is called upon to deal with as the 'Boots' of an inn, and the individual character of their unseen owners—owes something to Dan Weller, the shoemaker/mender across from Mr Dodd's, especially as there was a public house named the Marquis of Granby in nearby Percy Street.[38]

Another important shop on Mr Weller's side of the street was the pawnbroker. John Cordy Baxter's shop occupied the top corner of Norfolk Street (at the junction with Union Street) diagonally across from Mr Dodd's house. Mr Baxter's was a busy establishment. His premises consisted of two shops, providing storage space for all the pledges, and housing for his own family and several assistants. Dickens had experience of pawnbrokers in his childhood: Forster mentions him having to pawn family belongings from the house in Gower Street, before the family went into the Marshalsea. To be made forcibly to let go of familiar things one is fond of is painful, and the fear of never being able to redeem them must hurt, too, along with the idea that someone acquiring them for their money value would have no conception of their deeper meaning, would not see their real character, would not recognize their *biography*. Dickens invests life in objects, recognizes their human echoes, resonances, meanings, to an extraordinary degree, and in his early *Sketch*, 'The Pawnbroker's Shop', it is clear that he pities the poverty that brings people to the pawnshop, and recognizes the memories and meanings special objects can hold, and respects the understandable reluctance to part with them. The voice is that of an observer, but one who sorrows and understands.

Just after the child is born in the first chapter of *Oliver Twist*, Dickens describes the power of the old calico workhouse dress to transform the naked newborn infant from the multi-potent child into 'the orphan of a workhouse'. He uses the imagery of pawnbroking to explain how the clothes work their effect: 'he was badged and ticketed, and fell into his place at once'. Pawnbrokers' storerooms are complex filing systems which allow for the swift disposal and retrieval of objects. In a pawnbroker's shop every item deposited is ticketed, and according to Dickens's own description, often land on the floor before being taken to the storeroom, and appropriately deposited on labelled shelves.[39] This ties up with Dickens's strikingly memorable use of similar imagery when he described his own creative process: 'I never commit thoughts to paper until I am obliged to write, being better able to keep them in regular order, on different shelves of my brain, ready ticketed and labelled, to be brought out when I want them.'[40]

Objects taken in by a pawnbroker are 'pledges', a word that has the old biblical meaning of a solemn promise or something given as a guarantee of good faith, and with the sentiment associated with love-tokens (and indeed children) being 'pledges' of love. Of course a baby swaddled up does look a bit like a small parcel—one can see the physical association, too. The language of pledging is very prominent in *Oliver Twist*—one of the chapters is entitled '*The time comes for Nancy to redeem her pledge to Rose*', and in addition to Nancy several characters—Noah Claypole (ironically), the Doctor, and Harry Maylie all pledge themselves in one way or another. Here a biblical word is also used in pawnbroking, and in both places it is also associated with the notion of redemption. This is not just a literary conceit: Dickens employs the language of pledging in his own voice, in his own life, especially in the early letters: in conjunction with assorted serious commitments to write, to publish, to get away to see Catherine, *not* to write for Bentley during an altercation, and to give his word; he even pledges his 'veracity'.

As a boy Dickens had evidently visited one pawnbroker's shop frequently enough, according to Forster, to develop a good relationship with one of the staff:

a good deal of notice was here taken of him by the pawnbroker, or by his principal clerk who officiated behind the counter, and who, while making out the duplicate, liked of all things to hear the lad conjugate a Latin verb and translate or decline his musa and dominus. Everything to this accompaniment went gradually.[41]

This particular pawnbroker would presumably not have been in Mr Baxter's shop, as this story dates to about 1822/3 when the family was living some distance away. The experience seems to have been important for Dickens: not only did he tell Forster about it, but the relationship with the shop man seems to have humanized for him the sad business of losing belongings, and perhaps softened the shame of needing to enter such a place, and also allowed him to see that a shopkeeper might be educated enough to know some Latin.

In his *Sketch* 'The Pawnbroker's Shop' Dickens places the shop in Drury Lane, but as we know, he likes to cover his tracks, and he may have been making a nod to Hogarth when he did so. The essay was published in June 1835, so he had been researching the subject, observing carefully, and perhaps making notes the year before he started *Oliver Twist*. It may be that he knew more about pawnbroking than Forster has told us: the business of it looms very large in *Martin Chuzzlewit,* and the pawnbroker's shop man carries the same first name as David Copperfield. Cruikshank's image for Dickens's *Sketch* is an interesting view taken from behind the counter, inside the shop, which certainly feels true to the spirit of the *Sketch*. Dickens's interest in the backstage stories of pawnbroking lasted all his life: the very last entry he ever made in his little book of memoranda not long before his death in 1870 was: 'The pawnbroker's account of it?'[42]

The assistants in the Drury Lane pawnshop of Dickens's early *Sketch* are described as treating customers without much respect: deliberately filling in duplicates slowly, talking between themselves, and making them wait. But the entry of the boss, in a grey dressing gown, is a breath of different air: he has an authoritative manner, firm but humane: taking charge to refuse money to a violent drunkard, telling him to send his wife to receive the money instead.

I like to think this might be a sketch of Mr Baxter, the pawnbroker in Norfolk Street, partly because it would be good to get a glimpse of him, and partly because he was an interesting man. I have found him on one occasion donating the large sum of 30 guineas to a special appeal fund to open two new wards at the Middlesex Hospital, an amount greater even than that given by the aristocratic patroness of the appeal, the Duchess of Buccleuch.[43] His name appears, too, alongside that of the artist John Constable, who lived nearby in Charlotte Street, on a petition to Parliament in 1831 in support of 'Assisting the Cause of Reform'.[44] So it is not possible to perceive Baxter as a mere money-grasper of a pawnbroker: he was an altogether more complex, thoughtful, and humane man.

Dickens's portrayals of pawnbroking as a trade are mixed, for although he knew that money obtained on household goods often went on drink, he also understood the pathos of the need to raise pennies on household belongings, especially before weekly paid wages arrived at the end of the week. He knew that while pawnbrokers exacted high rates of interest and ultimately often took as forfeit precious goods that could not be redeemed, they also performed an important doorstep banking service for the poor, and that sometimes the money lent could provide a lifeline.[45] In 1837, while *Oliver Twist* was still appearing in monthly parts in *Bentley's Miscellany*, Dickens (the Editor of the journal) published an anonymous poem which expressed this ambivalence, under the generic term for a pawnshop, 'My Uncle':

> ...Above his door
> Invitingly were hung three golden balls,

FIGURE 37. A pawnbroker's shop interior, said to have been in Drury Lane. The view is taken from a privileged position behind the counter. In the open public part of the shop on the left, an assistant publicly assesses the value of a garment. The private boxes were for those seeking greater privacy in their transactions. Recent ticketed goods for warehousing are seen on the floor. The shop door shows that like Mr Baxter's, this pawnbroker's was situated on a corner. If this image was reversed in printing, the position of the private entrance and the shop window would match Baxter's shop too. Etched by George Cruikshank for *Sketches by Boz,* 1836.

As if to say, 'Who pennyless would go?'
Here is a banking-house, whence every man
Who has an article to leave behind,
May draw for cash, nor fear his cheque unpaid.
Ah me! Full many an ungrateful wight
In this same store, without a sigh or tear,
Parted his bosom friend, altho' he knew
That friend must dwell among the unredeemed.[46]

Mr Baxter has been examined with attention here, because I have a hunch that his shop may be central to *Oliver Twist*, in which the plot hinges upon the fate of a locket, secretly taken from the body of Oliver's mother after her death in childbirth. This locket is the key to Oliver's real identity, and its fate is fundamental to the entire story. It is described as a small gold locket, engraved with his mother's name 'Agnes', with space left for a surname, and a date less than a year before Oliver was born. It contained two locks of hair and a plain gold wedding ring. In the book, Oliver's malevolent half-brother Monks gets hold of the locket from the workhouse Matron, and drops it through a trap door into a rushing millstream, thinking he has destroyed the evidence of Oliver's parentage.

But Dickens allows Oliver's champion, Mr Brownlow, to establish the chain of evidence without this precious object itself. Two very elderly women from the workhouse, who are brought before Monks and the Matron in chapter 51, report that they had overheard the conversation between the workhouse Matron and the dying pauper nurse, Old Sally, who long before had nursed Oliver's mother, laid out her body, and purloined the locket. These elderly women announce that they had seen the Matron take the pawn ticket from the dead woman's closed hand, and that they had watched her go to the pawnbroker's the next day. Their testimony indicates that a pawnbroker's shop was in very close proximity to, indeed visible from, the workhouse. So it may be highly important that Mr Baxter's shop stood diagonally opposite from the Cleveland Street Workhouse,

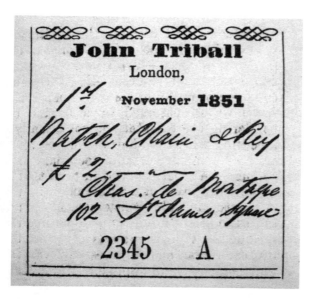

FIGURE 38. A nineteenth-century pawn ticket. Illustration to an essay entitled 'My Uncle' by Henry Wills (edited/retouched by Dickens himself), which originally appeared in *Household Words* in 1851. The fate of such a ticket is crucial to the plot of *Oliver Twist.* Reproduced in Wills's *Old Leaves.* New York, Harper, 1860.

and was also clearly visible from Dickens's front windows of No. 10 Norfolk Street. Mr Baxter's shop on the corner at 15 Norfolk Street is gone, but from the street corner outside his shop door, one can still look north up Cleveland Street and see the Workhouse, and south down Norfolk Street to Dickens's family home.

There is a wonderful moment in *Oliver Twist,* after the old women have given their evidence about the origin and fate of the locket, when Mr Brownlow's friend Grimwig asks the discomfited Mr and Mrs Bumble and Monks: 'Would you like to see the pawnbroker himself?'—and motions towards the door. It is almost as if that *eminence grise,* John Cordy Baxter, was waiting in the hall.[47]

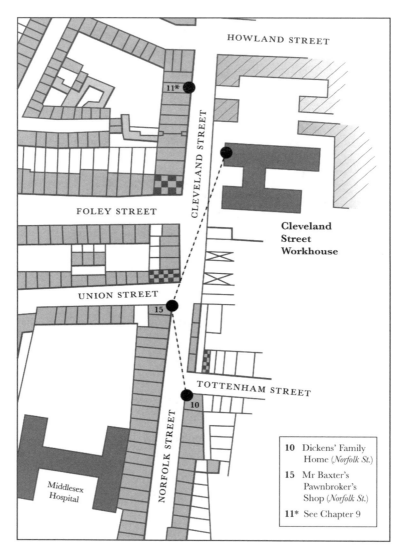

HOWLAND STREET

11*

CLEVELAND STREET

FOLEY STREET

Cleveland
Street
Workhouse

UNION STREET

15

TOTTENHAM STREET

10

NORFOLK STREET

Middlesex
Hospital

10 Dickens' Family
    Home (*Norfolk St.*)

15 Mr Baxter's
    Pawnbroker's
    Shop (*Norfolk St.*)

11* See Chapter 9

FIGURE 39. Sightlines between the Workhouse and Mr Baxter's corner (15–16 Norfolk Street) and Dickens's home. No. 11 Cleveland Street stands obliquely above the northern boundary of the Workhouse site.

In the *Pickwick Papers,* Sam Weller tells Mr Pickwick that he was originally apprenticed to a carrier. Curiously, the trade list of public carriers in the *London Directory* yields the following Dickensian-sounding names: Sikes, Sykes, Sugden, Tubbs, Siggs, Ruggles, Noah, Tugwell, Medlock, Bundle, Catchpole, and Diggens.[48] But one of the key figures in *Oliver Twist* probably did not come from this list. Perhaps the most telling instance of Dickens's use of a name from a local shop board, and one which provides evidence of an unquestionable association between *Oliver Twist* and the Cleveland Street Workhouse, is that of the shopkeeper at No. 11 Cleveland Street. He was an oilman, who sold tallow and oil for lamps and perhaps for paints, and whose first proud appearance in the London *Commercial Directory* of 1836 coincided with that of Dickens himself: 'Dickens, Charles—Reporter for the *Morning Chronicle*'. This man's shop faced the Workhouse, and his name was Mr William Sykes.[49]

The variant spelling of his surname may have appealed to Dickens for the book because it served to deflect identity from the shop-keeper, and perhaps protected Dickens himself (useful if the oilman was as malevolent in appearance as the real Bill Sikes!); and possibly too from the irony that it was shared with a very well-heeled firm of City bankers, at the Mansion House.[50]

In 1818 the shop at No. 11 Cleveland Street had been occupied by a different wax and tallow-chandler called Biddle, so the name is not a childhood memory. Sykes was a relatively new arrival, as he was not the ratepayer in 1828, so his shop board might have been spruce and bright, attracting attention to itself.[51] Further research will be necessary to try to pin down when Bill Sykes actually arrived in Cleveland Street. But he was certainly there in 1836–7 while Dickens was planning and writing *Oliver Twist.*[52]

FIGURE 40. Cast pewter regulation button from the Strand Union Workhouse. Manufactured for the Guardians of the Strand Poor Law Union by W. H. Norton of 249 Strand in the mid-nineteenth century. Found in the 1980s on the foreshore of the Thames.

CHAPTER 10

The Most Famous
Workhouse
in the World

TRUTH AND FICTION

W HEN HE WAS writing the final parts of *Oliver Twist* in 1838, Dickens was on a meteoric trajectory of success. With a wife and family of his own, plus servants, he had taken a lease on a fine house in Doughty Street, a genteel gated road a dozen or so blocks east, and parallel to, Norfolk Street.

He had designed an important chapter to lie near the end of the book, between Sikes's desperate pursuit into Jacob's Island, and Fagin's last night alive. It was one of those intervening chapters which earlier in the book he had likened to the layers in streaky bacon: allowing a release of tension after Sikes's terrible death, and a gentler interlude with the atmosphere of the fresher air outside

275

central London, before the dramatic scene inside the dark confinement of the condemned cell at Newgate.

Chapter 51 of *Oliver Twist* contributes in an important way towards the conclusion of the novel: it serves to tie up loose ends within the plot, and brings the story back full circle to its opening scenes. It features the great showdown with Monks, in which the now adolescent Oliver is at last allowed to understand his own identity, and comes to know about the pillaging and pawning of the locket from his mother's corpse. To get us to that scene, Dickens carries the reader on a journey through countryside, towards Oliver's birthplace.

In the carriage during the journey, there's a conversation between Oliver and Rose Maylie, which serves to remind the reader that Oliver is returning to the scenes of his childhood in markedly different circumstances from those in which he left it: he is now loved, happy, safe, and prosperous. Oliver expresses a longing to see his poor friend Dick at the branch workhouse, who had given Oliver a blessing as he began his flight to London near the start of the book. Rose comforts him by gently taking Oliver's hands between her own—a rare moment of kindly human touch for him. She observes—and I think Dickens wanted readers to sense a kind of mutual comfort and contentment here—that Oliver will be able to share with Dick news of his good fortune, and can be even happier because he will be able to help his friend. Rose's suggestion is expressed in a Victorian do-gooding sentimental tone, with which it is difficult for the modern reader to empathize: but we can nevertheless recognize what Dickens was trying to say for his own contemporaries, who were more habituated to expressions of this kind.

Oliver's return to the scenes of his childhood conveys some of the strangeness the adolescent Dickens might have felt returning again to live in Norfolk Street in 1829, after the gap of a dozen years. It would not be surprising if, while he was writing, Dickens had thought himself back into the time of his own return there: the place much the same, but himself irrevocably altered:

> they approached the town, and at length drove through its narrow streets...There was Sowerberry's the undertaker's just as it used to be, only smaller and less imposing in appearance than he remembered it—there were all the well-known shops and houses, with almost every one of which he had some slight incident connected—there was Gamfield's cart, the very cart he used to have, standing at the old public-house door—there was the workhouse, the dreary prison of his youthful days, with its dismal windows frowning on the street—there was the same lean porter standing at the gate, at sight of whom Oliver involuntarily shrunk back, and then laughed at himself for being so foolish, then cried, then laughed again—there were scores of faces at the doors and windows that he knew quite well—there was nearly everything as if he had left it but yesterday.[1]

Taking Oliver back to these scenes of his growing up, Dickens in Doughty Street was carrying many-layered memories of that parallel thoroughfare not far away, memories dating from childhood, from his return there as a young man, and—to judge by his use of Sykes's shop board—from more recent visits. The street and its vicinity held his life in a grasp, enclosing the Marshalsea years like bookends, in a way nowhere else did: from his early childhood to his young adulthood, the start of his own present success. The years between—the family's slide towards the Marshalsea and the blacking factory and the uncertain climb back out—were like the layers in streaky bacon: those years had taught him what impoverishment and hunger were like, how easily one might fall into poverty, how grim it was to be stuck in it, and how painfully uncharitable the society was in which he was beating a path to success.

Oliver has been traumatized, orphaned, alone, starved, maltreated, bullied, kidnapped, and inveigled into the orbit of a murderous London criminal underworld. He thinks back to his old self: 'a poor houseless, wandering boy, without a friend to help him, or a roof to shelter his head'. Now, safe from all this, comforted and cared for by loving friends, he arrives at the realization that he has the power to help others who yet remain in the bleak clutches of the workhouse system. If one was led to ponder why Dickens chose to confront the workhouse system in *Oliver Twist*, Rose Maylie's comment about little Dick suggests a powerful motivation: 'in all your happiness you have none so great as the coming back to make him happy, too.'[2]

Dickens's decision to create this novel at the height of his success with *Pickwick*, it would seem, bears a marked affinity to Oliver's resolution to help his pauper friend.

One of Cruikshank's illustrations to *Oliver Twist* shows Mr Brownlow and his housekeeper cosseting Oliver back to health, after his fever. He sits comfortably by their cosy hearth. There are signs of food having been eaten, and he's warm and safe. Over the mantelpiece in this domestic setting, above a clock and a vase of flowers, is a framed image of the Good Samaritan, which looks to have been inspired by Hogarth's famous painting. It's a small detail, but a significant one, and it feels as if it is likely to have been asked for by Dickens himself.

The image underlines a central theme in *Oliver Twist*, which concerns the workings throughout society of the *opposite* of Christian charity, the obverse of the Samaritan impulse: a pervasive culture of predation. Pickpocketing and burglary were among its best-known forms, but so, in Dickens's book, was the workhouse system.[3] It may be that something he had read in Smollett's translation of *Gil Blas* had lodged in his mind: 'everyone loves to prey upon his fellows; it is an universal principle, though variously exerted.'[4]

Oliver Twist begins, we discover, with predation from a workhouse corpse by an old pauper nurse. The purloined locket is pawned, and the old nurse's corpse is itself preyed upon by the workhouse Matron; then she herself is preyed upon by the villain, Monks. Dickens reveals the food chain. The child Oliver and his fellows are starved by the woman employed under the Poor Law to 'farm' the children, to benefit herself. Gamfield the chimney sweep would prey upon the child, and the Poor Law authorities (personified by the man in the white waistcoat) would indeed invite it, by advertising a financial inducement for him to be removed from the House. The undertaker hopes to use the boy as a mute to prey upon the gullibility of the public, and so the book continues: kidnapping, burglary, prostitution, spying, murder, all of them predatory.

At the lowest and least defended end of the social pecking order is the orphan child: starved, punished, used as cheap labour, provoked, inveigled, and kidnapped, used as a tool by criminals, his identity stolen, in danger at every turn, but finally saved by good fortune and the power of kindness, by the parallel determination of Mr Brownlow and the bookshop proprietor not to pass by on the other side.

It's a grim story, with an upbeat conclusion, but not a happy ending: the domestic happiness at the very end of the book is tempered by irreparable losses (Oliver's mother, Dick) and the knowledge of the existence of real evil at loose in the world, not just among criminals but in the institutional cruelties inflicted on vulnerable human beings by the workhouse system. The novel works rather as a political parable, a modern fairy tale. No one in power at the time, and few ordinary readers, wanted to think about the real fate of such a child: it was only through fiction that Dickens was able to invite them imaginatively to do so. The workhouse passages in *Oliver Twist* develop into a melodrama of enormous power, dealing with contemporary issues of crime, punishment, and reclamation by goodness. When the young Queen Victoria recommended the book to the Prime Minister, Lord Melbourne, he gave it up as distasteful.[5]

The power of the story is evident in our own culture: we celebrate *Oliver Twist* in plays, stories, musicals, adaptations for film and TV, where Oliver and Sikes, Fagin, Nancy, and the Artful Dodger are almost bywords. But a London doctor writing factually at exactly the same time about the actual treatment of real parish children by the Poor Law system—a contemporary of Dickens—is almost unknown and unread.

Dr Thomas Pettigrew is one of the unsung medical heroes of London's past. He was a surgeon working at the Charing Cross Hospital, which was then a new building in the West Strand. Towards the end of 1836, Pettigrew wrote a courageous and principled remonstrance against the pauper farming system then being used against the children of the parish of St James Piccadilly.[6] Dickens was probably finalizing his plans for *Oliver Twist* at the time. Pettigrew described the regime of malnutrition and effective starvation under which the parish children of St James (the same place as the Palace, not a poor parish) were reared from 6 weeks to 7 or 8 years of age, in a private establishment six miles south of London, in the village of Norwood.[7] Pettigrew's title page carried a sad verse which provides an image of the state of the children he had witnessed:

> The vigour sinks, the habit melts away,
> The cheerful, pure, and animated bloom
> Dies from the face; with squalid atrophy
> Devour'd, in sallow melancholy clad.[8]

At the inquest of George Coster, a parish boy, it had become clear to Pettigrew that the children at Norwood were being systematically starved, that economies of scale (the fee to the parish for each child was four shillings and threepence a week) were economies at the expense of child lives: victims, he said, of amalgamated parsimony and negligence. Pettigrew believed Coster's inquest had been rigged to exonerate the parish, so as to prevent the true verdict of neglect and starvation to be found. At Norwood, he said, over 300 children were crammed into one room, several to a bed, eighty of them profoundly emaciated, seventeen of them seriously ill. In modern times, we have seen news films and photographs of orphanages abroad exposing child neglect and malnutrition: Pettigrew was doing equivalent reportage then, but without being able to document the emaciation and dereliction of these children's lives on film. Children's welfare, he urged, should be the parish's prime responsibility: 'no temptation should be placed in the way of individuals to make money or derive a profit upon such a subject as the support of the poor.'[9] Pauper farming was an 'incentive to traffic in humanity', he argued. Pettigrew accused the parish of trying to burke enquiry into excess deaths in the parish. The Poor Law Commissioners, he said, were not unbiased public servants: most especially Dr Mott, who Pettigrew alleged was actually financially involved in a business farming out paupers in an establishment at Brixton. *The Morning Chronicle* (for which Dickens was working at that time) accused Pettigrew of spreading false and scandalous allegations, but he was supported by several other doctors, who validated his statement concerning the real cause of young Coster's death.

Dickens and Pettigrew were later friends, but in 1836, Dickens was probably already disgusted by the position taken by his own newspaper, which preferred to malign the messenger rather than hear the message concerning the terrible death of a child. The *Chronicle*'s coverage of the issue may have provoked one of Dickens's clashes with his own Editor, and would certainly have made him painfully conscious of the conflict between his own interests as a salaried journalist and his humanitarian views. One can appreciate why he left the newspaper with such alacrity as soon as he had signed the contract with Bentley to become an Editor himself, and appreciate too, why he started almost immediately on *Oliver Twist*.

In fact Pettigrew was ignored by both St James's parish and by the Poor Law Commissioners, and rather than being closed down, the proprietors of these south London 'farming' establishments were allowed to expand their facilities greatly, eventually leading to hundreds of unnecessary deaths.[10]

In the opening chapters of *Oliver Twist*, Dickens addresses closely similar issues to those raised by Pettigrew—especially the starvation and maltreatment of parish children, and the ugly profiteering the Poor Law system encouraged on the part of the proprietors of such establishments. But compared to the real inhumanity of the system Pettigrew described, Dickens's criticism is understated, achieved by satire, using ridicule, laughter, and a tone of voice that engenders ironical disbelief, rather than (like Pettigrew) by direct confrontation. An anonymous reviewer in a contemporary journal, *John Bull*, recognized immediately the subversive power of the ridicule, observing apropos of the opening chapters:

The second number of *Bentley's Miscellany* has appeared, and contains an exceedingly good article by Boz... called 'Oliver Twist', and casts the bitterest satire upon the New Poor Laws that can well be imagined. Upon political questions it is always agreeable to find a coadjutor who can strengthen by the force of ridicule the powers of opposition to Whig tyranny.[11]

Dickens certainly captures the spirit of the new dietary, when he allows the reader to discern Oliver's thoughts on the nature of the workhouse soup. Rescued from the aggressive magistrate by Mr Brownlow, the kindly housekeeper Mrs Bedwin serves up a bowlful of good broth to help Oliver recover from his near-fatal fever. Looking at it, he thinks it strong enough 'to furnish an ample dinner, when reduced to the regulation strength, for three hundred and fifty paupers, at the lowest computation'.[12] Of course this is Dickens's thought rather than Oliver's, yet the pertinence of the irony was not lost upon his contemporaries. Kathleen Tillotson has noted a report in his old newspaper, the *Morning Chronicle*, during the serialization of *Oliver Twist*, which serves to illustrate contemporary perceptions of the book's powerful effect: 'Boz has produced so strong an impression… that in Chelsea, for instance, people have gone about lecturing for the purpose of counteracting the effect of his writings.'[13]

The portrayal of the workhouse in *Oliver Twist*, and the poor child's desperate request for more, was fiercely topical when it was written, and the book's relevance, if anything, increased with time. As the Poor Law continued longer in force, the truth of Dickens's perception of the real inhumanity of the workhouse system became increasingly evident. Much suffering went on behind closed doors, but sporadic evidences of the system's inhumanity reached public consciousness through the national newspapers: for example, the revelations concerning the workhouse in Andover (Hampshire) in 1845–6, where paupers were so starved that they fought each other for the rancid meat on bones they were employed to crush for fertilizer; and the disastrous events of 1849, in which hundreds of neglected and malnourished London workhouse children died when cholera broke out at an overcrowded and insanitary baby farm run by a private contractor, Drouet, at Tooting, south London.[14]

Dickens was already famous when he wrote the 'autobiographical fragment' in the 1840s, having already published *Sketches by Boz*, *Pickwick*, *Oliver Twist*, *Nicholas Nickleby*, *The Old Curiosity Shop*, *Barnaby Rudge*, and *Martin Chuzzlewit*, and then being engaged in writing *Dombey and Son*.[15] He must surely have been conscious of having used materials from his own life in his writings. From what we now know, it is possible to suppose that his silence about Norfolk Street in the 'autobiographical fragment' is likely to reflect a knowing discretion in the adult Dickens, not a failure of memory.

In a letter to Forster while he was writing *David Copperfield*, Dickens mentions that he had devoted a long week to the 'very complicated interweaving of truth and fiction', spending a great deal of thought on what from the Marshalsea era he could properly use in the novel.[16] After finishing *Little Dorrit*, Dickens went back to Southwark in 1857, to look at the prison itself:

Went to the Borough yesterday morning before going to Gadshill, to see if I could find any ruins of the Marshalsea. Found a great part of the original building — now 'Marshalsea Place.' Found the rooms that have been in my mind's eye in the story. Found, nursing a very big boy, a very small boy, who told me how it all used to be. God knows how he learned it (for he was a world too young to know anything about it), but he was right enough.... There is a room there — still standing, to my amazement — that I think of taking! It is the room through which the ever-memorable signers of Captain Porter's petition filed off in my boyhood. The spikes are gone, and the wall is lowered, and anybody can go out now who likes to go, and is not bedridden; and I said to the boy 'Who lives there?' and he said, 'Jack Pithick.' 'Who is Jack Pithick?' I asked him. And he said, 'Joe Pithick's uncle.'[17]

In the case of the Marshalsea, Dickens was balancing family pain and the danger of revealing his social origins, with his own time-tempered view of the place and the desire to write his novel. He had to consider besides that he had already featured Mr Pickwick in a debtors' prison. The creative process of hiding biography in obvious places—what Forster called 'taking the world into his confidence'— is one at which Dickens was adept.[18] But he really hid things too, and not only in his fiction. During the writing of *Oliver Twist*, he had been asked by a German admirer to provide some information about his own biography for publication in Germany. His letter had ended 'I have said more about myself in this one note than I should venture to say elsewhere in twenty years', which serves to show how careful he had been with personal information. His summary is interesting because it shows that at that stage he was either hazy about the details of his own childhood, or that he had already begun knowingly to obscure parts of it:

I was born in Portsmouth, an English Seaport town...on the 7th February 1812. My father holding in those days a situation under the Government in the Navy Pay Office, which called him in the discharge of his duty to different places, I came to London, a child of two years old, left it again at six, and then left it again for another Sea Port town—Chatham—where I remained some six or seven years, and then came back to London with my parents and half a dozen brothers and sisters, whereof I was the second in seniority. I had begun an irregular rambling education under a clergyman at Chatham, and I finished it at a good school in

London—tolerably early, for my father was not a rich man, and
I had to begin the world.[19]

Dickens describes arriving in London at the age of 2 and leaving it
at 6—which seems to double the two years he is actually known to
have been in London as a child, and which differs markedly from
the brief version in Forster's later biography. The contemporary
documentation concerning his father, John Dickens's, working
career at the Navy Office has been well excavated: after two years
in London, the family went to Sheerness early in 1817 when Dickens
was not quite 5 years old.[20] The dating error suggests that Dickens
was mistaken, or that he felt subjectively that those two years in
Norfolk Street were much longer than they really were. Alternatively, he may have been trying to add a couple of years somewhere
to conceal the Marshalsea/blacking factory period which—as we
would expect—he did *not* share with his German correspondent.
The mistake of the double departure in this letter (he leaves, and
leaves again) may indicate that Dickens was discomfited by having
to write a direct untruth, fictionalizing his own past.

While the Marshalsea and the blacking factory are perfectly understandable silences, the omission of Marylebone, despite its focal
importance in his own biography, and that of his family, is altogether
less explicable. It may be noteworthy that Dickens doesn't elaborate
here about *where* in London his roots were. London is a very large place
in which to locate oneself without any further detail: it's a collection
of villages, and most Londoners will usually tell you without asking
whereabouts in London they're from. Dickens was very well aware of
this: there's a lovely moment, for example, in *Pickwick*, where a servant
girl's behaviour is explained by the fact that she was 'brought up

among the aboriginal inhabitants of Southwark'.[21] In another passage from the same book, Mr Weller senior, trying to persuade his son *not* to write verses in a Valentine to his sweetheart, says delightfully:

> I never know'd a respectable coachman as wrote poetry, 'cept one, as made an affectin' copy o' werses the night afore he wos hung for a highway robbery; and *he* wos only a Cambervell man, so even that's no rule.[22]

Dickens looks to have decided quite early on in his literary career to keep his own counsel: not just about the prison and the factory, but also about his own family back story in east Marylebone. But why this should be so currently remains mysterious. I am not entirely convinced that it was simply about concealing his social background—if that is all it was, why should Bayham Street and Somers Town (which were meaner streets) and even the shameful Marshalsea, nevertheless be known to and discussed with Forster? At this stage, alternative explanations—that Dickens had used too many stories from the street as inspiration, had grievously offended someone, or perhaps was protecting someone—are entirely conjectural. There must be a reason, but it is completely obscure. Just a shadow of a clue may perhaps reside in a reference in *Oliver Twist*; when Monks and the workhouse matron are about to discuss the locket, Monks says: 'if a woman's a party to a secret that might hang or transport her, I'm not afraid of her telling it to anybody.'[23] It is just possible that the locket story at the heart of *Oliver Twist* was derived from some real event associated with the Cleveland Street Workhouse, and/or the local pawnbroker's shop in Norfolk Street, and that the locality of the workhouse would have revealed the guilty party Dickens had hoped to conceal in fiction. An object like a gold locket and a gold ring stolen from a dead body might indeed have merited transportation.[24]

The depiction of the workhouse in *Oliver Twist* is fictional, but the real long-term effects of the Poor Law continued well into the twentieth century. What the Poor Law Commission's own doctors had known in the early years of the 'great economical experiment' of the New Poor Law—that most of those needing support from the system were not work-shy, but elderly, sick, or dependent—was ignored and overlooked for more than a generation. J. P. Kay, reporting to the Poor Law Commission back in 1838, had observed: 'The metropolitan workhouses chiefly contain aged paupers, more or less infirm,' and he recognized and recommended then, in 1838, the need for proper nursing.[25] While poor children were farmed out to places like Drouet's at Tooting to starve and die, the Poor Law Commissioners delayed the provision of decent healthcare or nursing provision for the sick and the elderly until well after Florence Nightingale's work in the Crimea, and in the process, rendered many lives and many deaths profoundly wretched, desolate, and agonizing.

When in the late 1840s Louisa Twining visited the Workhouse in Cleveland Street, to see an elderly woman she had known from her own parish, who had begged not to be forgotten, Miss Twining found it more depressing than a prison.[26] The master and matron ran what she described as 'a reign of terror' within the institution, which no one in authority would end because 'they kept order and

FIGURE 41. Louisa Twining, a portrait photograph *c*.1860, from her autobiographical *Recollections of Life and Work*. Miss Twining was the instigator of the 'Workhouse Visiting' movement, which took her years of dogged lobbying to organize, in the teeth of relentless official opposition.

were economical'. Miss Twining's hope of being able to organize regular visits for all those who might benefit was declined, and she was shuttled between the Strand Guardians and the Poor Law Board, each fobbing her off with official objections to 'interference'. Miss Twining wrote letters to the press, and eventually became a key figure in the establishment of the Workhouse Visiting Society, the women of which went determinedly into workhouses to carry flowers, prayers, and pictures to the poor creatures inside, and to witness, supported from behind by funds from Miss Burdett Coutts, the philanthropist with whom Dickens worked closely for many years.

In the aftermath of the Crimean War it at last became obvious that nursing reform was not only a military matter. Florence Nightingale's efforts to train nurses had their greatest effects at the outset in the charitable 'voluntary' sector of hospital care. Even in the 1860s, most of the workhouses of London employed not a single trained nurse: all the nursing—as in the days of *Oliver Twist*—was still being done by paupers themselves. Louisa Twining, like Florence Nightingale, Frances Power Cobbe, and many other women pushing at the same door believed that sickness transformed a pauper into a patient, that sickness and poverty—as the Marylebone Dispensary philanthropists had so eloquently put it in the 1790s—was 'complicated Misery' deserving aid.

At about the same time as Miss Twining's efforts, in the mid-1850s, Dr Joseph Rogers was appointed as Medical Officer at the Workhouse in Cleveland Street. For the Guardians at the Strand, the appointment was a genuine mistake: Rogers, a deeply humane and dedicated doctor, was to prove a determined and successful champion of the poor, and for his fellow doctors. As far as is known, Rogers is also the only Poor Law Medical Officer who left a published memoir, so the Cleveland Street Workhouse is unique in having the testimony of its own doctor concerning its internal governance, for the period he was there. No other workhouse in the country has an insider's memoir to match it.[27]

When Rogers arrived at the Workhouse, only two of the twenty wards at Cleveland Street were officially designated for the sick, but he found elderly infirm, sick, and dying patients in every ward. In his estimate, only 8 per cent of inmates were well. He also

FIGURE 42. Dr Joseph Rogers, the humane Poor Law Medical Officer at the Cleveland Street Workhouse in the 1850s and 1860s, and author of important *Reminiscences*. It was Dr Rogers who read aloud Dickens's letter to the inaugural meeting of the Association for the Improvement of the Infirmaries of London Workhouses in March 1866.

discovered unmarried mothers in the lying-in ward suffering from extreme exhaustion, being on a 'starvation dietary'. Rogers was told that the lying-in ward was not under his jurisdiction. Assuming that the punitive diet was official policy, he wrote to the Poor Law Board at Whitehall to urge a more humane diet, and was informed that the Medical Officer had the power to specify the dietary: 'a power which', he later wrote, 'I did not hesitate to use'. His kind efforts were censured by the Guardians, who had devised the starvation dietary themselves to discourage other such women from giving birth there. This was the first of many difficulties with the Guardians, who supported the Master to the hilt, even when he was deliberately obnoxious or provocative towards Rogers.

It is interesting to discover from the Guardians' *Standing Orders* that it took Rogers less than two years to persuade them to remove the chains of restraint in the ward assigned to pauper lunatics, something I cannot find mentioned in his *Reminiscences*. Rogers seems to have managed this humane act by finding an authority beyond the Poor Law Commission, namely the Lunacy Commission, to enforce the change. The *Standing Orders* of the Strand Union Workhouse record in 1857: 'That the chains by which the strap is fastened to the iron bedstead used for violent lunatics be substituted by leather to meet the recommendation of the Commissioners in Lunacy.'[28] The bleak and barbarous atmosphere of the Cleveland Street Workhouse during the time Rogers worked there is well described in his book: the overcrowding was so bad that patients could get out only at the end of their beds; in 1866 556 people were sharing 332 beds. The cubic footage of space available per person was half that of the London prisons. But these were closed institutions, with no democratic oversight.

Rogers describes a rather Dickensian event inside the Cleveland Street Workhouse in 1857, when Mr Catch, the vile workhouse master who ran what Louisa Twining had described as the 'reign of terror' was finally dismissed. He had conspired to provoke Rogers into being sacked for dereliction of duty, but his plan backfired. 'So intensely tyrannical and cruel had been the rule of this man' said Rogers, that as he and his wife were leaving the building, the entire Workhouse 'rose up in open rebellion', and erupted in a noisy celebration of rough music, bashing any implement they could lay hands on to make a clamour, 'old kettles, shovels, penny trumpets', creating a celebratory cacophony that would have been audible up and down Cleveland Street, echoing along the nearby alleys, and in the streets around.[29]

Real reform was very slow in coming, but Dickens did live to see its beginnings before his death in 1870.

After the death of Thomas Wakley, the founding Editor of the medical journal *The Lancet* and a campaigning MP, the journal decided to appoint its own medical Sanitary Commission to investigate the condition of workhouse infirmaries. Wakley had long been an implacable parliamentary opponent of the Poor Law Commission, describing the law under which it acted as 'odious, detestable, and detested'.[30] *The Lancet* began publication of its Sanitary Commission's findings in the journal itself during the early summer of 1865, creating such a sensation in the press that the government soon intervened to announce its own enquiry.[31]

Rogers was personally abused and vilified by the Guardians at the Strand Union, who believed that he had written the Commission's *Report* on the Cleveland Street Workhouse himself. But he was quite able to prove them in error, when the author, Dr Francis Anstie, challenged them to show where, in his *Report*, he had departed from the truth. The press had a field day with the various revelations. The immediate upshot of the Commission's exposures was that—with wide and eminent support—a new association came into being. At the inaugural meeting of the Association for the Improvement of the Infirmaries of London Workhouses, Dr Rogers as Secretary read out to the cheers of the audience a letter of support from Charles Dickens. Apologizing for being unable to attend, Dickens wrote:

> My knowledge of the general condition of the sick poor in workhouses is not of yesterday, nor are my efforts, in my vocation, to call merciful attention to it. (Cheers) Few anomalies in the land are so horrible to me as the unchecked existence of many shameful sick wards for paupers, side by side with a constantly recurring expansion of conventional wonder that the poor should creep into corners to die rather than fester and rot in such infamous places. (Cheers)[32]

When Dickens referred in this letter to his efforts in his own vocation to call merciful attention to the shortcomings of the Poor Law, he meant not only in *Oliver Twist*. He had created, or commissioned and published in the journals he had founded, over a period of almost thirty years, a remarkable and remarkably consistent output of stories, characters, and articles on the theme of the Poor Law. Among the most recent of these had been the character of Betty Higden in *Our Mutual Friend*, who takes to the road rather than die in a workhouse. The book was the last novel Dickens completed before his death, published in parts over the period 1864–5—just ahead of and in parallel with the Lancet Sanitary Commission's *Reports*. The words the audience at the great meeting heard Rogers read aloud referring to the poor creeping into corners to die rather than fester and rot in workhouse wards, refer to those—young and old—who preferred to sleep out under the stars rather than enter those hateful places, and to the incomprehension which met their deaths. Dickens's creation Betty Higden addresses this incomprehension, by way of explaining the self-respect that refused to be browbeaten by the coercive humiliation of applying for help to the workhouse. 'It is a remarkable Christian improvement', Dickens says regretfully, 'to have made a pursuing Fury of the Good Samaritan; but it was so in this case, and it is a type of many, many, many.'

Betty Higden is an extraordinary character, whose thoughts Dickens presents almost in a stream-of-consciousness: 'afeerd that I'm a growing like the poor old people that they brick up in the Unions'. Sewn in the breast of her gown, Dickens explains:

> the money to pay for her burial was still intact. If she could wear through the day, and then lie down to die under cover of the darkness, she would die independent. If she were captured previously, the money would be taken from her as a pauper who had no right to it, and she would be carried to the accursed workhouse.... Most illogical, inconsequential, and light-headed, this; but travellers in the valley of the shadow of death are apt to be light-headed; and worn-out old people of low estate have a trick of reasoning as indifferently as they live, and doubtless

would appreciate our Poor Law more philosophically on an income of ten thousand a year.[33]

The critics of the workhouse system were vindicated when the government's own official enquiry was published in 1866. The inspector reported that most workhouses lacked light, ventilation, and space. Beds were too close together, and there was insufficient sanitation, often with no privacy or toilet paper provided. He recommended that several—including the Strand—be closed immediately.[34] The following year, the retiring President of the Poor Law Board, Gathorne Hardy, carried his Metropolitan Poor Act of 1867 through Parliament, establishing new infirmaries in London for the sick poor, quite separate from workhouses. A new body, called the Metropolitan Asylums Board, was created to cope with infectious diseases and insanity. The next decade saw the construction of twenty new hospitals around London, totalling 10,000 new beds. Many of these sites still serve as the core for newer hospitals currently in use under the National Health Service.

The old Workhouse in Cleveland Street also eventually became part of the National Health Service, but by a unique route, having new 'Nightingale' wards added at the back in the 1870s when it became the Central London Sick Asylum, and remaining in use as a public infirmary almost until the very end of the Poor Law era.

In the mid-1920s, however, it was acquired by the nearby Middlesex Hospital, and was comprehensively modernized into a

THE CLEVELAND-STREET
MATRON.

FIGURE 43. The Matron at the Central London Sick Asylum (as the Work-house building in Cleveland Street was then known), looking rather glum in 1883. She was sketched during a meeting by Charles Chambers Eames, a member of the governing committee. Florence Nightingale had hoped to influence the ap-pointment of the matron, but was resisted. The Matron's unhappiness probably derived from her unsupported predicament, and the lack of trained staff.

'voluntary' hospital, with brand-new surgical operating theatres and maternity facilities. The Middlesex Hospital itself was badly in need of rebuilding at that time, and the added space provided by the Workhouse (now called the Annexe) allowed the Hospital to decant first its own east wing into the modernized Workhouse

FIGURE 44. Middlesex Hospital Annexe. This fine inter-war photograph looking northwards up Cleveland Street shows the Workhouse on the right, rejuvenated and modernized. The new front wall dates to 1926. The busyness of the street further north gives an idea of what the area might have been like in Dickens's day, before the Telecom Tower was built on the next block. Had the unknown photographer turned to look south, Dickens's old home would have been easily visible from the same vantage point.

building—while that entire half of the Middlesex's own fabric was demolished and rebuilt—and then to repeat the process for its west wing. The complete rebuilding was done with barely any disruption to the Hospital's services. The Middlesex had acquired almost all the Georgian shops along its own eastern flank, the same shops of the old Norfolk Street, which young Dickens had looked out upon from his upper window from Mr Baxter the pawnbroker's down to Charles Street. These were now demolished to allow the whole Hospital to expand its footprint, so that it re-emerged from this process on a somewhat grander scale. So in a way, the Workhouse holds within its walls not only its own long story, but also the history of the Middlesex Hospital.

When the Middlesex Hospital had been completely rebuilt, the Workhouse building became its Outpatients' Department, and at the end of the 'voluntary' hospital era, along with the Middlesex Hospital itself, it was adopted into the National Health Service. The Cleveland Street Workhouse therefore continued to serve sick Londoners from the Appointed Day at the creation of the National Health Service in 1948 until the twenty-first century. It only closed with the closure of the Middlesex Hospital itself in 2005/6.[35] The Cleveland Street Workhouse is the only Georgian workhouse in the London region which has survived so many changes of administration since the 1770s, while nevertheless continuing with the core function of housing the sick and infirm of the metropolis. It is a unique survival, and deserves to be appreciated and celebrated as such.[36]

There are many reasons why the old Workhouse in Cleveland Street should be recognized as a key source of inspiration for the most famous workhouse in the world: the one featured in *Oliver Twist*. The most weighty is that for more than four years of his life before he wrote that celebrated novel, Charles Dickens lived nine doors from the Workhouse gates. As Peter Higginbotham, an expert on workhouse history and author of the *Workhouses* website, has observed: 'Over the years, a number of other workhouses have vied for the recognition as being the one that inspired *Oliver Twist*.

However, until now, the most obvious and convincing candidate has been overlooked.'[37]

Evidence presented in this book shows how closely *Oliver Twist* fits the regime at Cleveland Street, and shows too that a number of echoes in other of Dickens's writings (*Sketches by Boz*, *Pickwick Papers*, and *Barnaby Rudge* among others) parallel his use of local knowledge in *Oliver Twist*. The brown cloth of Oliver's pauper uniform in the novel is the same regulation colour as that in use at the Cleveland Street Workhouse, the meagre dietary and the apprenticeship system for pauper children fits, too. So too does the connection with the 'branch' workhouse baby farm in rural Hendon, seven (not seventy) miles away, the mistress of which is named Mann in the novel, but Merriman in reality.

We must not forget, either, the identity of purpose between the Strand Union Guardians and the Poor Law Commissioners. The Italian Boy—the personification of the victim child—was buried in the Workhouse graveyard, while Mr Weller sold shoes opposite Dickens's home, only a stroll from the 'Marquis of Granby' in Percy Street.[38] Goodge and Marney worked in nearby Berners Mews. Miss Havisham and Mr Bumble, or someone very like them, passed Dickens's front door. Signor Billsmethi lived in Mr Dodd's house, while Mrs Maylie's namesake was buried in the local churchyard; Corney, Bardell, and Rudderforth were other local names, and the undertaker Sowerberry's surname looks to have been inspired by that of a local publican. The location of the pawnbroker's shop in Norfolk Street, visible from both the Workhouse and from Dickens's old home, sustains the central plot line of the stolen locket. Ultimately, no better confirmation could be wanted than that the shop across from the workhouse gates was run by Bill Sykes.

An anecdote is told of a London stroller in the 1860s, who went into a junk shop in Seven Dials to enquire about a picture he'd noticed, in among the odds and ends in the grimy shop window. After examining it, and agreeing a price of five shillings with the shopwoman, he was surprised by a question from behind:

'May I look at the drawing?' said a voice.

'Certainly,' returned the purchaser: when to his surprise, he discovered that the request had come from none other than Charles Dickens, who was sitting unobtrusively, notebook in hand, in the corner of the shop. After scanning the watercolour for some moments, he handed it back to the owner, observing:

'T' (meaning Turner).

'Yes,' replied Mr Roe.

'I congratulate you,' said Dickens.[39]

The shop was a dusty junk shop in a down-at-heel part of London, but in the window there was a Turner, and in a corner inside was Dickens. What an extraordinary stroke of luck for that stroller! No wonder the encounter was told, and told again. The tale is worth looking at, because it reveals something of importance about the way Dickens worked, which may be why the author Gladys Storey repeated it. The Turner for five shillings was the stroller's gem, while the sight of Dickens is also ours: we can see him as he was not expecting to be seen, in his maturity, notebook in hand, sitting in the dark corner of an obscure junk shop, observing and taking notes.[40]

To occupy that position, there must presumably have been an arrangement of some kind with the shop woman, who had allowed him to be there: some agreement that he might sit there quietly to observe and listen to whatever might pass.[41] He had evidently been there long enough to become part of the furniture, remaining unnoticed until, through his own curiosity, he drew a stray customer's attention to himself. That dark corner might have been a happy place for Dickens, a celebrity in the 1860s and recognized everywhere.

I feel rather like that lucky stroller in Seven Dials. Entering the street to seek the history of the Workhouse, something caused me to turn and find, to my surprise, Charles Dickens, secreted so very unobtrusively that no one noticed he'd been there all the while, nine doors from the Workhouse gates.

HEAVEN & EARTH.
'Oh! it's very well to Live on the Taxes—but the devil to pay them.'

Appendix*

TABLE 1: CHRONOLOGY OF DICKENS'S MAJOR WORKS

Sketches by Boz	in various places	1833–6
Pickwick Papers	in monthly parts	1836–7
Oliver Twist	in monthly parts	1837–9
Nicholas Nickleby	in monthly parts	1838–9
The Old Curiosity Shop	in weekly parts	1840–1
Barnaby Rudge	in weekly parts	1841
Martin Chuzzlewit	in monthly parts	1843–4
A Christmas Carol	Christmas book	1843
Dombey and Son	in monthly parts	1846–8
David Copperfield	in monthly parts	1849–50
Bleak House	in monthly parts	1852–3
Hard Times	in weekly parts	1854
Little Dorrit	in monthly parts	1855–7
A Tale of Two Cities	in weekly parts	1859
Great Expectations	in weekly parts	1860–1
Our Mutual Friend	in monthly parts	1864–5
Edwin Drood	in monthly parts (unfinished at Dickens's death in 1870)	

* I thank Michael Allen, Norman Page, David Perdue, Peter Razzell, and Paul Schlicke for materials in these tables.

TABLE 2: CHRONOLOGY OF *PICKWICK*,
TWIST, AND *NICKLEBY*

	1836	1837	1838	1839
Pickwick	March———————October			
Twist			February—————April	
Nickleby			March——————————October	

TABLE 3: DICKENS'S SIBLINGS

1810 (August)	Fanny	(d. 1848)
1812 (7 February)	Charles	(d. 1870)
1814 (March)	Alfred Allen	(d. September 1814)
1816 (April)	Letitia	(d. 1893)
1818 (September)	Harriet	(d. August 1827)*
1820 (August)	Frederick	(d. 1868)
1822 (March)	Alfred Lamert[†]	(d. 1860)
1827 (October)	Augustus	(d. 1866)

* The date of Harriet Dickens's death has been discovered by Professor Bill Long, and is due to appear in W. F. Long, 'Defining a Life: Charles's Youngest Sister, Harriet Ellen Dickens (15.9.1818–19.08.1827)' *Dickensian*, forthcoming. I thank him for sharing his work with me prior to publication.

† The spelling of Lamert/Lamerte is inconsistent in the sources. Alfred's middle name lacked the 'e' at the end, whereas in the Chancery documents associated with the blacking factory which Michael Allen has discovered, Lamerte has the extra 'e' throughout. See M. Allen, *Charles Dickens and the Blacking Factory*. St Leonards, Oxford-Stockley, September 2011.

TABLE 4: WHERE DICKENS LIVED BEFORE 'BOZ'

age	year	address	
birth	1812	13 Mile End Terrace, Landport, Portsmouth	(christened at Portsea)
		16 Hawke Street, Portsmouth	
1	1813	Wish Street, Southsea	
2*	1814	Wish Street, Southsea	
3	1815	10 Norfolk Street, Marylebone	
4*	1816	10 Norfolk Street, Marylebone	
5	1817	Sheerness, then Ordnance Terrace, Chatham	
6*	1818	Ordnance Terrace, Chatham	
7	1819	Ordnance Terrace, Chatham	
8*	1820	Ordnance Terrace, Chatham	
9	1821	St Mary's Place, Chatham	
10*	1822	16 Bayham Street, Camden Town	
11	1823	4 Gower Street North	
12	1824	<u>FATHER ARRESTED FOR DEBT</u> Family in Marshalsea prison, then Lodgings	Blacking factory at Hungerford Stairs, then Chandos Street CD in Little College Street, then Lant Street

Where Dickens Lived before 'Boz'

age	year	address	
13	1825	29 Johnson Street, Somers Town	CD at School: Wellington House Academy (Camden Town)
14	1826	29 Johnson Street, Somers Town	CD at School: Wellington House Academy (Camden Town)
15*	1827	Family evicted from Johnson Street Lodgings in 17 Polygon	CD leaves school; clerk at Gray's Inn
16	1828	29 Johnson Street, Somers Town	CD clerk at Gray's Inn/Lincoln's Inn
17	1829	10 Norfolk Street, Marylebone	CD Doctors' Commons/ Freelance reporter
18	1830	10 Norfolk Street, Marylebone	CD Doctors' Commons/ British Museum Reader
19	1831	10 Norfolk Street, Marylebone	CD Doctors' Commons/ British Museum Reader
20	1832	Fitzroy Street + 70 Margaret Street + elsewhere	CD at *Mirror of Parliament, True Sun*
21	1833	18 Bentinck Street, Manchester Square	CD's 1st sketch published
22	1834	CD moves to Furnival's Inn	CD at *Morning Chronicle*
		CD LEAVES FAMILY HOME FOR GOOD	**FIRST PIECES SIGNED 'BOZ' PUBLISHED**

* sibling born

TABLE 5: DICKENS'S OCCUPATIONS IN RELATION TO HIS ADDRESSES

Home	Date	Age	Dickens's Occupation
Somers Town	1827	15	Gray's Inn office junior clerk Ellis & Blackmore
Somers Town	1828	16	Gray's Inn clerk + short period with attorney Charles Molloy
Norfolk Street	1829	17	Freelance reporter Police courts/law courts
Norfolk Street	1830	18	Freelance reporter + works in Doctors' Commons—BM Reader's ticket
Norfolk Street	1831	19	Doctors' Commons + Parliamentary Reporter *Mirror of Parliament*
Fitzroy Street	1832	20	Parliamentary Reporter *Mirror of Parliament* + *True Sun*
Bentinck Street	1833	21	Parliamentary Reporter *Mirror of Parliament*; First Sketch published
Bentinck Street	1834	22	12 Sketches published, *Mirror of Parliament* + *Morning Chronicle*
Furnival's Inn	1835	23	32 Sketches published + *Morning Chronicle* Staff Reporter
Furnival's Inn	1836	24	15 Sketches published + *Morning Chronicle* + *Pickwick* commissioned
Doughty Street	1837	25	*Pickwick* continues; begins publishing *Oliver Twist* in Bentley's Miscellany

NOTES

A Note on Sources

Materials on Dickens's biography owe much to the work of many Dickens scholars, and I should like to pay particular tribute to the work of Kathleen Tillotson, Paul Schlicke, Michael Allen, Michael Slater, David Paroissien, Andrew Sanders, John Drew, Peter Ackroyd, Malcom Andrews, Norman Page, Duane deVries, Fred Kaplan, Robert Patten, Harry Stone, Steven Marcus, and to the very recent work of Bill Long. I have also dug into the work of older biographers, especially Forster, but also the fine work of W. J. Carlton and Ada Nisbet, Una Pope-Hennessey and Gladys Storey, and have dipped into *The Dickensian*, although sadly not as much as I would have liked to have done. Dickens scholars worldwide will raise glasses when it becomes available (and searchable) electronically.

There are a number of really outstanding sources now available on the internet which have proved of enormous value, such as the Workhouses website, Old Bailey online, London Lives, David Perdue's Dickens Page, and the British Library's newspaper archives online, also BathSpa Greenwood Map of London, Project Gutenberg, John Johnson Collection online (Bodleian Library), The London Gazette, Archivemaps, MAPCO, The Pilgrim Letters online, Dickenslive, InternetArchive (Dickens Journals Online), LondonRemembers, Oxford Dictionary of National Biography, Openlibrary, Project Gutenberg, The Times archive online, Victorian Literary Archive Online Nagoya

University Japan (Dickens Concordance), VictorianLondon, IGI, The Partleton Tree, and The Word on the Street (National Library of Scotland). I thank all those involved in creating and sustaining these sites, most especially those which are freely available to everybody.

Abbreviations

Note. I have used very few abbreviations here. The main ones are as follows:

Forster, *Life* (Ley) refers to the edition of John Forster's *Life of Charles Dickens*, which was edited by J. W. T. Ley. London, Cecil Palmer in 1928.
LMA refers to the London Metropolitan Archives.
ODNB refers to the Oxford Dictionary of National Biography.
Pilgrim Letters refers to the 12-volume set of Dickens Letters published by the Clarendon Press, Oxford between 1965 and 2002, edited by Madeline House, Graham Storey, Kathleen Tillotson, W. J. Carlton and others. The entire set is now available online, and I am grateful to Oxford for making them available to me while I was researching this book.

Quotations from the novels are taken from the Oxford World's Classics series, except for those from *Oliver Twist*, which have been checked against the first edition. Those from *Sketches by Boz* are from the forthcoming Clarendon edition, edited by Paul Schlicke, to whom I am grateful for allowing me to use his corrected versions.
I have not noted the date on which I accessed the various websites used for the research on this book. The research and writing were being done between late October 2010 and late August 2011.

Introduction

1. See: M. Allen, *Charles Dickens, Warren's Blacking and the Chancery Court*. Podcast of a talk recorded 1 October 2010 at The National Archives. www.nationalarchives.gov.uk/podcasts/charles-dickens-

warrens-blacking-and-the-chancery-court.htm, and his newest book: *Charles Dickens and the Blacking Factory.* St Leonards, Oxford-Stockley, 2011. Also other papers by him: 'New Evidence on Dickens's Grandparents'. *Dickensian*, forthcoming; 'New Light on Dickens and the Blacking Factory'. *Dickensian*, forthcoming; also very recent work by Professor Bill Long on Dickens's younger sister, Harriet. W. F. Long, 'Defining a Life: Charles's Youngest Sister, Harriet Ellen Dickens (15.9.1818–19.08.1827)'. *Dickensian*, forthcoming.

1. Discovery

1. L. Staples, 'Two Early London Homes of Charles Dickens'. *Dickensian*, 1951: 198–200.
2. Forster's *Life of Charles Dickens* was first published in 1872–4.
3. Forster, *Life* (Ley): 2.
4. Ibid. 23–4.
5. The current whereabouts of Forster's interlined manuscript copy seems unknown.
6. www.lovecamden.org/hindsites-charles-dickens-walk accessed November 2010, unaltered August 2011.
7. That is, unless his story 'Mrs Lirriper's Lodgings' (located in Norfolk Street, Strand) can be thought of in such a way.
8. The 'autobiographical fragment' was apparently unfinished/incomplete when Dickens gave it to Forster, and so may not have reached as far as the years of Dickens's early adulthood. Dickens is said to have burnt the part covering his courtship with Maria Beadnell. The fragment may therefore have ended before Dickens's second period in Norfolk Street.
9. M. Slater, *Charles Dickens*. New Haven and London, Yale University Press, 2009: 96–7.
10. See Appendix A.
11. R. Richardson and B. S. Hurwitz, 'Joseph Rogers and the Reform of Workhouse Medicine'. *British Medical Journal*, 1989, 299: 1507–10.

12. Forster, *Life* (Ley): 34.
13. Since closed.
14. J. T. Smith, *A Book for a Rainy Day.* London, Bentley, 1861: 311.
15. M. Allen, *Charles Dickens' Childhood*. New York, St Martin's Press, 1988: 29–35. A new edition is due out for Dickens's 200th birthday in 2012.
16. *Pilgrim Letters*, i: Letter to John Macrone, 27 October 1835: n. 5.
17. Forster, *Life* (Ley): 36.
18. Paul Schlicke has pointed out that we have to be aware that Monmouth Street Seven Dials is not the same street as it was when Dickens was writing about it—the old name was given to another street nearby when Shaftesbury Avenue was built in the 1870s. Personal communication.
19. See e.g. C. Tearle, *Pilgrim from Chicago*. London, Longman, 1913: chapters 1 and 9 *passim*. In his Preface to the 1841 edition of *Oliver Twist*, Dickens ridiculed Sir Peter Laurie's silly assertion that Jacob's Island could not exist because it had appeared in a novel. See Kathleen Tillotson's Introduction to the 1966 Clarendon edition of *Oliver Twist*, 1966; J. E. Butt and K. Tillotson, *Dickens at Work*. London, Methuen, 1957: 191.
20. *Pickwick Papers*, chapter 13.
21. P. Fitzgerald, *Bozland*. London, Downie, 1895: 120–1.
22. *Pickwick Papers*, chapter 28.
23. Marylebone was famed for its poor road surfaces. See A Churchman, *A General Statement of the case of the Parishioners against the Select Vestry of St Marylebone*. London, Riebau, 1828.
24. See D. Paroissien, *Companion to Oliver Twist*. Oxford, Blackwell, 2008: 226–7.
25. 'New Year's Day'. *Household Words*, 1859, 19: 97.

2. Vicinity

1. Forster, *Life* (Ley): 2.
2. *Dombey and Son*, chapter 12.

3. M. Allen, *Charles Dickens' Childhood*, New York, St Martin's Press, 1988: 22.

4. T. Follini, 'James, Dickens, and the Indirections of Influence'. *The Henry James Review*, 25(3), 2004: 228–38.

5. G. Cruikshank, *The Fox & the Goose: or, Boney Broke Loose!* London, Whittle & Laurie, 1815 British Museum Prints and Drawings, British Museum Satires 12506.

6. This was the summer Frankenstein and The Vampyre were born in Geneva. See B. Hurwitz, R. Richardson, 'Somnambulism, Vampirism and Suicide: The life of Dr John Polidori'. *Proceedings of the Royal College of Physicians of Edinburgh*, 1991 (October), 21/4: 458–66.

7. J. Hanway, *Citizens' Monitor*. London, Dodsley, 1780: p. xvi.

8. J. P. de Castro, *The Gordon Riots*. Oxford, Oxford University Press, 1926: 194.

9. *Barnaby Rudge*, chapter 44.

10. Bill for damages 14 June 1780. L/RV/38:1779–80. London Metropolitan Archives. A large gang of rioters was caught in Seven Dials on 12 June 1780 after the riots were over. See de Castro, *The Gordon Riots*: 194.

11. See *Barnaby Rudge*, Preface.

12. The site is now under the Telecom Tower.

13. Michael Allen's work underpins this part of the chapter concerning Dickens's association with Marylebone. I thank him for his kindness and generosity on many points, small and large. His work on Oxford Street was shared with me prior to publication.

14. Lady Crewe had been a close friend of Georgiana Duchess of Devonshire, and was still alive when the Dickens family moved up to London in 1816. See n. 13 above.

15. G. Storey, *Dickens and Daughter*. New York, Haskell House, 1971: 33–4.

16. Ibid. 33.

17. Allen, *Charles Dickens' Childhood*: 31–4.

18. John Dickens was described as 'of this parish', so it seems that at that time he was living close to his work. See Storey, *Dickens and Daughter*: 35.
19. *Holden's Triennial Directory*. London, Holden, 1809: ii. 39.
20. Allen, *Charles Dickens' Childhood*: 18–19. The woman servant's wage of £14 per annum is mentioned in the case of Ann Darter, 17 April 1822: oldbaileyonline.org. Charles Barrow, had he been prosecuted, would probably have been transported to Australia as a convict.
21. Ibid.
22. St Marylebone: *Registers of Baptisms Marriages and Burials*, 1816. Microfilm at London Metropolitan Archives. For the baptism of William and John Dickens, see *Register* for 20 November 1785. See M. Allen, 'New Evidence on Dickens's Grandparents'. *Dickensian*, Forthcoming. Marylebone New Church, beside which Dickens would live later for several years in Devonshire Terrace, was consecrated in 1817.
23. Allen, *Charles Dickens' Childhood*: 11–13.
24. M. Slater, *Charles Dickens*. New Haven and London, Yale University Press, 2009: 618.
25. 'Forty years in London'. *All the Year Round*, 1865: 253–7. The piece is attributed to Wills by E. Oppenlander, *Dickens' All the Year Round*. Troy, NY, Whitston, 1984: 297.
26. De Quincey was speaking of London in about 1804, ten years previous to Dickens's arrival. See T. De Quincey, *Confessions of an English Opium Eater*. Part II, originally published in the *London Magazine*, October 1821. London, Routledge, 1886. Accessed on Project Gutenberg July 2011. I thank Bridget MacDonald very much for this reference.
27. The park was still private in 1815–17, but it was opened to the public in 1833 after the death of George IV.
28. *The Middlesex Farmer*. British Library: shelfmark 1161.b.14.

29. See the painting of a party of haymakers by John Glover, taken from the top of Upper Baker Street *c.*1820 reproduced in W. H. Manchee, 'Marylebone and its Hugenot associations'. *Proceedings of the Hugenot Society of London*, 1916, 11/1: 1–72. But hints of the fields hung on for a long time. I myself can remember my own astonishment hearing two old ladies talking together in a bus travelling south from Camden Town, in the 1970s, discussing the place near the junction of the Hampstead and Euston Roads where they had gathered watercresses when they were girls. Old maps show there was indeed a reservoir at the position of which they were speaking, just by Drummond Street.

30. D. J. Olsen, *Town Planning in London*. New Haven, Yale University Press, 1964: 145–8. Doughty Street was also a gated road.

31. Anon., *Plan of the Mary-le-bone General Dispensary*. London, The Dispensary, 1791.

3. Institutions

1. *Gentleman's Magazine*, 1857, 27: 7–8.
2. For the eighteenth-century culture of fund-raising see S. Lloyd, 'Pleasing Spectacles and Elegant Dinners: Conviviality, Benevolence and Charity Anniversaries in 18th century London'. *Journal of British Studies*, 2002, 41/1: 23–57. The Hospital was said to be 'in danger of being annihilated' in 1811, presumably from the impoverishment of the Napoleonic Wars. D. Lysons, *Environs of London*. London, Cadell, 1811: vi. 236.
3. J. Tallis, London Street Views. London, Tallis, 1839, part 65: 171.
4. J. T. Smith, *A Book for a Rainy Day*. London, Bentley, 1861: 215. The encounter is undated, but Sarah Banks died in 1818.
5. E. Walford, *Old and New London*. London, Cassell, 1878: iv. 467. The quotation from Mayhew is from his essay 'The London Street Markets on a Saturday night'. http://etext.virginia.edu/toc/modeng/public/MayLond.html. Accessed 30 July 2011.

6. Thackeray said that the man seemed to think he could prove his gentility by calling it 'that demned place'. J. O. Brookfield (ed.), *A Collection of Letters of W. M. Thackeray*. London, Smith Elder 1887: 116.

7. *Sketches by Boz*, 'The Hospital Patient'.

8. *Pilgrim Letters*, ii: Letter to Douglas Jerrold, 3 May 1843.

9. Report cut from an unidentified newspaper, pasted into a scrapbook in the British Library, shelfmark Crach.1.Tab.4.b.3.

10. It is referred to under this name in Westminster Archives H879 Trustees of the Poor—Meetings held at the Workhouse 1791.

11. D. Lysons, *The Environs of London*. London, Cadell, 1811: iii. 278.

12. Westminster Archives MS 9549 1775–92; and MS 9532A 1863.

13. St Paul Covent Garden Trustees of the Poor, Westminster Archives H879, 1 July 1791.

14. The tradition is probably very old, and may have derived from monastic institutions.

15. From G. Crabbe, *The Borough*. London, Hatchard, 1810.

16. St Paul Covent Garden: *Minute book of the Guardians & Overseers of the Poor.* Westminster Archives H883A 1768–95.

17. St Paul Covent Garden, Trustees of the Poor, Westminster Archives H879, 29 July 1791.

18. Westminster Archives H879, 23 December 1791, 16 December 1791.

19. Westminster Archives H879, 12 July 1793, 30 October 1795.

20. St Paul Covent Garden, Trustees of the Poor, Westminster Archives H879, 16 September 1791, 25 May 1792.

21. Ibid. H879, 16 September 1791–9, December 1791.

22. Ibid. H879, 9 December 1791.

23. Ibid. H879, 11 May 1792, 5 August 1796.

24. Ibid. H879, 21 April 1792.

25. Ibid. H879, 23 May 1794.

26. J. Brown, *A Memoir of Robert Blincoe*. Firle, Sussex, Caliban Books, 1977.

27. Anon., 'Sermons in Stone', *The Builder*, 11 September 1858: 613.

28. R. Schnebbelie, *View of the London Workhouse, Bishopsgate Street, 1819*. Museum of London Database, reference: 80.501/723.

29. For a photograph of such a workhouse bell, see P. Higginbotham, *Life in a Victorian Workhouse*. Andover, Pitkin, 2011: 11. Gordon McMullan tells me that the Georgian workhouse in Walthamstow, now the Vestry House Museum, has an inscription over its entrance, which reads: 'If any would not work neither Should he eat' (2 Thessalonians 3:10) and the date 1730 in Roman numerals.

30. J. Rogers, *Reminiscences of a Workhouse Medical Officer*. London, Fisher Unwin, 1889: 37.

31. J. P. Kay, *Poor Law Commission*, 16 July 1838 LMA WE/BG/ST/114: 122. See also Rogers, *Reminiscences of a Workhouse Medical Officer*: 4–5, 36.

32. The design and construction of the current wall and gates date to the mid-1920s.

33. Many years later, when Dickens rang at a workhouse to gain entry to speak to the workhouse master, he stepped inside smartly before the gatekeeper could keep him out. One has a strong sense from his own description that he was familiar with the manoeuvre from having witnessed it. See C. Dickens, 'A Nightly Scene in London'. *Household Words*, 1856, 13: 25–7.

4. Home

1. I have not emphasized the appearance of medical students in *Pickwick* and elsewhere, which might well be influenced by Dickens's familiarity with this locality.

2. I thank Paul Schlicke for this lovely quotation.

3. These three also have very delicate fanlights above their front doors, and corbels with stylized acanthus leaves, which the corner house lacks.

4. Westminster Archives, P1221.

5. These men were jointly involved in other building projects in other parts of London, such as Brompton Park House, whose site is now

part of the South Kensington Museums. See F. H. W. Sheppard (ed.), *Survey of London*, 38: 3–8. I have also found Horsfall building in Pentonville, and the original name of a great basin of the Regent's Canal now known as Battle Bridge Basin was Horsfall Basin. See the website of the London Canal Museum www.canalmuseum.org.uk/visit/virtualtour4.htm.

6. For the bomb damage see *The London County Council Bomb Damage Maps 1939–1945*. London, London Topographical Society, 2005. For Whitfield's Tabernacle, see D. Lysons, *Environs of London*. London, Cadell, 1811: vi. 257.

7. Norfolk Street contained 34 houses, plus the two corner buildings on Charles and Goodge Streets, so only 10 per cent of the street's original houses still exist, Dickens's home—luckily—being one.

8. There were a number of people by the name of John Dodd in the district at the time, and until serious genealogical work is undertaken it is not possible to be sure if he was related to any of the other Dodd families living in Marylebone at the time. He may have been one of several John Dodds whose baptisms at St Marylebone Old Church are recorded in the same register as William and John Dickens. John (b. 21 August 1785) and William (b. 21 September 1783) Dickens were baptized together on 20 November 1785. Close to the same opening in the register is recorded the baptism of James Dodd, son of Christopher and Jane Dodd, baptized 7 October 1785, whose older brother John Dodd, of the same parents, had been baptized 30 March 1783. So this pair of brothers were of similar ages to Charles Dickens's father and uncle. They had younger sisters too: Mary Dodd, baptized 20 June 1788 and Elizabeth Dodd, 2 December 1791. Another pair of brothers, John Dodd, baptized 10 February 1796, and Thomas Dodd, 4 December 1799, sons of John and Susanna Dodd, appear in the same volume. Dodd, Dickens, Beard, Oliver, Chipperfield, Wills, and Bacon are local names which crop up repeatedly in these registers. Of course the John Dodd of 10 Norfolk Street may well not appear in the Marylebone register at all:

he may have been a Nonconformist, not baptized until adulthood, of some other religion, or born and raised elsewhere. I understand Professor Bill Long is currently working on Mr Dodd.

9. M. Allen, *Charles Dickens' Childhood*. New York, St Martin's Press, 1988: 30 (citing Langton).

10. Mr Dodd is named in the *London Gazette* in 1815 and 1825. It is just possible that there were two Dodds, father and son of the same name.

11. See the notebook of William Marsh, of Marsh Sibbald & Co, bankers of Marylebone, noting losses in the banking crash of 1824–5. Mr J. Dodd of Norfolk Street, Middlesex Hospital, was a creditor to the amount of £101.0s.7d.; Westminster Archives. The same bank, whose offices were in Berners Street, had been the employer of Henry Fauntleroy, hanged in November 1824 for forgery and embezzlement. See Case of Henry Fauntleroy, 28 October 1824: oldbaileyonline.org.

12. *ODNB*: Dodd, Henry.

13. Ibid. Dodd, John and Thomas.

14. See the *London Gazette* website: http://www.london-gazette.co.uk

15. Sam Weller mentions 'red-faced Nixon', a book of prophecies, which sold for sixpence. See *Pickwick Papers*, chapter 42.

16. Hundreds of artists associated with the area are listed in A. Cox-Johnson, *Handlist of Painters, Sculptors and Architects associated with St Marylebone 1760–1960*. London, St Marylebone Public Libraries Committee, 1963.

17. Nollekens died there an old man in 1823. W. H. Holden, *Houses with a History in St Marylebone*. London, British Technical Press, 1950: 17–18.

18. *Johnstone's London Directory*, London, Johnstone, 1818. See also Gahagan on the website sculpture.gla.ac.uk.

19. Cox-Johnson, *Handlist of Painters, Sculptors and Architects associated with Marylebone 1760–1960*. Francis Danby lived at 10 Norfolk Street in the 1840s.

20. Ibid.

21. Or indeed of the famous embezzler, Dr Dodd, hanged at Tyburn in 1777. See *ODNB*: Dodd. Accessible on the British Museum Prints and Drawings Collection Database: *Roderick Random* 1780 (AN519029001), *Fatal Bridge* 1810 (AN518888001, Newgate Calendar) *Malefactors' Register* 1780 (AN789528001). Another Dodd engraved a bird's eye view of the Zoological Gardens in 1846, in the same collection (AN782540001).

22. Daniell's wife was the sister of the artist Richard Westall. How one wishes he had turned his eye to his own environment, and sketched the workhouse opposite!

23. *A Voyage round Great Britain.* London, Longman and Daniell, 1814–25.

24. A number of other prints in the British Museum Prints and Drawings collection were created there. See the British Museum online database. See also R. Engen, *Dictionary of Victorian Engravers.* Cambridge, Chadwyck Healey, 1979: 150.

25. Audubon is said to have danced for joy in Tottenham Street when he discovered the Havells. British Museum Prints and Drawings has a colour print of a bedroom at Hampton Court by Richard Cattermole, printed by Havell in 1816 while the Dickens family was in Norfolk Street. Richard's brother George Cattermole was later an illustrator of *The Old Curiosity Shop*.

26. See British Museum Prints and Drawings. Dixon had premises in Tottenham Mews. He also created a portrait of the Crewe sisters, one of whom was the employer of Dickens's Grandmother.

27. Now in the British Museum and believed to be of Derby manufacture.

28. When Dickens's family returned to Norfolk Street the theatre's name had been changed to The Prince of Wales, and other name changes followed subsequently, the best known being the most recent: The Scala. Tokens for entrance to the theatre gallery dating from *c.*1829 may be found in the Montague Guest Collection in the British Museum (item 339). The theatre has since been demolished.

29. British Museum Prints and Drawings. British Museum Satires 9916.

30. *Interior of the Regency Theatre.* R. B. Schnebbelie (artist), Cook (engraver). London, Wilkinson of Fenchurch Street. British Museum Prints and Drawings (AN837261001).

31. The theatre had many changes of name over its long lifetime, the last being near its end in 1903 when it was known locally as the 'Dusthole'. See G. Clinch, *Marylebone and St Pancras*. London, Truslove, 1890: 185. Other artists in the near neighbourhood of Norfolk Street included William Bewick (who lived in Nassau Street) and the miniaturist and portrait painter Frederick Cruikshank (sometimes given as Cruickshank), and a number of French artists. Romney's work had been displayed in the shop windows in Charles Street not long before—his famous portrait of Tom Paine (who had lived at No. 7 Marylebone Street, just around the corner from the Workhouse) was etched and printed in Charles Street. See Cox-Johnson, *Handlist of Painters, Sculptors and Architects associated with Marylebone 1760–1960*, who lists hundreds of artists who have lived in the area. Re: Paine, see also Barb Jacobson in Fitzrovia News: http://news.fitzrovia.org.uk/2010/11/17/thomas-paine-lived. It is not known if Dickens's *Pic-Nic Papers* had anything to do with the place. C. Dickens (ed.), *The Pic-Nic Papers*. London, Colburn, 1841.

32. The John Johnson Collection has a number of examples online. See http://johnjohnson.chadwyck.co.uk/home.do

33. These are all items listed on butter-papers in the John Johnson Collection, Bodleian Library. Other sidelines included being an agent for an insurance company. It is unlikely that Mr Dodd ran a small circulating library, as there was one already on Cleveland Street.

34. *London Gazette*, 13 February 1816: 16; 20 February 1816: 15. http://www.london-gazette.co.uk/

35. The bitterness of debtors whose insolvency resulted from such practices was expressed in a song 'Thus we insolvent debtors live | Yet we may boldly say | Worse villains often credit give | Than

325

those that never pay, | For wealthy knaves can with applause | Cheat on, and ne'er be tried | But in contempt of human laws | In coaches safely ride'. Prisoners' song sung by Mr Platt from *The Prisoners' Opera*, Sadlers Wells, *c.*1730.

36. See, for example, the little display in a pane of the shop window in Laurie and Whittle, *A Touch at the Times*, 1805. British Museum Prints and Drawings (AN511872001), showing two figures and the moon, with some unidentified goods on the shelf beside.

37. *The Mirror*, 1835, vol 25: 47. John Johnson Collection Bodleian Library. I would love to think that the cheesemonger was Mr Dodd!

38. *Oliver Twist*, chapter 17.

39. *Nicholas Nickleby*, chapter 32.

40. H. Heath, *What a treat*, and *I wish you may get it*. London, Gans, 1828. British Museum Prints and Drawings Collection (AN685774001).

41. *Sketches by Boz*, 'The Streets at Night'.

42. It is unlikely that each of the upper floors was self-contained, as they are today. Concerning the risks of upstairs living in London, see the case of Mary Ann Rycroft, 2 December 1824: oldbaileyonline.org.

43. Westminster Archives D.Misc.244.

44. *The Whip Club*. London, Fairburn, *c.*1815. British Museum Prints and Drawings Collection: British Museum Satires Undescribed.

45. I believe Cruikshank's image owes something to the Grimaldi one. He is known to have worked for Fairburn.

46. I thank my son Josh for his assistance in the transcription process.

47. *Pickwick Papers*, 'The Bagman's Story', chapter 14, and chapter 37.

5. Street

1. It is also possible that he needed extra money at that time, with bankruptcy impending, so may have let the main floor and the one above it, and moved his own household into the attics.

2. M. Allen, *Charles Dickens' Childhood*. New York, St Martin's Press, 1988: 29.

3. *Pickwick Papers*, chapter 12.

4. Allen, *Charles Dickens' Childhood*: 62–3. Aunt Mary was known in the family as Fanny, but I have used Mary here to prevent confusion with Dickens's older sister.

5. Alternatively Mr Dodd may himself have moved up to the attic storey so as to be able to ask a higher rent for the best floor, or the Dickens family may have had the attic, and spread through four rooms; or they may have rented an additional room on the inter-mediate floor. We simply do not know. In London it was common policy for a servant to sleep in the kitchen. There was more usable space on every floor in those days as there were no bathrooms. All water above the hand-pumped tank on the first floor landing had to be carried up in buckets.

6. Mr Pickwick on Goswell Road, who has two floors to himself, has his sitting room on the first floor front, and his bedroom on the second floor front. Paul Schlicke points out Dickens's wonderful description of the view of London from Todger's, in *Martin Chuzzlewit*, chapter 9.

7. In richer households, servants' quarters generally occupied the attics/garrets.

8. A photograph of Hawke Street, Portsea, is reproduced in H. S. Ward and C. W. B. Ward, *The Real Dickens Land*. London, Chapman & Hall, 1904: 13.

9. G. Sturt, *A Small Boy in the Sixties*. Cambridge, Cambridge University Press, 1932: 24.

10. *Pickwick Papers*, chapter 12.

11. For the street plan showing the original house numbers see Peter Potter's Map of Marylebone, Westminster Archives.

12. *Pickwick Papers*, chapter 37. The shop described belonged to Bob Sawyer, a newly established surgeon/apothecary, and interestingly, in the late 1830s there was a medical man in one of the shops across from 10 Norfolk Street, perhaps also with a similar red lamp to that Dickens describes as being the insignia of a medical practitioner.

13. See *Sketches by Boz*, 'The Streets—Morning'.

14. T. S. Eliot, 'Prelude'.
15. Case of William Baker, 24 November 1834: oldbaileyonline.org. Others kept rabbits.
16. The data presented here concerning the livelihoods of the inhabitants of Norfolk Street has been collected from a variety of contemporary London street directories consulted at the British Library and at the Bishopsgate Institute.
17. Results of a search for 'Tottenham Street' on oldbaileyonline.org.
18. *Oliver Twist*, chapter 10.
19. Ibid. chapter 37.
20. William Hogarth pictured the interior; Sheridan was married there.
21. Forster, *Life* (Ley): 3–4.
22. Her second son, Alfred Allen, had died as a baby in 1814.
23. In the 1840s, her mother, Granny Barrow, lived with family in Holloway, on the far side of Copenhagen Fields, but we do not know where she or they were at this date.
24. M. Slater, 'How many Nurses had Charles Dickens?' *Prose Studies*, 1987, 10/3: 250–8.
25. *Sketches by Boz*, 'The Tuggses at Ramsgate'.
26. L. Staples, 'Two Early London Homes of Charles Dickens'. *Dickensian*, 1951: 198–200.
27. It is very telling that Dickens felt he had to defend his portrayal of Nancy because commentators had doubted its veracity; yet no one seems to have doubted the truth of his picture of Bumble.
28. I myself can remember being sent to our local butcher in Portobello Road Market, with coins wrapped in a note, and bringing back the shopping alone. This must have been when my elder sister was home from school sick, or my mother busy with a new baby. This was before I could read, so I was about 4 years old. T. A. Trollope described long exploratory journeys round London with his brother, both of them under 10 years of age, and in parts of town which many people might now regard with

horror. See T. A. Trollope, *What I Remember*. 2 vols. London, Bentley 1887: chapter 1 *passim*.

29. My Grandfather once told me that fairies inhabited the little alcoves at the very top of the long wall, which only marginally improved it.

30. *Oliver Twist*, chapter 3.

31. M. and M. Hardwick, *Dickens's England*. London, Dent, 1970: 11.

32. And indeed Dicken's relationship with Ellen Ternan.

6. Calamity

1. The earliest letters of any real value post-date this period. I take account here of very recent discoveries by Michael Allen, which concerns the blacking factory period of Dickens's childhood. Michael Allen's new book, *Charles Dickens and the Blacking Factory*, Oxford-Stockley, 2011, was in press while I was writing this book. The spelling of Lamerte with a final 'e' comes from this research.

2. E. Johnson, *Charles Dickens: His Tragedy and Triumph*. Harmondsworth, Penguin, 1979: title of chapter 2.

3. M. Allen, *Charles Dickens' Childhood*. New York, St Martin's Press, 1988: 36.

4. Ibid.

5. D. DeVries, *Dickens's Apprentice Years*. Hassocks, Harvester, 1976: 4.

6. *Pilgrim Letters*, i: Letter to J. H. Kuenzel, [?July 1838].

7. M. Slater, *Charles Dickens*. New Haven and London, Yale University Press, 2009: 6.

8. For details of Dickens's siblings, see Appendix B.

9. Forster, *Life* (Ley): 9.

10. See Chronology of Dickens's siblings in Appendix B.

11. Forster, *Life* (Ley): 10.

12. 'Gone Astray', *Household Words*, 1853, 7: 553–7. This episode must, I think, if it actually happened, pre-date his father's imprisonment in the Marshalsea, because during the blacking factory period young Dickens would have known how to navigate alone between

Camden Town and Charing Cross, and Charing Cross and Southwark.

13. The house, the London home of the Percy family, appears in a famous painting of Charing Cross by Canaletto.

14. The essay appeared in the month of John Dickens's birthday, August, so he may have been in his son's thoughts. Dickens's second son, Walter, had reached the age Dickens himself had been when he was sent to work in the blacking factory. Dickens's tenth child had just been born. Michael Allen thinks the guide was young Lamerte, which is also possible.

15. Forster, *Life* (Ley): 47.

16. *Pickwick Papers*, chapter 20.

17. Allen, *Charles Dickens' Childhood*: 30.

18. The Collegiate School for Girls was founded in nearby Euston Square in 1843. See *Report*. London, Houghton/Collegiate School for Girls, 1876.

19. The shouting may have been a common experience for the Dickenses as they were often in debt.

20. Dickens's elder sister Fanny was studying at the Royal College of Music, and somehow managed to remain outside.

21. Forster, *Life* (Ley): 32.

22. Mrs Nickleby is said to be based on her.

23. Forster, *Life* (Ley): 34.

24. Bob Sawyer is a character from *Pickwick*. Ibid. 29.

25. Ibid. 29–30.

26. If the workhouse in *Oliver Twist* is redolent of the one in Chatham, this young woman's experiences may explain it.

27. Forster, *Life* (Ley): 30.

28. *Sketches by Boz*: 'A Little Talk about Spring, and the Sweeps'. Originally published in *The Library of Fiction*, 1836: 113–19.

29. M. Allen, 'New Light on Dickens and the Blacking Factory', forthcoming; personal communication.

30. Forster, *Life* (Ley): 38.

31. Ibid. 35.

32. *Pilgrim Letters*: Letter to T. C. Barrow, 31 January 1836.

33. Forster, *Life* (Ley): 35. Concerning his need to walk, Dickens once wrote to Forster: 'If I couldn't walk fast and far, I should just explode and perish'. *Pilgrim Letters*, vii: *c*.29 September 1854.

34. Ibid. 38–45.

35. Johnson Street is now called Cranleigh Street.

36. 'An Unsettled Neighbourhood', *Household Words*, 1854, 10: 289–92. It is not yet known if the two shopkeepers with the surname of Dickens on Chalton Street—Richard, a grocer, and Thomas, a tobacconist—were in any way related to the family. Dickens does not mention them, but the contiguity of Johnson Street and Chalton Street is certainly intriguing. See *Kent's Original London Directory*. London, Kent, 1818. Genealogical research may help here.

37. G. Cruikshank, *London going out of town*. 1829. British Museum Prints and Drawings Collection (AN708938001).

38. *Our Mutual Friend*, chapter 4.

39. Allen, *Dickens' Childhood*: 99.

40. Cases of Thomas Halfpenny, Edward Stevens, William Pratt, 25 October 1827: oldbaileyonline.org

41. News cutting *c*.February 1817 British Library shelfmark Crach.1.Tab.4.b.3. This story puts me in mind of the one told by Sam Weller in Pickwick about the man who fell in the canal: 'I rather think one old gentle-man was missin'; I know his hat was found, but I a'n't quite certain whether his head was in it or not.' *Pickwick Papers*, chapter 13.

42. News cutting *c*.1810, British Library Crach.1.Tab.4.b.3.

43. 'Our School', *Household Words*, 1851, 4: 49–52; Forster, *Life* (Ley): 38–45.

44. Ibid. 38–45.

45. Quoted ibid.

46. The reminiscences of Dickens's schoolfriends may be found ibid.

47. Ibid.

48. Dickens remembered: 'there were at that time a number of poor Spanish refugees walking about in cloaks, smoking little paper cigars.' *Bleak House*, chapter 43.

49. J. M. L. Drew, 'Dickens's Evolution as a Journalist', in D. Paroissien, *Companion to Charles Dickens*. Oxford, Blackwell, 2008: 174–85. For penny-a-liners, see also J. Grant, *The Great Metropolis*. London, Saunders & Ottley, 1837, ii: chapter 5. Accessed online 27 July 2011 at www.victorianlondon.org/publications/thegreatmetropolis2-5. htm.

50. Forster, *Life* (Ley): 38–45.

51. 'Wise child' is a chapter title from that fine book: S. Marcus, *Dickens from Pickwick to Dombey*. London, Chatto, 1965: chapter 2.

52. *Charles Dickens's Acount Book 1827–9*. Harry Elkins Widener Collection, Houghton Library, Harvard University HEW 2.6.5.

7. Young Dickens

1. Aunt Charlton lived at 16 Berners Street. His Uncle Thomas Barrow lodged above a bookseller in Gerrard Street, Soho. See M. Allen, *Charles Dickens' Childhood*. New York, St Martin's Press, 1988. He had other friends in the area.

2. The notorious Red-Barn murder, by William Corder, generated a plethora of broadsheets, chapbooks, and ballads as well as china figurines in 1827–8. See J. Flanders, *The Invention of Murder*. London, Harper, 2011: plate facing 173. It is extraordinary to think that Dickens might later have seen *Pickwick* mugs and loving cups there, when they were novelties. See B. Maidment, 'Pickwick on Pots'. *Dickens Quarterly*, 2011, 28/2: 109–18.

3. Mary Allen/Lamerte had died in 1822, not long after her marriage. See Allen, *Dickens' Childhood*: 68–9.

4. W. F. Long, 'Defining a Life: Charles's Youngest Sister, Harriet Ellen Dickens (15.9.1818–19.08.1827)', *Dickensian*. Forthcoming.

5. Weller was not in the street in 1820. He seems to have arrived, according to the rate-books, in 1828. Westminster Archives,

rate-books 1828, Norfolk Street Marylebone. See also *Robson's London Directory*, London, Robson, 1832; *Pigot's London Directory*, London, Pigot, 1838.

6. How important the family connections of his mother were to Dickens's professional success will be clear from this chapter.

7. *London Gazette*, 25 May 1832: 18.

8. *Ipswich Journal*, 27 July 1822. T. A. Smith, *A Topographical and Historical Account of the Parish of St Mary-le-bone*. London, Smith, 1833: 315.

9. *Sketches by Boz*, 'Shops and their Tenants'.

10. http://charlesdickenspage.com/dullborough_town.html

11. References in the *London Gazette* to Norfolk Street, Middlesex Hospital indicate that houses with insolvencies/bankruptcies between 1815 and 1840 include: 1, 2, 7, 8, 10, 17, 20, 22, 24, 27, 30, 34. Mr Dodd's house had a particularly high rate of four (Mr Dodd twice, Mr Dickens, and Mr Menzies, for whom see below).

12. M. Le Sage, *The Devil upon Two Sticks*. Edinburgh, Donaldson, 1762.

13. Ibid. Audrey Jaffe explores this subject with splendid insight in her *Vanishing Points: Dickens, Narrative and the Subject of Omniscience*. Berkeley, University of California Press, 1991.

14. *Oliver Twist*, chapter 5.

15. *Pilgrim Letters*, i: Letter to an Unknown Clergyman [?1837]. A footnote citing Dickens's friend Marcus Stone explains: 'in reply to a letter of protest, in which his correspondent expressed incredulity that such a thing could ever occur, CD wrote: "Thou art the man." His churchyard was near Chatham.'

16. *Pickwick Papers*, chapter 24.

17. See *Sketches by Boz*, 'Shabby-Genteel People'.

18. Le Sage, *The Devil Upon Two Sticks*: 4. *Consolation*. London, Laurie & Whittle, 1795. British Museum Prints and Drawings: Satires Undescribed (AN518717001). The lawyer is recognizably a very modern type: although his costume is old, the posture, facial

expression and attitude, the whole ensemble, is so modern it is extraordinary. One can almost hear the accent!

19. W. S. Holdsworth, *Charles Dickens as a Legal Historian*. New York, Haskell House, 1972.

20. *David Copperfield*, chapter 38.

21. G. L. Craik, *The Pursuit of Knowledge Under Difficulties*. London, Charles Knight/Society for the Diffusion of Useful Knowledge, 1830.

22. Women, of course, did not figure in this conversation.

23. J. Forster, *Life* (Ley): 297.

24. The card came to light during the campaign to save the Cleveland Street Workhouse. All I found at the outset during a lengthy trawl of the internet was a verbal reference to it from an old sale catalogue issued by an auctioneer in the West Country. Auction houses do not divulge the identity of buyers, so I wrote to all the libraries and archives with significant Dickens holdings that I could think of, enquiring whether they had been the purchasers, or if they knew who might have acquired it. None seemed to have any knowledge whatever about it. The auctioneers, Dukes of Dorchester in Dorset, were kind enough to send me a photograph of the calling card, and allowed me to use the image so long as I acknowledged them as its source. To see the diminutive little card, with its elegant script, and especially to see that great name printed before it was great, associated with that street address, was a genuine delight, not least because it provided perfect confirmation of the documentary research I'd done now had perfect confirmation. The Workhouse campaign was at its height at the time I received this photo, and it was highly important for the Workhouse that the card should be more widely known, especially to Dickensians. The current Editor of *The Dickensian*, Professor Malcolm Andrews, had kindly put me in touch with a Dickens aficionado in Philadelphia, Herb Moskovitz, who runs a Dickens e-newsletter called the electronic BuzFuz, after a character from *Pickwick*. Seeking support for

the Workhouse campaign I enclosed the auctioneers' photograph of the calling card for the newsletter, requesting that the kindness of the auctioneers should be acknowledged, since I did not know the identity of the card's current owner. To my astonishment an e-mail swiftly arrived in my in-box from the man who had actually purchased the card at the West Country auction. He is the Canadian Dickens collector Dan Calinescu: he had seen the BuzFuz newsletter! He has since proved a strong and a generous supporter of the campaign for the Workhouse, and for a blue plaque on Dickens's old home on the corner of Tottenham Street. Mr Calinescu believes that the card may represent the first time Dickens's name appeared professionally in print. Personal communication with Mr Calinescu, London, 2011.

As we have seen, until the Workhouse campaign, Norfolk Street had been a peculiar void in Dickens's biography, and the card provided clear evidence of his having firmly belonged there. To me, the calling card was an absolute clincher—it provided conclusive proof that Dickens had lived in Norfolk Street, and crucially, evidence of a kind that other people could witness for themselves. This became particularly important when a prominent London politician hostile to the preservation of the Cleveland Street Workhouse made the public statement in an interview in the national press that news of a Dickens connection was spurious. (See L. Bradbury, 'Oliver Twist's Workhouse Discovered'. *Daily Telegraph*, 20 January 2011.)

25. The owner of the *Morning Chronicle* lived on Fitzroy Square itself. It remains a prestigious address.

26. See Appendix D for a chronology of Dickens's occupations at his various London addresses between the years 1827 and 1837.

27. British Museum, London: Ledger 'Admissions to Reading Room 1827–1835'. 'Berner' is an error for Berners.

28. Further research is required to confirm whether or not Ward is related to the novelist Ann Radcliffe, née Ward, whose father was

a haberdasher, of London and Bath, and whose maternal uncle was the surgeon William Cheselden. Ward later moved to Percy Street, Bedford Square, and, later still, to Bath. His major work, *Practical Observations on Distortions of the Spine, Chest and Limbs* (London, Renshaw, 1840), was dedicated to Sir Astley Cooper, and lists Ward's qualifications as: MRCS, FRMed. and Chir, and corresponding Fellow of the Medical Society of London.

29. See *Pilgrim Letters*, i: 14 August 1837.

30. British Museum, London: Ledger 'Admissions to Reading Room 1827–1835'.

31. J. Grant, *The Great Metropolis*. London, Saunders & Ottley, 1837, ii: chapter 5. Accessed online 27 July 2011 at www.victorianlondon. org/publications/thegreatmetropolis2-5.htm.

32. W. J. Carlton, 'John Dickens, Journalist'. *Dickensian*, 1957: 5–11. The newspaper's failure pre-dated the eviction from Johnson Street, Dickens leaving school, and his sister's withdrawal from the Royal College of Music.

33. J. Britton, *Autobiography*. London, published for the Author, 1850: 102.

34. See M. Slater and J. Drew, *Dickens' Journalism*. London, Dent, 4 vols., 1996–2000.

35. Aunt Charlton's husband was a clerk in the Prerogative Office, Thomas Charlton worked in the Vicar General's Office in Bell Yard. See L. C. Staples (with A. T. Butler, A. Campling, R. Straus and W. J. Carlton), *The Dickens Ancestry: Some New Discoveries*. London, Dickens House, 1951. Thomas Charlton is listed as a proctor in *Robson's London Directory*. London, Robson, 1832: 2.

36. J. M. L. Drew, *The Pride of Mankind*. Oswestry, Hedge Sparrow Press, 2005.

37. Fairburn often added this direction to his publisher's byline.

38. Pailthorpe is considered a reliable informant by the Editors of the Pilgrim edition of Dickens's Letters, in confirming Dickens's involvement with Cruikshank's *The Loving Ballad of Lord Bateman*. See *Pilgrim Letters*, i: Letter to George Cruikshank, 29 March 1839

and footnote. John Drew mentions Pailthorpe's assertion concerning the Italian Boy chapbook, but does not elaborate. See J. M. L. Drew, *Dickens the Journalist*. Basingstoke, Palgrave Macmillan, 2003: 196n.

39. For a chronology and narrative of these events see R. Richardson, *Death, Dissection and the Destitute*. Chicago, Chicago University Press, 2000: chapter 6 *passim*.

40. Ballads were sung in the streets, like this one purporting to be the voice of Mrs Wilson, the mother of one of Burke and Hare's victims, Daft Jamie, who was an Edinburgh street character:

> Cruel monsters, they had eyed you,
> And had marked you for their prey;
> To their horrid den decoyed you,
> *And* with whisky paved the way.
>
> O, my heart how it does shudder
> At the deeds confessed and done,
> That have been committed by them,
> Monsters in the human form.
>
> Who could for the love of money
> Turn the living into dead,
> And thus prepare for the dissector
> Subjects to supply his need.
>
> You who bought and used his body,
> Surely you was much to blame,
> In concealing thus a murder,
> For you must have known the same.

Extracted from 'Lines supposed to have been written by Mrs Wilson, Daft Jamie's Mother'. Accessed online on the Word on the Street website of the National Library of Scotland: http://digital.nls.uk/broadsides/broadside.cfm/id/15224/transcript/1

41. See the cases of John Druitt, Jane Druitt, and Jane Reeve, 5 April 1832: oldbaileyonline.org. Note also the use of pawn tickets in this case.

42. Richardson, *Death, Dissection and the Destitute*: chapter 8 *passim*.

43. The faces of the three men tried for the Italian Boy's murder on the unsigned fold-out frontispiece to the Fairburn chapbook may be from the hand of Isaac or Robert Cruikshank, or the younger Percy. The bodies and shadows look to have been prepared in advance by the well-known caricaturist Phillips ('Sharpshooter'), who also worked extensively for Fairburn, and the sketches of Carlo Ferrari and of the men murdering another victim at the rear of Nova Scotia Gardens may be drawn or engraved by another hand. The use of several artists on one image was not at all unusual, especially for swift work, and remained common in Fleet Street through much of the nineteenth century. R. Richardson and R. Thorne, *The Builder Illustrations Index 1843–83*. Institute of Historical Research, 1995: Introduction.

44. See a similar case reported by Kathleen Tillotson concerning Seymour, *Dickensian*, 1958: 11–12.

45. Fairburn had given other young authors a start on the literary ladder. See J. Britton, *Autobiography*. London, Printed for the Author, 1850: i. 103–5. Dickens's friend Maclise also sketched courtroom portraits.

46. For an earlier instance, however, see Anon., *Trial of James Leary*. London, Fairburn, 1813: title page.

47. *Bleak House*, chapter 11. See also J. Larson, *Dickens and the Broken Scripture*. Athens, University of Georgia Press, 1985. Victorian Web online text accessed July 2011.

48. *Oliver Twist*, chapter 52. See also S. Wise, *The Italian Boy*. London, Cape, 2004.

49. *York Herald and General Advertiser*, 10 December 1831. The trial had taken place on 2 October 1831.

50. D. DeVries, *Dickens's Apprentice Years*. Hassocks, Harvester, 1976: 4.

51. Anon., *Narrative of the Total Loss of the Rothesay Castle Steam Vessel*. London, Fairburn, 1831.

52. *Shipwreck! Charles Dickens and the Royal Charter*. Anglesey, Anglesey Books, 2011.

53. Anon., *Extreme cruelty to Children, MURDER!* London, Fairburn, 1829.

54. The children at the manufactory were so starved that they stole food from the scraps kept for pigs. Brownrigg was so infamous, and so very topical because of the Hibner case, that Douglas Jerrold adopted the pen name Charles Brownrigg at about this time, as a nom de plume for a hen-pecked husband. See M. Slater, *Douglas Jerrold*. London, Duckworth: chapter 5 *passim*.

55. Case of Esther Hibner, 9 April 1829: oldbaileyonline.org.

56. The first, Frances Colpitts, had also died from the effects of her maltreatment. Fairburn's pamphlet says she had been exhumed, as her body had already been secretly buried by a corrupt under-taker, whose premises were said to have been on the New Road. His name was Mr Hamp, and indeed there is a Henry Hamp, furnishing undertaker, of 7 Phoenix Rd, Somers Town in the *Post Office Directory*, London, Kelly, in 1846. Might this be the derivation of Gamp? And might he have been the employer of the young sweep with whom Dickens had spoken?

57. Dickens gave evidence against an omnibus driver for cruelty to a horse in 1838. Nils Erik Enkvist, 'Charles Dickens in the Witness Box'. *Dickensian*, 47, part 4, Autumn 1951: 201. Thanks to Robert Newsom and other friends on the Dickensforum for help in tracing this reference.

58. *Leigh Hunt's London Journal*, 11 June 1834: 87. Hunt was quoting F. K. Arnay.

59. *Sketches by Boz*, 'A Visit to Newgate'.

60. The latter is a corner shop, and is still there: now called the 'Charles Dickens Coffee House', on the south-east corner of Tavistock Street and Wellington Street.

61. Richardson, *Death, Dissection and the Destitute*: 197.

62. *Pilgrim Letters*, v: Letter to John Forster, [?1846–1848]; see also For-ster, *Life* (Ley): 530.

63. Ibid. 60.

8. Workhouse

1. See *Morning Post*, 12 May 1834; 14 May 1834.

2. See F. H. W. Sheppard, *Local Government in St Marylebone*. London, Athlone Press, 1958: 276.

3. These figures date to 1835. See *Second Annual Report of the Poor Law Commissioners for England and Wales*. London, Clowes, 1836: 632.

4. See T. Jones, *Select Vestry Comforts*. London, Fores, 1828. The British Museum's copy of this caricature has the names of several of those present added by hand. British Museum Prints and Drawings. BM Satires 15527. The impact of such caricatures could be very serious indeed: Baron Graves committed suicide in 1830 after the publication of caricatures satirizing his wife's affair with the Duke of Cumberland. See *ODNB*: North, Thomas.

5. The Act (7 Geo. III c. 39, 1767) was introduced through the good offices of the philanthropist Jonas Hanway. Prior to Hanway's Act, hundreds of children died annually from inadequate care. See also *ODNB*: Hanway, Jonas.

6. *Oliver Twist*, chapter 2.

7. *Oliver Twist*, chapter 8.

8. I thank Peter Higginbotham for this important insight, which is crucial to an understanding that the workhouse in *Oliver Twist* belongs to a central London parish. His workhouses.org website is a splendid source of data on Poor Law history across the UK. See P. Higginbotham, Hanway's Act. http://www.workhouses.org.uk/MetInfChildren.

9. *Oliver Twist*, chapter 4.

10. The Battle of Barnet was in 1471, during the Wars of the Roses. Hendon village is now part of the London Borough of Barnet.

11. LMA WE/BG/ST/110/1: Letter re the delivery of coals to the proprietor, Miss Merriman, Infant Poor Establishment, Burroughs Lodge, Hendon: 6 July 1836. The place was close to the farm on which Mark Lemon, the Editor of *Punch* lived as a child.

12. F. Whishaw, *Map of the Whole Manor of the Parish of Hendon*. London, Whishaw, 1828. British Library Maps. In the list of subscribers to this magnificent map is a Dr Lee, who worked in Doctors' Commons.

13. Dickens was very familiar with North End, and he mentions that he has been at Hendon on more than one occasion in letters. See *Pilgrim Letters*. For being often seen there, see N. B. James, *The Story of Hendon Manor and Parish*. Hendon, Warden, 1932: 114.

14. *Oliver Twist*, chapter 48.

15. *Oliver Twist*, chapter 2.

16. L. F. Cody, 'The Politics of Illegitimacy in an Age of Reform: Women, Reproduction, and Political Economy in England's New Poor Law of 1834'. *Journal of Women's History*, 2000, 11/4: 131–56.

17. 'W.R.' writing in *Leigh Hunt's London Journal*, 1834: 211. The line in William Blake's *Songs of Experience*: 'And is that little cry a song?' springs to mind.

18. *Messrs Fry & Fitch's Southwark Female Farmed Poor House, Southwark*, 1830. From the records of St James Garlickhithe. Museum of London.

19. See E. Murphy, 'The Metropolitan Pauper Farms 1722–1834'. *London Journal*, 2002, 27/1: 1–18; E. Murphy, 'Samuel Tull's Net Manufactory'. Unpublished MSS. I thank Elaine Murphy for her kindness in sharing these papers with me.

20. The first part of the novel's serialization was in February 1837.

21. See D. Green, 'Icons of the New System'. *London Journal*, 2009, 34/3: 264–84. See also K. Hollingsworth, *The Newgate Novel*. Detroit, Wayne State University Press, 1963, App. B: Date of the Action of *Oliver Twist*: 232–3. Hollingsworth dates the action to between 1828 and 1831, so: after the 'Select Vestry Comforts' caricature, and up to and including the first 'revision' of the parish Workhouse in Cleveland Street.

22. *Reports of the Sub-Committee appointed by the Committee of Management of the Parish of St Paul Covent Garden, for the Revision of their Workhouse.*

London, Parish of St Paul Covent Garden Committee of Management, 1831.

23. See E. Murphy, 'The Metropolitan Pauper Farms 1722-1834'. *London Journal*, 2002, 27/1: 1–18; E. Murphy, 'Samuel Tull's Net Manufactory'. Unpublished MSS. See note 19.

24. I have not found Mr Dodd submitting tenders to supply the Workhouse.

25. *Pilgrim Letters*, i: Letter to Mary Anne Leigh, 7 March 1831: n. 3, citing a speech of 1865.

26. J. M. L. Drew, 'Dickens's Evolution as a Journalist'. In D. Paroissien, *Companion to Charles Dickens*. Oxford, Blackwell, 2008: 174–85.

27. Fairburn's Italian Boy chapbook was published during the 1831 parliamentary recess.

28. *Pilgrim Letters*, i: Letter to Thomas Mitton, [?21 November 1834] and footnote.

29. The various addresses that are known from letters appear in the Pilgrim edition of Dickens's letters. John Dickens was named in the *London Gazette* in November that year as an insolvent debtor, and his previous addresses given in series: Norfolk Street, George Street, North End, and Belle Vue Hampstead—so his flight is clear. *London Gazette*, 22 November 1831: 28. Only two letters from Charles Dickens seem to survive from the whole of 1831, the first dated 7 March, from George Street, Adelphi (off the Strand), the second from Belle Vue, Hampstead, both relating to Miss Beadnell. Dickens's mother is known to have returned to the George Street address when another debt crisis hit late in 1834, so it is possible that the household in Norfolk Street had broken up in late February or March 1831, or that his father had gone to ground alone. I thank Michael Allen for helpful discussions about these matters.

30. The next letter in the Pilgrim edition volume dates to the following year, and is written from North End, Hampstead, *c.*April 1832. Possibly Dickens had nowhere else reliable to fix upon. Mr Dodd was suffering financial difficulties at the time, too.

31. *Pilgrim Letters*, vii: Letter to C. P. Roney, 2 May 1853. See also W. J. Carlton, 'A Companion of Copperfield Days'. *Dickensian*, 1953: 7–16.

32. His parents' financial difficulties might have been exacerbated by the loss of his income to the family budget.

33. *Pilgrim Letters*, i: Letter to Thomas Beard, 2 February 1833. This was probably a happy event, but the publication of John Dickens's insolvency (and his Marshalsea prisoner status) in the *London Gazette* that May was perhaps the last straw for the Beadnells, and Dickens at last saw the hopelessness of his courtship. *London Gazette*, 7 May 1833: 20.

34. Forster, *Life* (Ley): 62. See also Drew, 'Dickens's Evolution as a Journalist': 174–85.

35. Forster, *Life* (Ley): 64.

36. N. C. Edsall, *The Anti-Poor Law Movement*. Manchester, Manchester University Press, 1971: 7.

37. *Oliver Twist*, chapter 4.

38. R. Richardson, *Death, Dissection and the Destitute*. Chicago, Chicago University Press, 2000: App. 4, 291–2.

39. Burke and Hare were discovered in November 1828. A Parliamentary Select Committee had already reported in July 1828, before the discovery. The first Anatomy Bill was introduced on 12 March 1829. It was thrown out by the Lords, 5 June 1829. See Richardson, *Death, Dissection and the Destitute*: 157, 337. An anachronism appears in *Pickwick Papers*, which is set in 1827: a reference to burking, from Mr Pickwick: see chapter 31. The matter was clearly still on Dickens's mind.

40. Richardson, *Death, Dissection and the Destitute*: 157.

41. It also accomplished something else: it forced the poor to provide for their own funeral costs, or risk dissection. See ibid. chapter 11 *passim*.

42. 'Paul Pry' [i.e. William Heath]: *A Few Illustrations for Mr Warberton's Bill*. London, McLean, 1829. British Museum Prints and Drawings Collection: Satires 15777. The King's Bench debtors' prison is where Mr Micawber is incarcerated in *David Copperfield*, and also features in

Nicholas Nickleby and *Little Dorrit*. Interestingly, the same caricature shows a black servant buying human meat from a street stall for his master Dr Rawhead, carrying very prominently a basket and a large key—exactly the props Nancy is given when she is sent out to the Police office to seek out news of Oliver, in *Oliver Twist*, chapter 25.

43. *Oliver Twist*, chapter 4. Readers interested in the ways other writers' works were influenced should look at Tim Marshall's fine work, *Murdering to Dissect: Grave-robbing, Frankenstein and the Anatomy Literature*. Manchester, Manchester University Press, 1995.

44. Richardson, *Death, Dissection and the Destitute*: 266.

45. The swift entry appears to have been something he knew about already, perhaps from having witnessed how easily others were excluded.

46. C. Dickens, 'A Nightly Scene in London'. *Household Words*, 1856, 13: 25–7.

47. *True Sun*, 1 December 1832. See also Richardson, *Death, Dissection and the Destitute*: 234–5.

48. M. Slater, *Charles Dickens*. New Haven and London, Yale University Press, 2009: 37.

49. John Drew calls this 'politicised prose'. See Drew, 'Dickens's Evolution as a Journalist': 174–85.

50. *Oliver Twist*, chapter 7.

51. P. Schlicke, 'Bumble and the Poor Law Satire of Oliver Twist'. *Dickensian*, 1975: 149–56.

52. M. Slater, *Charles Dickens*. New Haven and London, Yale University Press, 2009: 51.

53. John Drew says: 'he developed a sideline in more imaginative free-lance work'. See Drew, 'Dickens's Evolution as a Journalist': 174–85.

54. W. J. Carlton, *Charles Dickens Shorthand Writer*. London, Palmer, 1926: 111.

55. *Oliver Twist*, chapter 1.

56. *Oliver Twist*, chapter 2.

57. *Oliver Twist*, chapter 13.

58. Letter to the Revd Richard Burgess, Rector, 44 Cadogan Place, London, re: Case of Ann Nugent. LMA WE/BG/ST/110/1. Other material mentioned below comes from this source.

59. LMA WE/BG/ST/110/1, 2 July 1836.

60. Some of the Strand Guardians did endeavour to soften this edict. See LMA WE/BG/ST/110/1, 1836–7.

61. See this volume, Chapter 3.

62. LMA WE/BG/ST/110/1.

63. See for example, the case of Elizabeth Clinch LMA WE/BG/ST/110/1.

64. My notes are taken from WE/BG/ST/110/1 series of records of the early Strand Union, held at the London Metropolitan Archives. This is an impressionistic account only, from a relatively swift examination the materials available. I am keenly aware that the picture is more complex than I have been able to outline here.

65. D. R. Green, *Pauper Capital*. Farnham, Ashgate, 2010: 126. Mott was writing in 1838.

66. See R. Neate, *St Marylebone Workhouse*. London, St Marylebone Society, 2003: *passim*.

67. LMA WE/BG/ST/110/1. Other prospective employers, one a carrier, another the keeper of an 'insane establishment', were to have a 'choice' of boys. Others included a tailor, a calico printer, and a solicitor (for a servant-girl).

68. See J. M. White, *Some Remarks on the Statute Law affecting Parish Apprentices*. London, Longman, 1829. The parishes of St Giles and St George were sending boys to the Sea Service in 1829. See *Papers relating to the Parishes of St Giles and St George*. London, Parish: 1829. Marylebone parish was still regularly sending boys to the Sea Service in the 1850s. See R. Neate, *St Marylebone Workhouse*. London, St Marylebone Society, 2003: 30. In fact boys from Cleveland Street were being sent to the Sea Service in the 1840s, so the initial enthusiasm for Chadwickian factory discipline does not seem to have lasted. See LMA WE/BG/ST/101.

69. *Oliver Twist*, chapter 17.

70. LMA WE/BG/ST/110/1.

71. No data corresponds in *The Times* online database, the British Library Newspaper Collections online, or the Gale Newsvault, searched August 2011.

72. LMA WE/BG/ST/110/1 Strand Union: Election of Guardians, 1836. Dickens occasionally used the Piazza Coffee House as an address, and his Shakespeare Club met there. See *Pilgrim Letters*, i: Letter to Macready, 26 January 1839; footnote to Letter to Forster, 30 March 1839. Dickens certainly knew Cuttriss, but the evidence we have is of a later date. See *Pilgrim Letters*, iv: Letter to Frank Stone, 7 May 1846. A further possibility, though less likely, is that Dickens gained news from Hansard, printer of Dickens's *Sketches* for Macrone. The Hansards were important figures in the parochial management of St Giles and St George. This notion would not explain the matched details from the Strand, unless the Hansards were exceptionally well informed, which they might have been. They would also have been unsympathetic to Dickens's view of the Poor Law, and their relationship was not of the best, so this route seems unlikely. A further possibility is that he met someone at the offices of the *Morning Chronicle*, which—being pro-Poor Law—was the newspaper favoured with adverts for new staff from the Strand Union Guardians. See LMA WE/BG/ST/110/1:12.7.1836.

73. It looks as though Mr Dodd moved away in the 1830s, but so far exactly when is uncertain.

9. Works

1. Furnival's Inn was sited where the 'Prudential' Building now stands in High Holborn, at the southern end of Leather Lane. According to Darton's Map of London of 1817 (MAPCO online) the City boundary went through the middle of Furnival's Inn. Field Lane was at the junction of Saffron and old Holborn Hills, where the road ran steeply down towards the valley of the River

Fleet, and was largely destroyed in the building of Holborn Viaduct. Bleeding Heart Yard still stands, very changed, between Greville Street and Ely Place. When Dickens was living in Furnival's Inn, most of what is now Greville Street was called Charles Street. Michael Allen's new book, *Dickens and the Blacking Factory*, addresses important new data he has discovered concerning Dickens's associations with the area of Field Lane.

2. The first series of *Sketches by Boz* appeared on 8 February 1836, the second, on 17 December 1836, both published by Macrone. See Paul Schlicke's authoritative edition of *Sketches by Boz*. Oxford, Clarendon, 2012. I am very grateful to Professor Schlicke for allowing me access to parts of his manuscript in advance of publication.

3. Proposal and agreement made in February 1836; see *Pilgrim Letters*, i.

4. M. Slater, *Charles Dickens*. New Haven and London, Yale University Press, 2009: chapter 4 title.

5. *The Spectator* 26 December 1836: 1234–5. I thank Paul Schlicke for bringing this fine review to my attention.

6. Dickens signed the contract to edit *Bentley's Miscellany* on 4 November 1836, and resigned from the *Morning Chronicle* on 5 November 1836. See Paul Schlicke's edition of *Sketches by Boz*: Chronology.

7. Charles Dickens jun. was born 6 January 1837. The first issue of *Oliver Twist* appeared in Bentley's in the February issue of 1837. It continued appearing in parts until April 1839.

8. Slater, *Charles Dickens*: 45. Late in 1835 they were at 18 Upper King Street, Bloomsbury. See *Pilgrim Letters*, i: Letter to Catherine Hogarth, [?September 1835] plus footnote.

9. For Dickens's various addresses in Marylebone see the volumes of the *Pilgrim Letters*. Edward Street lay between Duke Street and Marylebone Lane.

10. A. Cox-Johnson, *Handlist of Painters, Sculptors and Architects associated with Marylebone 1760–1960*. London, St Marylebone Public Libraries Committee, 1963.

11. *Pilgrim Letters*, i: Letter to Laman Blanchard, 23 December 1838.

12. Cox-Johnson, *Handlist of Painters, Sculptors and Architects associated with Marylebone 1760–1960* (also the artist Richard Dadd, possibly an inspiration for Jonas Chuzzlewit). See also Marylebone General Dispensary: *List of Subscribers*. London, Dispensary, 1785. Thomas Hood and the Jerrolds lived in St John's Wood, a more distant part of Marylebone parish.

13. *Pilgrim Letters*, iii: Letter to William Mitchell, 16 February 1842. The play had been performed on 24 February 1834.

14. *ODNB*: A'Becket, Gilbert.

15. J. A. Megelin, 'Feminism or Fetishism'. In L. Garafola (ed.), *Rethinking the Sylph*. Hanover and London, Wesleyan University Press, 1997: 69–90.

16. See *Pilgrim Letters*, i: Letters to Kolle, 3 December 1833 and [?10 December 1833].

17. It received its Royal assent on 4 and 5 August 1833; William IV, c.76.

18. R. St Clair, *The Pauper Boy*. London, Newman, 1834: 44.

19. Ibid. 77.

20. *London Gazette* 1840: Insolvent Debtor 16 October 1840: 27.

21. Fludyer Street was an old street of small houses south of Downing Street, since obliterated by government buildings. No. 10 was at the St James's Park end of the street. This sounds fashionable to us now, but that part of Westminster then was known for its slums, and the marshy nature of the land. Dickens knew Wakefield Street, because it ran into Henrietta Street, where some of his siblings had gone to school.

22. Dickens knew where Menzies had moved to, and the outcome of the breach of promise accusation. The *Sketch* was written before Menzies's insolvency, but after the Dickens family had left Mr Dodd's.

23. Gissing, for example, says: 'In truth, away from London he was cut off from the source of his inspiration; but he had a memory stored

with London pictures. He tells us, and we can well believe him, that, whilst writing, he saw every bed in the dormitory of Paul's school, every pew in the church where Florence was married. In which connection it is worth mentioning that not till the year 1855 did Dickens keep any sort of literary memorandum-book. After all his best work was done, he felt misgivings which prompted him to make notes. A French or English realist, with his library of documents, may muse over this fact—and deduce from it what he pleases.' G. Gissing, *Charles Dickens—A Critical Study*. London, Gresham, 1902: 57.

24. F. Kaplan, *Charles Dickens' Book of Memoranda*. New York, New York Public Library, 1981 [facsimile].

25. Quoted in R. J. Dunn, *David Copperfield: An Annotated Bibliography*. Garland, 1981: 179.

26. *Pilgrim Letters*, i: Letter to John Macrone, [?27 October 1835]. The appearance of this paragraph makes me think of Mr Jingle in *Pickwick*, but so do many paragraphs in *Leigh Hunt's London Journal*.

27. Kaplan, *Charles Dickens' Book of Memoranda*.

28. H. Stone, *Dickens' Working Notes for his Novels*. Chicago, University of Chicago Press, 1987: 139.

29. Nollekens died there an old man in 1823. W. H. Holden, *Houses with a History in St Marylebone*. London, British Technical Press, 1950: 17–18. See E. Topham, *The Life of Mr Elwes, the celebrated Miser*. London, Brewman, 1796.

30. For Marleybone see for example P. Potter, *Plan and Section of Proposed Aqueduct from the River Thames through by or near . . . Marleybone*. London, *c.*1830. The local shopkeeper named Marley was at 87 Titchfield Street. See *Kelly's Post Office Directory*, London, Kelly, 1846.

31. Pepys's Diary, 7 May 1668, quoted in W. H. Manchee, 'Marylebone and its Hugenot associations'. *Proc. Hugenot Soc. Lond.*, 1916, 11/1: 1–72. The female professor dates to 1838 in Norfolk Street: more research will be required to see if she was there earlier; she was a

lodger, so evidence may be difficult to find. *Pigot's London Commercial Directory*, London, Pigot, 1838.

32. *David Copperfield*, chapter 10. Rudderforth is listed in the local ratebooks, and can also be found in the street directories. For Jonah Dennis, see St Pancras Ratebooks 1815. Thanks to John Richardson for his splendid transcription of these ratebooks. There was also a Dennis who was a publican in Cursitor Street, and another householder there was called Tubman.

33. She was the wife of Thomas Malie, MD, and was buried in 1827 in the St Marylebone churchyard ground on the south side of Paddington Street. See T. Smith, *Topographical and Historical Account of the Parish of St Marylebone*. London, Smith, 1833. This name might also have come from a playful use of the name of one of Dickens's go-betweens in the courtship with Miss Beadnell, Miss M. A. Leigh, but I think not, as it seems Dickens did not much like her. See *Pilgrim Letters*, i: Letter to Miss M. A. Leigh, 7 March 1831.

34. 'Where We Stopped Growing'. *Household Words*, 1 January 1853: 362–3.

35. E. Walford, *Old & New London*. London, Cassell, 1878: iv. 467.

36. H. Stone, *Dickens and the Invisible World*. London, Macmillan, 1980: 279–93. I am very grateful to Paul Schlicke for directing me to this work.

37. *Kelly's Post Office London Directory*, 1846. For Lord Haversham see F. H. W. Sheppard (ed.), *Survey of London*, 33–4 [St Anne Soho]: 82–3.

38. The Marquis of Granby, a very important public house name for *Pickwick Papers*, stood (indeed still stands 2011) at the end of Percy Street, it carried the same name in the 1830s.

39. A. Backhouse, *The Worm-Eaten Waistcoat*. Backhouse, Upper Poppleton, 2003: *passim*. See also W. F. Sayer, *The Warehouse Boy*. London, Jackson, 1849.

40. *Knickerbocker Magazine*, New York, as 'in a recent letter to us', 1839, 14: 196;. Quoted in *Pilgrim Letters*, i: June/July 1839.

41. J. Forster, *Life* (Ley): 15.

42. Kaplan, *Charles Dickens' Book of Memoranda*: 25.

43. *The Times*, 22 February 1820: 1.

44. *The Times*, 9 May 1831: 1.

45. The proffered lifeline was not only for the poor: in 1840 Dickens and Forster both had to pawn their gold watches in Birmingham when a holiday journey to Stratford-on-Avon had proved longer and more expensive than expected. See Forster, *Life* (Ley): 158.

46. Anon., 'My Uncle'. *Bentley's Miscellany*, 1837, 2: 175.

47. It is not yet clear whether John Cordy Baxter was related to John Cordy Jeffreason, one of Dickens's correspondents (see *Pilgrim Letters*). The more I have pondered this offstage appearance, the more I have wondered if it indicates the source of the tale.

48. *Robson's London Directory*, London, Robson, 1832: 84. Dickens does not use all these names in his work, it is the charm of them that is noteworthy. They were originally in alphabetical order. Mr Pickwick's surname was originally that of a stage-coach proprietor at Bath.

49. Dickens and Sykes both appear in *Pigot's London Alphabetical and Classified Commercial Directory*. London, Pigot, 1836. 11 Cleveland Street was the 8th shop after the 'King & Queen' public House, going north. The original building has since been replaced.

50. See *Robson's Improved London Directory for 1820*, London, Robson, 1820.

51. See *Johnstone's London Directory*, London, Johnstone, 1818; Westminster ratebooks: Cleveland Street, 1828.

52. See *Pigot's Alphabetical and Classified Commercial Directory*, London, Pigot, 1836. Sykes was still there in 1838; see *Pigot's London Commercial Directory*, London, Pigot, 1838.

10. The Most Famous Workhouse in the World

1. *Oliver Twist*, chapter 51.

2. Ibid.

3. In his later works, also the Law.

4. M. Le Sage, *Gil Blas*, trans. T. Smollett. London, Walker, Johnson & Richardson, 1809: chapter 5.

5. See Kathleen Tillotson's Introduction to the Clarendon edition of *Oliver Twist*. Oxford, 1966: 400, quoting Queen Victoria's Letters, 1838–9.

6. The new Hospital had been opened in Agar Street, just off the Strand in 1834, at the western end of Chandos Street. T. J. Pettigrew, *The Pauper Farming System: A Letter to the Rt. Hon. Lord John Russell on the Condition of the Pauper Children of St James Westminster as demonstrating the necessity of abolishing the Farming System*. London, Rodd, 1836.

7. Dickens was familiar with this area, as his uncle John Barrow lived there.

8. The poet was John Armstrong.

9. Pettigrew, *The Pauper Farming System*.

10. D. R. Green, 'Icons of the New System: Workhouse Construction and Relief Practices in London under the Old and New Poor Law'. *London Journal*, 2009, 34/3: 264–84.

11. *John Bull*, 6 February 1837.

12. *Oliver Twist*, chapter 12.

13. K. Tillotson, Introduction to the Clarendon edition of *Oliver Twist*, Oxford, 1966: p.xvi. Workhouse soup became a passionate issue: in York Poor Law Union the workhouse soup was subject to chemical analysis in 1839. See *York Herald*, 14 September 1839. See also a ballad of the era: *The Workhouse Boy*. Sharp, printer, *c*.1840. National Library of Scotland: APS4.8510. It concerns a hungry boy who went missing, and who, it was discovered later, had fallen into the workhouse soup copper. Although this ghastly occurrence is not elaborated, he presumably became an ingredient of the workhouse soup, and was devoured by the unwitting workhouse inmates.

14. See www.workhouses.org/Drouet where four excellent articles Dickens wrote on the disaster are available online.

15. I am using Forster's date for the 'fragment' of 1847 here, when Dickens would have been 35. But, there is debate as to whether it possibly belongs to an earlier period.

16. M. Slater, *Charles Dickens*. New Haven and London, Yale University Press, 2009: 293.

17. *Pilgrim Letters*, viii: Letter to Forster, 7 May 1857.

18. The biographer Diane Middlebrook perceived this process in the work of both Ted Hughes and Ovid. Personal communication, London 2003–7.

19. *Pilgrim Letters*, i: Letter to J. H. Kuenzel, [?July 1838].

20. The best source for this early chronology is Michael Allen's beautiful book *Charles Dickens' Childhood*. New York, St Martin's Press, 1988. A new edition is planned for 2012.

21. *Pickwick Papers*, chapter 31.

22. *Pickwick Papers*, chapter 33.

23. *Oliver Twist*, chapter 38.

24. Professor Tim Hitchcock, historian and a key figure in the creation of the Old Bailey Online website agrees that transportation would have been a likely punishment for the theft of an article the value of a gold locket and ring. Personal communication 28 August 2011. There would also have been the matter of a fraud on the Poor Law authorities, as the child's parentage was obscured as a result of the theft, which had long-term cost implications.

25. J. P. Kay, Poor Law Commission 16 July 1838 LMA WE/BG/ST/114:122.

26. L. Twining, *Recollections of Life and Work*. London, Arnold, 1893.

27. Anyone wishing to understand the importance of the Cleveland Street Workhouse in the history of the Poor Law, in addition to its place in relation to Dickens, ought to read Dr Rogers's book. J. Rogers, *Reminiscences of a Workhouse Medical Officer*. London, Fisher Unwin, 1889. It is available free online: www.archive.org/details/josephrogersmdreooroge See also R. Richardson and B. S. Hurwitz, 'Joseph Rogers and the Reform of Workhouse Medicine'.

British Medical Journal 1989, 299: 1507–10. Online: www.bmj.com/content/299/6714/1507.full.pdf

28. WE/BG/ST/101 Strand Union: *Standing Orders*: 17 March 1857. LMA This seems to immediately pre-date the period when John Forster became Secretary (1858) and then Commissioner (1861) at the Lunacy Commission, but he and Rogers may well have come in contact over other such issues at some later stage.

29. See J. Rogers, *Reminiscences of a Workhouse Medical Officer*. London, Fisher Unwin, 1889: 21. Catch later committed suicide when (like Mr Bumble in *Oliver Twist*) he was faced with having to enter the workhouse himself.

30. *Hansard*: *House of Commons Debates* 19 March 1841, 57: 400. Wakley had been proposing to invite the House of Commons to abolish the Poor Law Commission. *The Lancet*'s new Commission undertook its work in his memory.

31. *Lancet* Sanitary Commission. *The Lancet*, 1865, 2: 14, 73, 131, 184, 240, 296, 355, 513, 575, 711; 1866, 1: 66, 104, 173, 376; 2: 235.

32. *Pilgrim Letters*: to E. Hart, late February 1866. The meeting took place on 3 March 1866. 'The land' has been read elsewhere as 'England'.

33. *Our Mutual Friend*, chapter 8.

34. E. Smith, *Report on the Metropolitan Workhouse Infirmaries and Sick Wards*. British Parliamentary Papers 26 June 1866, 61: 372.

35. The chronology has been somewhat simplified here: there was a period during the Second World War when the building was an emergency first aid centre.

36. We argued this point in our campaign report to government: happily it was heard.

37. Peter Higginbotham quoted during the campaign to save the Workhouse: see David Perdue's Dickens page http://charlesdickenspage.com/

38. Two local allusions stand out in *Pickwick*, both associated with the Wellers: the church in Langham Place appears on Sam Weller's

Valentine in chapter 33, and Tony Weller's reference to the 'Regency Park', in chapter 44, a wonderful confabulation of the Regent's Park up the road, and the old Regency Theatre on Tottenham Street.

39. G. Storey, *Dickens and Daughter*. London, Muller, 1939: 116–17.

40. His surviving book of 'Memoranda' does not seem to be the notebook Dickens had in the shop, as it has little which looks to have been composed in a junk shop, unless it be a conversation between two men about Gibbon's *Decline and Fall*. The so-called 'Book of Memoranda' looks to me to be a secondary-level notebook, where thought-through ideas were stored at a stage later than running note-taking.

41. Walter Bagehot once described Dickens as a 'correspondent for posterity'. R. Barrington (ed.), *The Work and Life of Walter Bagehot*. London: Longmans, 1915: 3.

INDEX

Note: CD = Charles Dickens, London Places are listed under London, and Dickens's novels and characters are listed under Dickens: works

357

Index

Index

Index

Index

Index

Index

snobbery, about London addresses 53, 57, 68, 189, 321 n.25
Soho Bazaar 32–5
soup, in workhouses 220
Sowerby, Marylebone publican 259
Spectator, on 'Boz' 247
sponging houses 101, 223
St Clair, Rosalia, pseud.: *The Pauper Boy* 253
Stamp, Mr, of Norfolk St 133, 174
Staples, Leslie 5–6, 316 n.1, 329 n.26, 337 n.35
starvation dietaries 216–17 , 281, 283, 292–3
Stevens, Valentine, Poor Law Guardian 244, 347 n.72
Stone, Frank 347 n.72
Stone, Harry 262–3
Stone, Marcus 334 n.15
Storey, Gladys 302, 314
Strand Poor Law Union 218, 237–45, 290
Strand Union Workhouse, *see* Cleveland Street Workhouse
streaky bacon 105, 275, 278
sweeps, workhouse children 155–9
Sykes, bankers 273
Sykes, William 273–4, 277, 301

Tallis, John: *Street Views* 62–5, 124–7
tallow chandler 107
Taylor's Buttons 86–7
tea, in workhouses 220, 222, 250
Ten Hours Act, 1847 108
Ternan, Ellen 29
Thackeray, William Makepeace 68
third world parallels 216, 280–4
Tillotson, Kathleen 284
traditional tales, chapbooks 95
transportation 145
Trollope, Thomas Adolphus 329–330 n.28
True Sun 231–3
Turner, J.M.W. 302
Twining, Louisa 289–91, 294

undertaking 79, 134, 228, 232, 235, 240, 279, 340 n.56
University College School 151
unmarried mothers
    starvation dietary 292–3
    yellow gown 240

Vampyre, see *Frankenstein*
vestry gluttony caricatured 210–12
violence against children, *see* child cruelty
voluntary hospitals and medical charities 58, 291

Wakley, Thomas 294, 355 n.30
Ward, William Tilleard 190
Warren's blacking, *see* Allen; Dickens: life; Drew; Lamerte; London: places: Hungerford Stairs/Chandos Street
water closets 115–19, 175
Waterloo, Battle of, 1815 40–1, 43
Weller, Daniel, of Norfolk Street 175–6, 264, 301
Weller, Mary, Dickens family servant 145–6
West, Benjamin 183
Westall, Richard 325 n.22
Westminster Archives 22, 25, 91, 110
Westminster, University of 242
White Woman of Berners Street 260–4
Whitechapel workhouse, poor outside 229–30
Whitfield's Tabernacle 92, 135
Wilkin, Margaret 243–4
Wills, William Henry 55, 271
Wilson, James, 'Daft Jamie' 338 n.40
Wilson, Mary 80
Wollstonecraft, Mary 170
Woodward, John 242
Workhouse Boy 353 n.13
workhouse children:
    apprentices 203–5, factory hands 8, 80–1; servants 146–7, 155–6; sweeps 155–9; *see also* sea service
    starvation/maltreatment 203–5, 281–4
workhouse infirmary building programme of 1870s 297
Workhouse Visiting Society 290
Workhouses, *see* Cleveland Street Workhouse; Poor Law
Workhouses, website 300, 341 n.8

year without a summer, 1816 42
yellow gown 240
York Herald 201–2

Z: pen-name of John Dickens 192